Israel on the Road to Peace

Israel on the Road to Peace

Accepting the Unacceptable

Ziva Flamhaft

WestviewPress

A Division of HarperCollins*Publishers*

Copyright © 1996 by Westview Press, Inc., A Division of HarperCollins Publishers, Inc.

Published in 1996 in the United States of America by Westview Press, Inc., 5500 Central Avenue, Boulder, Colorado 80301-2877, and in the United Kingdom by Westview Press, 12 Hid's Copse Road, Cumnor Hill, Oxford OX2 9JJ

A CIP catalog record for this book is available from the Library of Congress.
ISBN 0-8133-2414-9 (hc) — ISBN 0-8133-2774-1 (pbk)

The paper used in this publication meets the requirements of the American National Standard for Permanence of Paper for Printed Library Materials Z39.48-1984.

10   9   8   7   6   5   4   3   2   1

To the memory of my parents,
Haya and Tsvi Backman

Peace can in fact be assured only if one or more of the interested powers will make concessions to each other, by lowering their demands or discarding their mutual suspicions. If neither will consent to do this, I do not believe that human wisdom can evolve a scheme to prevent the competing forces from eventually clashing together.

—Otto von Bismarck, memorandum (undesignated),
October 20, 1876

Diplomatists are naturally so conservative that, even if once a century they are compelled to take a step forward, they spend a great deal of time and ingenuity in assuring themselves and the world that they have been standing still.

—Leonard Woolf, *International Government*

Contents

Tables

Acknowledgments

In the process of writing this volume, I benefited from the assistance of a number of individuals. Special thanks are due to Professors Dankwart A. Rustow and Asher Arian for their support and scholarly guidance and to Professors Abraham Bargman and Irving Markovits for their comments and suggestions. I am grateful as well to Ambassador Seymour M. Finger and Professors Benjamin Rivlin and W. Ofuatey-Kodjoe for their remarks.

I also thank Brigadier General (res.) Aharon Levran; Ambassador Samuel Lewis; former assistant secretary of state for Near Eastern and African affairs Richard Murphy; the former Israeli health minister and current mayor of Jerusalem, Ehud Olmert; member of Knesset and current foreign minister of Israel, Shimon Peres; former member of Knesset and current president of Israel, Ezer Weizman; and Professor I. William Zartman, who were kind enough to take time from their busy schedules to speak with me.

I owe particular thanks to my husband, Stephen, and my daughter, Odellia, without whose patience, support, and understanding I could not have taken on this project.

Ziva Flamhaft

Prologue

This book went to press shortly after the tragic assassination of Prime Minister Yitzhak Rabin at a Tel Aviv peace rally on November 4, 1995. The killer, a twenty-five year old Israeli hard-liner, was reportedly a member of Eyal, an obscure, Jewish, right-wing, underground militant group founded in 1990 by members of the Kach movement, the latter banned in 1994. The horrendous act of the assassin, which apparently enjoyed the blessing of a number of ultra-nationalist rabbis, induced tremendous outrage against extremist groups in Israel and enormous support for the peace process. Evidently, the assassination was meant to stop the implementation of the Israeli-Palestinian Interim Agreement on the West Bank and Gaza Strip, also known as Oslo II, which was approved by Rabin's cabinet on September 27, 1995, signed in Washington on September 28, and ratified by the Knesset on October 6 by a vote of 61 to 59. If implemented, it would relinquish less than one-third of the West Bank to Palestinian control.

The agreement was structured to broaden Palestinian self-rule in the West Bank for an interim period not exceeding five years from the signing of the Gaza-Jericho agreement (no later than May 1999). It set the timetable for the permanent status negotiations to begin no later than May 1996, two months after the Israeli Defense Forces are scheduled to complete their redeployment from the last West Bank city. In his comprehensive speech to the Knesset upon the agreement's ratification, Rabin reassured the country that, among other things, the permanent solution would ensure that greater Jerusalem would remain united under Israeli sovereignty and that the borders of the State of Israel would extend beyond the 1967 lines to include most of the Land of Israel as it was under the rule of the British mandate. He admitted, however, that withdrawal from the 1967 lines was necessary in order to preserve the Jewish and democratic nature of the State of Israel and its security.

Will Rabin's vision prevail after his untimely death? Can the peace process survive the deep cleavages appearing in Israeli society? Can the Labor government implement its agreement with the PLO amid the shock and grief engulfing the country? No, say those who believe that Rabin, the warrior who led the IDF to its stunning victory over the Arab armies in 1967 and the defense minister who did not hesitate to use the harshest of measures to quell the *intifada*, was the only Labor leader who had sufficient credibility to trade territory for peace with the PLO. Additionally, they argue that Israeli society, already so divided over the peace process, has been further wrenched apart by Rabin's assassination. Moreover, the massive campaign of terror launched by Hamas as Israel and the PLO move closer to the permanent status negotiations has jeopardized the future of the peace process altogether. Others, however, believe that since peace remains the only option for both Israel and the Palestinians, the assassination will draw many indecisive Israelis toward the Labor government and that the peace process will be enhanced in spite of the setback inflicted by the Hamas reign of terror. I share this view.

It is not clear whether, or to what extent, Rabin's murderer was influenced by the venomous rhetoric that has characterized the controversy over the peace process since the signing of the Declaration of Principles in September 1993. But if it is possible that the virulent language that consumed the political discourse in Israel legitimized the use of violence against Israeli officials, and Rabin's murder in particular, many Israelis would consider it a moral imperative to realize Rabin's objectives. And although some members of the Israeli right would argue that Rabin provoked settlers and other right-wing nationalists by alienating them, most Israelis must question why they remained silent when the right's criticism of the Labor government's policies turned into personal and vicious attacks against the prime minister, including accusations of being a "traitor" and "murderer," deserving punishment by death. Similarly, most Israelis must question why they remained apathetic when Rabin, the soldier and statesman who had faithfully served his country since before independence, was portrayed as an Arab or even as a Gestapo officer—the worst insult in a country that was created out of the ashes of the Holocaust. Indeed, 74 per cent of those Israelis who were surveyed on November 10, 1995, by *Yediot Aharonot* less than a week after Rabin's murder supported the continuation of Rabin's policies in the peace process.

In the wake of Hamas's terrorism similar accusations have been voiced against Prime Minister Shimon Peres by agitated Israelis. But this time the public cannot remain silent, not only because of the tragic consequences such silence bore when Rabin was attacked but because Israelis know that Hamas seeks to harm them through the demise of the peace process. As for the credibility issue, we must consider the record of Peres. A former defense ministry director-general, deputy defense minister, and defense minister, Peres has expertise that must not be underestimated. As deputy defense minister in the 1960s, Peres was largely responsible for the establishment of Israel's weapons industry and nuclear program. And it was Shimon Peres who first envisioned a peaceful and integrated Middle East, a concept that is actually coming to life.

The Israeli public might also envision the fruits of peace and conclude that these must not be lost. In diplomatic terms, for example, Israel, by agreeing to recognize the PLO and to take the risks involved in implementing the Declaration of Principles, gained international acceptance it had not known since the aftermath of the 1973 war. Its relations with many Third World countries in Asia, Africa, and elsewhere—some of which, including a number of Muslim states, severed diplomatic relations with the Jewish state in the 1970s—have been greatly improved. In 1994 the Vatican opened diplomatic ties with Israel, and Pope John Paul II accepted Rabin's invitation to visit the Jewish state. In the UN too, where Israel has long been spurned by the Arab states and their allies, Israel's status has been steadily improving. Currently Israel maintains diplomatic relations with 155 of 185 UN members.

In economic terms, peace with the Palestinians has provided Israel with unprecedented opportunities. The implementation of the Declaration of Principles will continue to improve the business climate in the Middle East, stimulating investment and growth, which in Israel have already reached an annual rate of 7 per cent—the highest in the industrial world. For Israel these developments are bound to attract large-scale investment and trade and to open markets that until the Declaration of Principles were completely closed off to Israel. It may also foster the creation of a Common Middle East market and will certainly encourage tourism throughout the region. And although the primary Arab boycott against Israel has not yet been lifted, other Arab countries may follow the example of Morocco, Tunisia, and Qatar, which have deviated from the guidelines of the Arab League on the boycott. Additionally, Israel is already benefiting from the lifting of the secondary and tertiary boycotts, which is more important to its economy. After the December 1994 Middle East Economic Conference at Casablanca, Israeli corporations received dozens of enquiries from business groups in Egypt, Jordan, Morocco, Algeria, Tunisia, and Lebanon, which proposed joint ventures. In September 1995 a second regional economic conference convened in Amman, attracting more foreign investors and further improving regional economic ties.

In military terms, peace with the Palestinians would relax tension on Israel's boundaries and in the territories and would enable the IDF to tighten border security, intensify its war against terrorism, and shrink its defense forces. Potentially, progress towards peace with the Palestinians would lead to a comprehensive Arab-Israeli peace, enabling Israel to focus on serious threats from more distant enemies supported and trained by Iran. Above all, peace with the Palestinians would end the Israeli occupation, helping Israel to strengthen the democratic process and the rule of law that have been its guiding principles since the Jewish State was established.

1

Introduction:
Israel, the Stubborn Partner

On September 10, 1993, after decades of mutual animosity, Yitzhak Rabin, the prime minister of Israel, and Yasir Arafat, chairman of the Palestine Liberation Organization (PLO), exchanged letters of mutual recognition. Three days later, against the backdrop of the White House, the two former archenemies shook hands on the occasion of the signing of the Israeli-Palestinian Declaration of Principles. These historic events could be the beginning to an end of a century of bloodshed between Arabs and Jews, Palestinians and Israelis.

Their mutual recognition and the subsequent agreement Israel and the PLO signed were the outcome of months of secret talks that took place in Oslo. The swift success of the Oslo negotiations presents a sharp contrast to the failure of repeated U.S. attempts in the 1980s and early 1990s to continue the Camp David peace process. These attempts involved serious efforts to influence Israel to begin negotiations with Jordan and the Palestinians.

A number of diplomatic trends and international events seemed to suggest the opportunity for peace. First, the 1982 Lebanon war demonstrated the limitation of armed conflict as a method of achieving political aims. The Lebanon invasion taught Israel that military victories create more problems than solutions; the war weakened the PLO and drove the organization further away from Palestine than ever, from Lebanon to Tunisia.

Second, the Arab League began to deviate from the famous three nos of the Khartoum summit of 1967—no recognition of Israel, no negotiations with Israel, no peace with Israel. This became apparent in September 1982 when the league initiated the Fez plan, which implicitly accepted the existence of Israel.

Third, by 1984—when Egypt had begun its reentry into the Arab world—the Arab boycott to punish Egypt for the Camp David agreements and the peace treaty with Israel had failed. Notably, by May 1989, ten years after its expulsion, Egypt was allowed to rejoin the Arab League without abrogating the peace treaty with Israel.

Fourth, the Iran-Iraq war proved that Israel was not the only threat to the Arab world. Yet it was not until the end of the Cold War and the aftermath of the Gulf war that Israel finally entered the Madrid peace conference, in October 1991. Even so, not until the reemergence of Labor as the leading political party in Israel in June 1992 did diplomacy become truly effective.

Israel avoided negotiations in the decade that followed the Lebanon war because of the political change that occurred in the country in 1977: the replacement of Labor by the Likud as the dominant party in Israel and the emergence of a number of right-wing parties. These "territorial parties," which are committed to keeping all of the occupied territories, together with other territorial bodies, managed to frustrate any peace efforts that might have involved territorial concessions. That changed in 1992, when a considerable number of Israeli voters no longer deemed the issue of land crucial.

If mediation is to succeed, not only the diplomatic and international settings but also the domestic political situation has to be right, particularly when one of the parties to the conflict is a democracy. This volume provides an in-depth study of the effect Israel's internal struggles had on the Arab-Israeli peace process as the country reacted to various peace proposals from the early 1980s until the momentous events of September 1993. I also demonstrate how the return of the Labor Party to power in 1992 produced a breakthrough in negotiations.

This narrative also covers the tireless efforts of the United States to promote a comprehensive peace in the Middle East; the evolving ideas of Palestinian representation to the Middle East peace talks; an evolving Middle East international peace conference; the PLO's gradual acceptance of Israel; the role of the Jewish settlement movement in Israel in thwarting the peace process; Israel's gradual acceptance of the PLO; and, above all, a remarkable democracy at work.

Israel's refusal to take advantage of mediation efforts from 1982 to 1991—when it was all but forced to join the Madrid conference—was peculiar in view of a number of dramatic regional developments that could normally induce negotiations. These events included the outbreak of the *intifada* in December 1987; King Hussein's cutting all legal and administrative ties to the West Bank in favor of the PLO in July 1988; and the Palestine National Council's (PNC) recognition of United Nations Resolutions 242 and 338[1] in November 1988 and the opening of a U.S.-

PLO dialogue that December. The collapse of the Israeli National Unity government over the peace process in March 1990, the defeat of Likud in June 1992, and the various steps that the new Labor government took to revive talks made the study of the peace process all the more intriguing.

Scholars who deal with the subject of mediation often neglect to point out how ineffective third-party mediation can be when negotiations are not supported domestically. I show that the stronger domestic support is, the better the chance mediators have in fulfilling their goal. Conversely, lack of domestic support, or domestic opposition to negotiations by important groups, impedes the ability of the third-party to mediate a negotiated solution to a conflict even when regional and international conditions are favorable.

This is not to deny the potential role of third parties in resolving regional conflicts. As the Camp David process and the Oslo negotiations showed, third-party mediation can be instrumental when the sides directly involved want to negotiate but cannot do so on their own. Indeed, faced with enormous difficulties during the first stages of the Camp David talks, President Anwar el-Sadat and Prime Minister Menachem Begin would not have continued their dialogue without the active involvement of the United States. Similarly, without the diplomatic skills and atmosphere the Norwegians provided, Israel and the PLO might have found it much harder to agree on mutual recognition and self-rule arrangements in Gaza and Jericho. Yet without the initial determination of the adversaries to bring their disputes to an end, neither the United States nor Norway could have been effective in their mediation efforts. As Norway's late foreign minister graciously acknowledged, the Israeli-PLO agreement was "the outcome of the two parties. It is theirs and they will defend it."[2]

The period I examine in this volume begins with the announcement of the Reagan peace plan of September 1, 1982, the first serious attempt since Camp David to continue the Arab-Israeli peace process. I end with the September 13, 1993, signing of the Declaration of Principles on Interim Self-Government Arrangements between Israel and the PLO. The main players in my study are the United States and Israel. During the period I cover here, no other outside power dominated the Arab-Israeli peace process more than did the United States, although other actors—the European Community, the Arab League, King Hassan of Morocco, the former Soviet Union, and Romania—tried to influence the negotiations. Only the United States was vigorously and systematically involved. By 1991 the United States, as the only remaining superpower, was the single force believed to be able to influence the post-Gulf war peace process.

Israel, the only stable democracy in the Middle East, was nearly evenly split between those who supported territorial compromise in the name of peace and those who opposed any territorial compromise even for peace. On the international level Israel is a modest power, greatly dependent on the economic, military, and political support of the United States. Yet it exercised a great degree of independence in foreign policy. On the regional level Israel is the only functioning democracy and the only non-Arab and non-Muslim state in the Middle East. The country is surrounded by four Arab states—Egypt, Jordan, Lebanon, and Syria—three of which were hostile to it throughout most of the period I examine. Nonetheless, during most of this time Israel saw no urgent need to end its conflict with the Arabs.

On the domestic level Israel is divided between hawks and doves, the devout and the secularists, Sephardim (the descendants of Middle Eastern and North African-born Jews) and Ashkenazim (the descendants of European and North American-born Jews), and 18 percent of the Israeli population is Arab. Yet Israel is a thriving democracy capable of applying the principle of pluralism to the national debate over peace, security, and relations with the Arabs.

Israel's reaction to the various peace proposals provides an excellent case study in conflict resolution: It involves a persistent diplomatic attempt by a superpower to persuade much weaker regional players to resolve their conflict, a prolonged resistance to resolving one of the most protracted regional conflicts since World War II (in itself a source of potential global instability), and the element of domestic political change.

Notes

1. United Nations Security Council Resolution 242, adopted on November 22, 1967, called for the withdrawal of Israeli forces from territories occupied in the Six-Day War. Resolution 338, adopted on October 22, 1973, called for an immediate ceasefire, an implementation of Resolution 242, and direct negotiations between the concerned parties under appropriate auspices.

2. Johan Jorgen Holst, speaking before the National Press Club, Washington, D.C., October 4, 1993.

PART ONE

The Peacemakers

2

International Interests in a Stabilized Middle East

International efforts to solve the Arab-Zionist conflict began in the 1930s when the flight of European Jews to Palestine agitated Palestinian Arab nationalists, who feared that Arabs would soon become a minority in Palestine. But it took some sixty years before the warring parties finally agreed to come to the negotiating table at the Madrid conference.

One general pattern in negotiations in the Arab-Israeli conflict is unmistakable: Earnest mediation attempts always emerged at a time of or immediately following a crisis. These attempts involved both private individuals and officials from various governments, as well as United Nations dignitaries—occasionally all at the same time.

But there are three primary interveners in the Arab-Israeli conflict: Britain, which during the mandate period (1920–1948) had made several attempts to impose a solution on the parties but never succeeded; the United Nations, which between 1947 and 1949 and in 1967 could at best achieve cease-fire agreements; and the United States, which from the mid-1970s onward assumed the role of near exclusive mediator.

Yet neither Britain nor the United States nor the United Nations, to whom both the Arabs and the Zionists frequently turned to help determine the future of Palestine, could bring the parties together, even when the only alternative was war. Often this was because Arab and Zionist leaders were governed by public opinion in their own communities.[1]

These failures included one of the most serious mediation attempts in 1939–1943, involving such figures as the prominent Zionist leader Chaim Weizman; the Saudi king Ibn Sa'ud; Prime Minister Winston Churchill and Foreign Secretary Anthony Eden of Britain; and President Franklin Roosevelt and officials in the U.S. Department of State. The initiatives fell through in part because of the failure of some Zionist leaders to promote it, in part because Ibn Sa'ud feared being labeled a "traitor."[2]

From the termination of the British mandate and the establishment of Israel in 1948 to the Camp David agreements in 1978, other mediation efforts failed as well. This failure was often the result of the discrepancy between the Arab and Israeli positions and the tenacity with which both held on to these positions.[3] And while the Camp David negotiations and the Egyptian-Israeli peace agreement that followed marked the first successful mediation efforts in the Arab-Israeli conflict, as Saadia Touval observed, this rare achievement was the result of the momentous concessions Egypt and Israel made (for Israel, the return of the Sinai; for Egypt, the recognition of Israel and a separate peace) rather than the unique features of the Camp David mediation process—that is, President Jimmy Carter's personal involvement; his use of pressure and threats on the one hand and attractive incentives on the other; and the guarantees he offered. Perhaps most significant, the compromises Egypt and Israel made had been agreed upon before mediation began and were brought about by other factors.[4]

Since 1948 the Arabs and Israelis have fought five major wars of attrition and terrorism, turning the Middle East into one of the most explosive regions in the world. During the Cold War especially, the intervention of outside powers has resulted in periodic international tensions, at times severe. Why have third parties—the United States in particular—been so persistent in trying to bring an end to the Arab-Israeli conflict when these efforts have caused so much frustration?

The international quest for Arab-Israeli peace during and after the Cold War was the result of a number of specific goals and interests; the most important was to prevent a superpower confrontation that could result from an Arab-Israeli war. Other motives included the desire to diminish the influence of the Soviet Union in the Middle East, the need to ensure the uninterrupted flow of oil to the Western allies and Japan, the prevention of strain in U.S. relations with its Western allies and Japan, the protection of the existence of Israel, and the promotion of human rights for the Palestinians through Palestinian self-determination.[5]

Preventing Superpower Confrontation[6]

At the end of World War II, the Middle East had become an area of great contention between the two emerging superpowers. In geopolitical terms the Middle East connects the three continents of Asia, Africa, and Europe, and it contains the largest amount of the world's oil reserves. It is also a major market for arms and heavy military equipment. It thus became a target for Soviet expansionism, which the United States took all necessary measures to contain.

The vehicle that enabled the superpowers to intervene in the Middle East as part of their global balancing act during the Cold War was the Arab-Israeli conflict. The duration of that conflict and its cyclical crises made intervention all the more possible through political, military, and economic support to local states. Ironically, the superpowers' supply of weapons to the two sides helped to make the Arab-Israeli conflict militarily unwinnable, turning the search for peace into a more effective instrument of intervention.

The existence of ultrasophisticated nuclear weapons in the hands of the United States and the former Soviet Union reduced the likelihood of an uncontrolled escalation of tension between the superpowers, though the Arab-Israeli conflict always had the potential of turning into a direct U.S.-Soviet confrontation. The October 1973 Arab-Israeli war, for example, developed from a regional conventional crisis involving three states into a potentially nonconventional global crisis involving the superpowers. That near confrontation was the result of U.S. and Soviet intervention on behalf of their client state, as Washington aided Israel and Moscow aided Egypt and Syria.

The war began on October 6 and lasted thirty-eight days. On the third day of the war, it became apparent to Washington that the Israeli losses were far greater than previously estimated. Since the United States could not permit the Soviet-equipped Arab armies to win the war, President Richard Nixon decided to approve arms shipments to Israel in accordance with an earlier Israeli request. Moscow in turn enticed Jordan and Algeria to enter the war, promising them full diplomatic support.

On October 10 Moscow started a massive airlift to Syria and at the same time proposed a cease-fire.[7] Washington rejected the proposal: Because Israel had not yet recaptured territory it had lost, a cease-fire would have meant a clear victory for the Soviet-supplied Arab forces and severely impaired the United States in negotiating postwar settlements.

The Nixon administration soon learned that in addition to conducting an airlift, the Soviets had placed seven airborne divisions on military alert. The United States gave clear warning that it would resist any Soviet military intervention. When Israel expressed willingness to proceed with a cease-fire agreement because of its shortage of military equipment, Nixon decided on an immediate airlift to Israel—a move meant to counter the Soviet airlift to its Arab client state. Indeed, the astounding magnitude of the airlift was intended to outdo Soviet supply efforts.

The tide began to turn on October 14, when the Egyptians suffered a heavy setback in the Sinai. Israeli forces then crossed to the west bank of the Suez Canal and destroyed the Soviet-made surface-to-air missiles there. By October 16, as the Israeli forces threatened the Egyptian Third Army, the Soviets again attempted to arrange a cease-fire.

On October 20, at the invitation of Soviet leaders, Secretary of State Henry Kissinger arrived in Moscow for consultations. During the visit Kissinger proposed a plan to which the Soviets agreed. That plan became the basis for United Nations Resolution 338. The cease-fire went into effect on October 22, 1973.

But a day later the Israeli forces made further advances, partly surrounding the Egyptian Third Army. On October 23 the Security Council passed Resolution 339, calling on the parties to return to the October 22 lines. United Nations observers were to be sent immediately to supervise the cease-fire, which was to go into effect on October 24. On October 25 the Israeli forces encircled the Egyptian Third Army, cutting it off from supply lines.

On October 24 President Sadat requested that U.S. and Soviet forces be sent to the Middle East. Although the Soviets favored his proposal, the United States refused to admit Soviet troops to the region. Soviet leader Leonid Brezhnev threatened to send troops unilaterally if the United States refused Sadat's proposal. He also placed his air mobile forces in Europe on alert. Moreover, reports circulated that a Soviet vessel carrying nuclear material arrived at Alexandria on October 22.

In reply Washington issued a military alert of U.S. forces (the state of alert reached DefCon III—increased readiness without the conviction that war is likely) and warned Sadat that the appearance of Soviet troops on Egyptian soil would have to be resisted. When the United States estimated that the Soviets were capable of lifting 5,000 troops daily into Egypt, it bolstered the number of U.S. forces in the eastern Mediterranean, reinforced the previous alert, and placed its armed forces around the world on nuclear alert. Kissinger publicly warned the Soviet Union that a nuclear war might result from a Middle East confrontation.

A few hours later Egypt withdrew the request for a joint Soviet-U.S. force, asking instead that the Security Council dispatch to the area an international force. Such a force customarily excluded troops from the five permanent members of the council. It was created that same day through Resolution 340.

The 1973 Arab-Israeli war was the second crisis in which the United States and the Soviet Union reached the brink of armed confrontation. The only other comparable situation occurred during the 1962 Cuban missile crisis. Although the Cuban missile crisis was far more serious than the 1973 Middle East crisis, the latter did demonstrate the risk that the Arab-Israeli conflict imposed on the superpowers when they pursued similar interests in the area.

Reducing Soviet Influence in the Middle East

Analysts of Soviet policy in the Middle East during the Cold War are usually divided into two schools of thought. One school views Soviet Middle East policy as primarily defensive, believing the Soviets were interested mainly in preventing the region's use as a base for attack on the Soviet Union. The second school considers Soviet policy essentially aggressive, aiming at the removal of Western influence from the strategically important oil-rich region.[8]

Wherever the truth lies, there is no question that the Middle East was of great strategic value to the Soviets. First, it protected their southern border—a strategic concern that became significant with the creation of the North Atlantic Treaty Organization (NATO) and the Middle East Treaty Organization (METO), also known as the Baghdad Pact. Second, the area contains an important "warm-water" route for the former Soviet Union. Third, as an oil-rich region, the Middle East could free the Soviet Union from the burden of supplying oil to East European countries and allow it to profit from Arab oil boycotts against the West.[9] There is little wonder, then, that Moscow used the Arab-Israeli conflict to exert its influence in the Middle East.

Although Soviet aspirations in the eastern Mediterranean intensified after World War II, Moscow's intervention in the region started much earlier, as part of its attempts to combat British imperialism. In 1920, at the Baku Congress of the People of the East, the Soviet Union allied itself with Arabs oppressed by colonialism and semicolonialism, and in 1921 it concluded treaties of friendship with Turkey and Iran. At the end of World War II the Soviets demanded that Turkey cede several Turkish districts lying on the Russian-Turkish border, revise the Montreux Convention (governing the Bosporus and the Dardanelles) in favor of a joint Russo-Turkish administration of the straits, sever ties with Britain, and conclude a Soviet-Turkish treaty by which Moscow would acquire naval and land bases in the Dardanelles for joint defense. In 1946, as Britain and the United States withdrew most of their forces from Iran, the Soviets refused to remove their own forces from the country, demanding instead oil concessions similar to those the British had secured. The Soviets also supported a rebellion of the Azerbaijani population in northern Iran at approximately the same time they tried to gain control of the Dardanelles.[10] They ultimately withdrew from Iran that year and exercised much less influence in the area until 1955.

Like the United States, the Soviet Union attempted to extend its influence in the region as part of its global objectives. And like the United States, the Soviet Union focused its Middle East policy on the Arab-Israeli conflict. Until 1950 Moscow tried to influence the Middle East through diplomatic and military aid to Israel. Yet by the end of 1948, a shift in Moscow's attitude toward Israel was evident after Golda Meir, first minister to Moscow, raised the question of the emigration of Soviet Jews to Israel.

The years between 1950 and 1967 marked a progressive decline in Soviet-Israeli relations and the culmination of a Soviet-Arab coalition. More precisely, relations between the two countries began to worsen in 1949, when David Ben-Gurion, the first Israeli prime minister, outlined Israel's foreign policy, indicating the country's neutrality in the Cold War. Then in 1950 Israel sided with the United States on the invasion of South Korea.

When Nikita Khrushchev replaced Joseph Stalin in 1953, the Kremlin played up its split from Israel to court potential Arab allies, paying particular attention to Egypt. Khrushchev understood the potential of revolutionary regimes in the Middle East. After all, Gamal Abdul Nasser had not only emerged the winner of the internal power struggle in Egypt in 1952, but he also continued to play a progressive role in the battle against imperialism: He challenged the British in the Suez Canal, openly supported the Algerian National Liberation Front (FLN) against the French, and in 1955 surfaced as a charismatic leader at the first conference of the nonaligned countries at Bandung. And as Nasser prospered as the Pan-Arab leader, the Soviets could extend their friendship to the rest of the Arab world through him.

The year 1955 constituted an important milestone in Soviet relations with the Middle East, as Moscow managed to balance the gains the West had made in the area by befriending the Arabs and their allies in the nonaligned movement. It was also in 1955 that the Soviet Union and its satellites began a massive military and economic aid policy in the Middle East, extending low-interest loans and technical assistance to Egypt, Syria, and Yemen. Of particular importance was the Soviet-Czech arms deal with Egypt, the magnitude of which was unprecedented in the history of arms sales.[11]

Although Moscow did not aid Egypt during the 1956 Suez campaign, the war enabled the Soviets to strengthen their ties with Egypt and Syria. The Soviet undertaking to build the Aswan High Dam in 1960 marked a further improvement in Soviet-Egyptian relations. And even though their relations sharply deteriorated from 1958 to 1960, in the period preceding the 1967 Arab-Israeli war, Soviet support for the Arabs reached an unprecedented level, playing a significant role in provoking the Six-Day War. During that time the Soviet Union intensified its ties with Syria and encouraged the Syrians to carry out anti-Israeli military activity under Soviet protection. When Nasser ousted the UN peacekeeping forces from the Sinai and proclaimed a blockade of the Strait of Tiran, Moscow used UN debates as a forum for its anti-imperialist propaganda.

Humiliated by the poor performance of the Soviet-equipped Arab armies during the Six-Day War, Moscow broke off diplomatic relations with Israel and stepped up support of its Arab clients. Egypt, by now completely dependent on the Soviets for the resupply of arms, became more vulnerable to Soviet penetration and began to serve as a route for Russian infiltration to Yemen, South Arabia, and Africa and as a channel for Moscow's increased influence on socialist movements in various Muslim countries. By the late 1960s the Soviet Union completely identified itself with Arab nationalism and with the Arab struggle against Zionism and Western imperialism. In 1972, however, the Soviets suffered an embarrassing setback in the Middle East when President Sadat expelled from Egypt all Soviet advisers. Ironically, that defeat helped the Soviets penetrate deeper into the Middle East: Moscow now sought to maintain its influence in the region through stepped-up political, military, and economic aid to Syria and, for the first time, through direct military aid to the PLO.

In the 1973 Yom Kippur War, Egypt was still receiving massive military aid from Moscow. As a result of the impressive performance of the Egyptian and Syrian Soviet-trained forces, Soviet influence in the region mounted. But Sadat's desire for economic aid from the United States and U.S. mediation in the Arab-Israeli conflict after the 1973 war—in itself the birth of the peace process—shifted the political balance of power in the region in favor of the United States.

The demise of the Soviet Union has since terminated the influence of the former superpower in the Middle East and elsewhere. Russia has reestablished diplomatic relations with the Jewish state, and it appears unlikely that Russia will try to regain some of the old Soviet influence in the Middle East by interfering in the region's politics.

Protecting Oil Supplies
to the Western Allies and Japan

Until the end of the Cold War, the free flow of oil from the Middle East to the industrial world was second in importance to East-West relations. But oil has been widely considered to be the lifeblood of the industrial countries since the mid-1950s, when it began to replace coal as the most important source of energy. Since 1989 the protection of oil supplies has become a primary concern.

Between the mid-1950s and the early 1970s, the world's consumption of oil tripled, and the international trade of oil increased nearly fivefold.[12]

By 1991 the International Energy Agency (IAE) projected that in the year 2005 world oil consumption would approach 4.15 million metric tons (mmt) oil equivalent. Of this, 1.97 million mmt oil equivalent will be consumed by the industrial democracies.[13]

Indeed, the commodity has been especially vital for the nations of Western Europe and Japan and to a lesser degree the United States. From 1960—the year the Organization of Petroleum Exporting Countries (OPEC) was founded—to 1975, Western Europe and Japan depended almost entirely on imported oil for their energy needs. During this period the importance of oil to the United States rose sharply, leaving the country unable to meet its energy requirements with indigenous resources—and unable to act as emergency oil supplier to the NATO allies and Japan.[14] Access to oil in the Middle East has thus become all the more necessary to the United States, which hopes to maintain a broad-based network of friendly ties in the area.[15]

Because of the large amounts of oil in the Middle East—the region contains almost 75 percent of the oil in world trade, and there is no prospect of any lessened importance for this oil in the near future[16]—it is there that the price of oil is set. This, coupled with the unique dependency of the industrial countries on oil, has enabled the oil-exporting countries to use petroleum as a political and economic weapon by restricting exports to oil-dependent countries and manipulating the price of oil.

The first incident to indicate the effect the Arab-Israeli conflict can have on Western access to oil from the Middle East occurred between November 1956 and March 1957. At that time the Suez Canal—the route by which nearly half of all the oil from the Persian Gulf reached its markets—was closed as a result of the 1956 Sinai campaign, a corollary of President Nasser's nationalization of the canal. His action invited the retaliation of Britain, France, and Israel.[17]

But it was the aftermath of the 1967 Six-Day War that provided the Arab oil-producing countries with the opportunity to turn oil into a purely political weapon. In August 1967, Arab finance and oil ministers met in Baghdad and agreed to create the Organization of Arab Petroleum Exporting Countries (OAPEC). The organization was formally established in January 1968 in Beirut by Saudi Arabia, Kuwait, and Libya. Abu Dhabi, Algeria, Bahrain, Dubai, and Qatar joined in 1970; Egypt, Iraq, and Syria in 1972.[18]

On October 16, 1973, six Gulf states agreed on a 70 percent price increase. The next day the Arab members of OPEC agreed to cut their oil production by 5 percent and to continue to do so by an additional 5 percent every month until Israel withdrew from all occupied Arab territories. On October 18 Saudi Arabia announced a deeper production cut until Arab demands were met. On October 19 President Nixon asked

Congress for $2.2 billion to help Israel pay for U.S. military equipment. The following day Saudi Arabia declared a total embargo on oil shipments to the United States. Arab members of OPEC subsequently extended the embargo to the Netherlands and Portugal, the two European countries who supported the U.S. policy in the Middle East. In December the Arab oil ministers decided to continue the embargo against the United States, the Netherlands, and Japan. The embargo was lifted on March 18, 1974, but in June Saudi Arabia announced a 35 percent increase in its rate of share in the Aramco oil concession, retroactive to January.[19]

Although the embargo had limited practical impact, its psychological effect was significant: Fear that the embargo might be extended and that Arab oil production might be reduced even more prompted a wave of panic buying in Europe and Japan, which in turn constrained supplies and drove prices even higher.[20] It also caused a strain in the relationship between the United States and its Western allies and Japan.

The next oil crisis came about because of the 1979 revolution in Iran.[21] That crisis spurred the West to build up an unequaled surplus for future crisis situations. Still, as the Carter Doctrine indicated, the Middle East remained vital to the industrial democracies.[22]

In 1980 another local conflict imposed yet another threat to the supply of oil from the region. The Iran-Iraq war, which began in September, did not lead to a serious oil shortage because of the huge stockpiles the West had created. However, the escalation of hostilities coupled with the tanker war in 1984 enticed the United States to help secure the transport of oil from the Persian Gulf. The safety of the supply of Middle Eastern oil to the industrialized world was an important reason for U.S. involvement in the Gulf war—although it was not one of President George Bush's declared goals to justify the U.S. response to the Iraqi invasion of Kuwait in August 1990. Instead, Bush expressed concern with the establishment of regional security and stability in the Gulf and the necessity of maintaining the integrity of Saudi Arabia, reflecting U.S. awareness of the strategic value of this region. Indeed, a decisive outcome of the Gulf war was denying Saddam Hussein control of oil supplies and ensuring the free flow of oil from the Middle East at reasonable prices.[23]

As an immediate reaction to the Iraqi invasion of Kuwait, Bush issued executive orders halting trade with Iraq and freezing Iraqi and Kuwaiti assets in the United States. Shortly thereafter, U.S. troops and aircraft, backed by various forces from European, Arab, and Asian countries, were dispatched to Saudi Arabia to protect the kingdom from an Iraqi attack.

After four UN Security Council resolutions failed to convince Saddam Hussein to withdraw from Kuwait, the United States increased its forces in the Middle East to 100,000. At the beginning of November 1990, U.S. troops in the region numbered more than 200,000, with another 400,000 to join them by early 1991 in order to guarantee an adequate offensive capability. This was the largest display of U.S. military power since the Vietnam War.

On January 12, 1991, Congress authorized Bush to use military force against Iraq, and on January 15 the president empowered the coalition forces to attack Iraq unless it began to withdraw from Kuwait soon after midnight of the UN deadline. On January 16, U.S. and allied forces began air attacks on military targets in Iraq and Kuwait, thus launching Operation Desert Storm. On February 27 Bush announced that the mission of liberating Kuwait was fulfilled. The war ended on March 2 with a UN Security Council resolution that set the terms for the end of hostilities.

Easing the Strain in U.S. Relations
with Its Western Allies and Japan

The existence of some important mutual interests does not preclude disagreements between the United States and its allies over conflicting interests. As Abba Eban has pointed out, the United States and Western Europe never entered into a contract to help or support each other in every crisis or confrontation. Rather, they simply agreed to protect one another in matters relating to the security of the North Atlantic area.[24] Still, in its pursuit of a globalist foreign policy, the United States cannot be indifferent to its allies' sentiments. For, as the Gulf war showed, without the support of the Western democracies and Japan, Washington may find it difficult to realize some of its global aims.

The Western Europeans and the Japanese have differed with Washington on a number of economic and political issues, including interest rates, relations with the Soviet Union, Central America, and the Middle East. The West European countries are involved in the Arab-Israeli conflict to a far lesser degree than the United States. Unlike the United States, they lack the power base from which to conduct an influential Middle East diplomacy, and their interest in the region is based on economic factors alone, not on geopolitical considerations.[25]

Because of their reliance on Middle Eastern oil, the Western European states have been willing to appease the Arabs, especially regarding the PLO. Indeed, since 1980 the European Community (EC) (which has since spawned the European Union, or EU) has recognized the PLO as a legitimate and instrumental partner in any Middle East diplomacy and urged its inclusion in peace negotiations even before the PLO accepted UN Resolutions 242 and 338. Furthermore, most European states interpreted Resolution 242 to mean total Israeli withdrawal from the 1967 boundaries, and most favor the creation of an independent Palestinian state in the

West Bank and Gaza. In return, the Arab oil-producing states have kept from intentionally injuring the economies of the European states.[26]

The first Western alliance crisis over the Middle East occurred in 1956, when Britain and France, in order to liberate the Suez Canal, mounted an attack on Egypt, prearranging the Israeli conquest of the Sinai that followed. Offended at not being consulted by his allies on the plans to invade Egypt and alarmed at the possibility that the invasion would drive the Arab world closer to the Soviet side, President Dwight Eisenhower put enormous pressure on the invading countries to stop the fighting and withdraw their forces from Egypt. The embarrassment of being defeated by Nasser—with the help of their U.S. ally—only added to the animosity Britain and France felt toward the United States.

The Suez affair, as Richard Barnet pointed out, seemed to signal that the bonds of alliance between Europe and the United States were loosening. The event that kept the Western alliance from falling apart altogether was the Soviet invasion of Hungary precisely at the time of the Suez crisis. The invasion reminded the British and French that Western Europe still depended on the United States for security.[27] The Six-Day War, too, strained relations among the allies. President Charles de Gaulle of France, who had an inherent contempt for the United States, blamed the war on the United States, turned against Israel, and presented himself to the world as the champion of Third World independence against U.S. imperialism.[28]

Unlike the United States, Europe did not view the Middle East in terms of Cold War competition. Led by France and the Federal Republic of Germany, Europe sought a more neutral and independent position on the Arab-Israeli conflict. Indeed, by 1973 the United States was the only Western supporter of Israel. During the 1973 Yom Kippur War, the NATO alliance experienced its most severe crisis since the Suez conflict of 1956. The European allies believed that the failure of the United States to press a settlement on Israel—a failure they blamed on U.S. domestic politics—led to the war, thereby putting at risk vital European interests. They displayed their irritation with Washington in refusing to cooperate in efforts to turn the tide to U.S. advantage.

When the 1973 war broke out, Britain and France rejected the U.S. suggestion for a cease-fire resolution that would urge the warring parties to return to the status quo ante. France later declined to participate in any diplomatic efforts to end the war.[29] On the sixth day of the war, Turkey refused to allow the United States to use U.S. air bases and other military facilities in Turkey for the war's objectives. Greece soon followed suit. Spain, which was bound to the United States by a treaty of friendship and cooperation, similarly prevented the United States from utilizing Spanish bases. Britain showed the same lack of cooperation when it declined the U.S. request to use British airbases. The Soviets, in contrast, were freer than the United States to use NATO airspace for their airlift.[30]

When Washington issued the military alert, the allies protested that there had been no prior consultation over a situation that involved U.S. troops stationed in Europe. West Germany, which had previously opened its ports to use by U.S. forces, refused to let the United States use any part of West German territory or air space—including U.S. bases there—for weapons delivery to Israel.[31] After the war, whereas Washington concentrated on a strategy of disengagement, the Europeans demanded an immediate Israeli pullback to the October 22 cease-fire line, to be followed by a withdrawal to the 1967 borders.[32]

The discrepancy between the U.S. and European positions on the conflict was the result of the different degrees to which the two sides of the alliance depended on Arab oil. In 1973 Britain imported about 59 percent of its oil from the Arab world, France 72 percent, and Germany 75 percent, while the United States imported only 16 percent of its total energy needs. Indeed, twice before the 1973 crisis—in 1948 and again in 1967—the Arabs had tried to use oil as a weapon against any nation that aided Israel. But in those two instances the tactic was ineffective: In 1948 Western Europe depended on oil for only 10 percent of its energy needs; only during the late 1960s did Western Europe convert to a petroleum economy.[33]

Again the alliance survived the crisis. Security was still a primary concern of its members, who made a deliberate effort to remedy the damage. And by fall 1974, the leaders of France, Germany, Britain, Japan, and the United States were swept from office, clearing the way for renewed friendship among incoming administrations.[34]

Since 1973 the Europeans have maintained a policy toward the Middle East independent of that of the United States. Combined with an oil glut and closer relations between the United States and a number of Arab Gulf states, that autonomy helped the Western allies survive the 1982 Lebanon war—the last Arab-Israeli war before the Declaration of Principles.[35]

Japan's involvement in the Middle East has been less extensive than that of Europe, though Japan's interest in a stable Middle East has likewise centered on a steady oil supply from the region: Japan depends on foreign oil for 90 percent of its energy requirements. The 1973 oil crisis thus hurt Japan even more than it hurt the West Europeans.

Although Japan's foreign policy had usually been compatible with that of the United States, by November 1973 Japan began to feel that its national interest might be jeopardized if it continued to identify with Washington's Middle East policy.[36] For the first time since the end of World War II, Japan openly broke with U.S. policy on an important global issue. In January 1974 the Japanese government announced a new pro-Arab policy. As a result, Tokyo concluded numerous bilateral deals with Arab states and offered them technical assistance and economic aid.[37] Japan still maintains good relations with the Arab states, as well as with the PLO, but it became friendlier to Israel in the early 1990s. Whether the extraordinary mood of cooperation that prevailed among the Western powers during the 1991 Gulf crisis can outlast another Arab-Israeli crisis is an open question.

Protecting Israel

Since the creation of Israel in 1948, the Western world has valued the existence of a sovereign democratic Western society in the Middle East. The United States has been more deeply concerned with the survival of Israel than has any other country. This concern grew especially strong after the 1967 Six-Day War and continued to receive wide public support even in the post-Vietnam era, when many U.S. citizens questioned the wisdom of their country's commitment to the security of other countries.[38] As Nadav Safran has pointed out, the U.S. commitment to Israel is a result of four factors: the strategic and economic interests the United States has had in the Middle East; the character of Israel as a beleaguered democratic, Jewish, immigrant state; and the deep attachment of 6 million American Jews to Israel.[39]

Of these, the strategic interests of the United States in the region are the most significant. Along with its close relations with Turkey, the United States used the support of Israel to penetrate the region and balance the Soviet influence there: After Washington failed to recruit the Arab countries into the Western camp for the purpose of using the Middle East as part of its global containment strategy (1948–1967), the United States adopted a new Middle East policy of stabilization and regional balance of power. To that end Washington could count on Israel's political stability as well as its military power. Thus, in the decade between 1957 and 1967, Israel became increasingly important as a regional ally. Additionally, Israel's stunning victory in the 1967 Six-Day War enabled the United States to mitigate Soviet influence in the Middle East, advance its own interests in the area, and use its new position to contain Soviet global expansionism.[40] From then on, the United States continued to benefit from it alliance with Israel, turning into the most influential external power in the region.[41]

Israel's pioneering spirit prior to and following the establishment of the state, its creation out of the ashes of the Holocaust, its democratic institutions, and its ability to stand up to huge hostile Arab armies all have aroused the idealistic sentiments of many Americans. Their commitment to Israel is further shaped by the Jewish lobby. The degree of that influence is often overstated, but the American Jewish community does have an impact on specific issues concerning Washington's policy in the Middle East. For example, it succeeded in pressuring successive administrations to reaffirm Kissinger's 1975 commitment not to negotiate with the PLO until a number of preconditions were met, and it had a noticeable affect on arms sales to moderate Arab countries and aid to Israel.[42]

The most forceful body to promote such policies was the American Israel Public Affairs Committee (AIPAC), which was formed in 1953 as an alternative to the U.S. Zionist Council—a pro-Israeli lobby that had a strained relationship with the Eisenhower administration. Although relations between AIPAC and the White House deteriorated in 1991 and early 1992 because of President Bush's position on a $10 million loan guarantee Israel had requested in order to help settle Jewish immigrants from the former Soviet Union, AIPAC remains the primary Jewish lobby in the United States.

Other pro-Israeli lobbies include about eighty political action committees (PACs) and the Conference of Presidents of Major American Jewish Organizations. The first are committees that make contributions to candidates running for federal elections; the second is an umbrella group that represents AIPAC and forty-four other organizations that deal directly with the White House and the State Department.[43]

Except during the Eisenhower and Bush administrations, the United States has been a strong supporter of Israel since its establishment in 1948. But not until the early 1960s, when it became apparent that the U.S. courtship of the Arabs had not reduced Soviet influence in the region, did Washington commit itself to balancing the Israeli military power against that of the Arabs. In 1962 the Kennedy administration agreed to sell Israel antiaircraft Hawk missiles to counter Soviet arms sales to Egypt, Syria, and Iraq.

President Lyndon Johnson deepened the U.S. commitment to Israel in response to the creation of an Egyptian-Syrian mutual defense treaty, the rise to power of a pro-Soviet Ba'athist regime in Damascus in 1966, and the Soviets' ongoing shipments of arms to radical Arab states. Facing these developments, the United States accepted Israel's request for additional military stockpiles. In 1966 the United States awarded Israel $92 million in military assistance, a sum that exceeded the total U.S. military aid to Israel since its founding.[44] Washington also agreed to sell Israel forty-eight Skyhawk bombers, in addition to the 210 tanks that it sold to Israel the previous year.[45]

But it was the Six-Day War that finally convinced the United States to become Israel's primary ally. The Soviet behavior that helped to provoke the war is well documented. This, together with the increased political and military dependence of Egypt and Syria on Moscow during and after the war as well as the French embargo on arms sales to Israel led the United States to step up political, military, and economic aid to Israel.

Political support was most evident in the United Nations, where the United States opposed any efforts to force Israel to withdraw from the occupied territories unconditionally. In terms of military aid, when the rearmament of the Soviets' Arab clients reached levels that threatened Israel's military superiority, the United States pledged to "keep Israel's military defense capability under active and sympathetic examination."[46] This decision, according to Safran, represented the first U.S. move to support by military means—not just diplomatic action—the premise that Israel should hold on to the territories it won in 1967 until the Arabs were prepared to make peace.[47]

Upon taking office, Nixon favored an evenhanded policy in the Middle East.[48] But when the Egyptians and the Soviets violated a U.S.-sponsored cease-fire agreement during the war of attrition, Nixon assured Israel of a speedy delivery of sophisticated military equipment. This was followed by a Senate concession giving the president almost unlimited authority to provide Israel with arms to counter the Soviet supply of weapons to Egypt.[49]

After the Soviets concluded a treaty of friendship and cooperation with the Egyptians in May 1971 and after intelligence reports indicated that the Soviets had reinforced their own troops in Egypt and were flying reconnaissance over the Sinai and the Sixth Fleet from bases in Egypt, Nixon pledged to help Israel in a long-term program to modernize its defense forces.[50] Between December 1971 and March 1973, the Nixon administration agreed to sell additional Phantom jets and Skyhawk bombers to Israel, concluded a memorandum of understanding to transfer technical information to Israel, assured Israel of assistance in modernizing its armed forces, and guaranteed the flow of financial assistance and military supply.[51]

The Yom Kippur War of 1973 was another occasion for the United States to deepen its commitment to Israel's security—yet with two important differences. First, in deciding to resupply the Israelis with military equipment lost during the first week of the war, the United States did not impose an arms embargo on all of the belligerent parties, its usual course of action in an Arab-Israeli conflict. Second, Nixon's request for $2.2 billion to cover the cost of the airlift was not only unprecedented in size and scope but a unique presidential request for aid to Israel.[52]

In 1974 Nixon promised future economic assistance and assured Israel of the United States' long-term commitment to provide military supplies.[53] After some initial friction with Kissinger that led to a U.S. policy "reappraisal," Israel's agreement to pull back from parts of the Sinai in

1975 resulted in a new level of U.S. aid to Israel: a foreign aid package that mounted to nearly $13 billion over a five-year period. The administration of Gerald Ford also agreed to consult regularly on Israel's long-term economic and military needs and to request such assistance in Congress annually. The agreement constituted the country's first formal written security commitment to Israel.[54]

The Camp David negotiations represented an even greater U.S. pledge to Israel. Immediately after the Egyptian-Israeli peace treaty was signed in 1979, the United States and Israel reaffirmed their 1975 agreement and all previous agreements and assurances. In addition the United States pledged to take diplomatic, economic, and military measures to remedy any violation or threat of violation of the treaty, including providing Israel with emergency supplies. Finally, Washington promised to support Israel's right to navigation and airspace through the Strait of Tiran and the Gulf of Aqaba.[55]

When Ronald Reagan entered the White House in 1981, his administration inherited all these guarantees. But his concerns about the Soviet threat in the region compelled him to expand the assurances even further. In November 1981 the administration signed the Strategic Cooperation Agreement with Israel, directed against the Soviet threat in the Middle East. When in December Israel annexed the Golan Heights, Washington canceled the agreement to protest the Israeli move but reinstated it in November 1983. Although the agreement was meant to counter increased Soviet involvement in the Middle East, in effect it simply deepened the U.S. commitment to Israel: It provided for joint U.S.-Israeli military cooperation, the repositioning of U.S. military supplies in Israel, and new military assistance grants and related privileges.[56]

In March 1984 the two countries formally agreed to cooperate on the development of selected defense equipment; in March 1985 the United States and Israel signed a free trade agreement designed to eliminate all tariffs between the two countries before 1995; in 1986 Congress named Israel "a major non-NATO ally"; and in December 1987 the two countries decided to expand the March 1984 agreement in a new memorandum of understanding.[57]

During the Gulf crisis Secretary of State James Baker reassured Israel that the United States remained committed to Israel's security if Israel were attacked by Iraq. In January 1991, after Iraq launched Scud missiles against Israel, the United States sent Patriot missile systems to Israel, and on March 22 Congress authorized $650 million in aid for Israel.[58]

But the guarantee that carries the most serious implications for the United States is the commitment to take military measures should the Egyptian-Israeli peace treaty be violated. It is possible that the United States would have to broaden this commitment in order to ensure a more comprehensive Arab-Israeli peace in the aftermath of the Israeli-PLO agreement of September 1993.

Promoting Human Rights for the Palestinians

If the protection of Israel's survival has been primarily an American concern, the promotion of human rights for the Palestinians, especially through self-determination, has been a European concern. But even though human rights have long been important to the Europeans, their support of Palestinian self-determination has been influenced more by the dependency on Arab oil than by altruism.

The Europeans did not begin to focus on the issue of Palestinian self-determination until 1973—when the oil-producing Arab states began to use oil as a political tool. In November 1973 the foreign ministers of nine EC countries who had met in Brussels to discuss the Middle East called for the recognition of the legitimate rights of the Palestinians.[59] This position was repeated on several other occasions over the next six years. But the most important EC document supporting Palestinian self-determination was the Venice Declaration of June 1980, issued at the conclusion of a two-day summit. The declaration corresponded with the position of the PLO on the national identity and specific rights of the Palestinian people and recognized the organization as the sole legitimate representative of the Palestinians. Paragraph six of the Venice Declaration specifically stated that "a just solution must finally be found to the Palestinian problem, which is not simply one of refugees. The Palestinian people, which is conscious of existing as such, must be placed in a position, by an appropriate process defined within the framework of the comprehensive peace settlement, to exercise fully its right to self-determination."[60] Paragraph seven insisted on the direct participation of the PLO in future negotiations for the achievement of these objectives. The EC endorsement of Palestinian self-determination was echoed in the Dublin and Madrid declarations of 1990 and 1991.

Except during the Carter administration, the United States has been less concerned about the promotion of Palestinian self-determination than has Europe. Nevertheless, the promotion of human rights in U.S. foreign policy serves two related purposes: It reflects the nation's own democratic standards in its global conduct and at the same time secures democracy at home. As an ethical precept, the principle of self-determination mirrors the traditional American anticolonial sentiment. As a pragmatic premise, self-determination is often believed to curb international conflict and promote international peace.[61] This indeed was the conviction behind the incorporation of the principle of the self-determination in the UN charter.

The only unambivalent endorsement of self-determination for the Palestinian people by a U.S. president came from Jimmy Carter in March 1977. Acknowledging their prolonged suffering, he declared that a homeland had to be provided for the Palestinian refugees. In a May press conference he repeated this notion, questioning whether there could be any hope for a settlement of the Arab-Israeli conflict without a homeland for the Palestinians.[62]

Carter formalized his personal ethical belief into policy during preparation for the proposed Geneva conference, when he dispatched Secretary of State Cyrus Vance to the Middle East in order to secure an agreement on five principles that he considered essential to any settlement. One of these principles was the creation of a nonmilitarized Palestinian entity with self-determination.[63]

Carter's concern for the rights of the Palestinian people reflected both the ethical and pragmatic aspects of U.S. foreign policy. As a moralist, he could not ignore the continued deprivation of Palestinian rights. As a pragmatist, Carter viewed the Palestinian question as an underlying problem of the Arab-Israeli conflict, in itself a potential global threat.[64]

In reality, however, bound by Washington's special relationship with Israel, neither Carter nor his Republican successors were able or willing to promote for the Palestinians any rights beyond self-rule, preferably under Jordanian administration. This was certainly the case with President Reagan: He was determined to alter the previous administration's political approach, which gave priority to human rights at the expense of security considerations. Reagan's preoccupation with security matters resulted in strategic cooperation with Israel, which barred any thought of Palestinian self-determination. Even President Bush, who tried to promote a more evenhanded Middle East policy, did not advocate any expression of Palestinian independence beyond self-rule. The administration of Bill Clinton does not endorse full Palestinian self-determination through statehood, instead regarding Palestinian self-rule as an interim arrangement before negotiations on the permanent status of the territories can begin.

■ ■ ■

The attainment of peace is rarely a goal in itself. Rather, when third parties seek to mediate in regional conflicts, they quite often have their own interests in mind. Because of the importance of the Middle East in global affairs, efforts to solve the Arab-Israeli conflict have involved a multiplicity of interests, some more vital than others. The problem with this approach is that the intermediary who is motivated by self-interest may neglect to take into account the concerns of the protagonists themselves, which in turn could deepen domestic opposition to mediation efforts. Such was the case in Israel with the Reagan initiative, the first U.S. mediation attempt since Camp David.

Notes

1. Neil Caplan, *Futile Diplomacy,* vol. 1: Early Arab-Zionist Negotiation Attempts, 1913–1931 (London: Frank Cass, 1983); vol. 2: *Arab-Zionist Negotiations and the End of the Mandate* (London: Frank Cass, 1986).

2. Ibid., pp. 133–138.

3. Saadia Touval, *The Peace Brokers* (Princeton: Princeton University Press, 1982), p. 319.

4. Ibid.

5. Jimmy Carter, *The Blood of Abraham* (Boston: Houghton Mifflin, 1985), p. 56; Henry Kissinger, *American Foreign Policy* (New York: W. W. Norton, 1977), p. 286.

6. Much of my description of the U.S.-Soviet encounter during the 1973 war is based on Henry Kissinger's *Years of Upheaval* (New York: Little, Brown, 1982), chs. 11–13.

7. Soviet leader Leonid Brezhnev initially attempted to arrange for a cease-fire with the Arabs on October 8.

8. Robert O. Freedman, "The Soviet Union and the Arab-Israeli Conflict," in Robert O. Freedman, ed., *World Politics and the Arab-Israeli Conflict* (New York: Pergamon Press, 1979), pp. 53–54.

9. Galia Golan, *Yom Kippur and After* (Cambridge: Cambridge University Press, 1977), pp. 7–8.

10. Walter LaFeber, *America, Russia and the Cold War, 1945–1990* (New York: McGraw-Hill, 1991), pp. 35–37.

11. George Lenczowski, *The Middle East in World Affairs* (Ithaca: Cornell University Press, 1980), p. 781.

12. Dankwart A. Rustow, *Oil and Turmoil* (New York: W. W. Norton, 1982), p. 107.

13. Richard N. Cooper, "Oil, the Middle East, and the World Economy," in Joseph S. Nye Jr. and Roger K. Smith, eds., *After the Storm: Lessons from the Gulf War* (Lanham, Md.: Madison Books, 1992), p. 149.

14. Melvin A. Conant and Fern Racine Gold, *The Geopolitics of Energy* (Boulder, Colo.: Westview Press, 1978), p. 12.

15. This conclusion is based in part on a conversation with former assistant secretary of state for Near Eastern and African affairs, Richard Murphy (currently senior fellow, Middle East, Council on Foreign Relations), New York, April 9, 1991.

16. Conant and Gold, *Geopolitics of Energy,* pp. 14, 26.

17. Rustow, *Oil and Turmoil,* pp. 101–102.

18. For the history of the political use of oil by the Arab states, see Don Peretz, "Energy: Israelis, Arabs, and Iranians," in Joseph S. Szyliowicz and Bard E. O'Neill, eds., *The Energy Crisis and U.S. Foreign Policy* (New York: Praeger, 1975), pp. 91–93.

19. Kissinger, *Years of Upheaval*, pp. 872–891. On December 22–23 the Persian Gulf members of OPEC announced a price increase of 128 percent. That meant 387 percent increase in the price of oil in two months. See Rustow, *Oil and Turmoil*, pp. 146–147.

20. Kissinger, *Years of Upheaval* pp. 873–874.

21. For the effect the revolution had on the price of oil, see Rustow, *Oil and Turmoil*, pp. 182–185.

22. The Carter Doctrine was announced on January 23, 1980, when Carter declared before a joint session of Congress that any attempt by an outside force to gain control of the Persian Gulf region would be regarded as an assault on the vital interests of the United States.

23. Martin Indyk, "The Postwar Balance of Power in the Middle East," in Nye and Smith, *After the Storm*, p. 84.

24. Abba Eban, *The New Diplomacy* (New York: Random House, 1983), p. 148.

25. Adam Garfinkle, "West European Peace Diplomacy in the Levant: But Will They Come?" in Willard Belling, ed., *Middle East Peace Plans* (New York: St. Martin's Press, 1986), pp. 118–120.

26. Ibid.

27. Richard J. Barnet, *The Alliance* (New York: Simon and Schuster, 1983), p. 170.

28. Ibid., p. 249.

29. Kissinger, *Years of Upheaval*, pp. 708–709.

30. Portugal, which sought to obtain U.S. military aid for its war in Mozambique and Angola, was the only European ally to provide the United States with transit rights. Ibid., pp. 520, 708–709.

31. Ibid., p. 714.

32. Ibid., p. 718.

33. Barnet, *The Alliance*, pp. 326–327.

34. Kissinger, *Years of Upheaval*, p. 723; Barnet, *The Alliance*, p. 333.

35. Since the signing of the Declaration of Principles, the European Union decided to strengthen the Middle East peace process. In December 1994 it canceled its embargo on arms shipments to Syria (the embargo was declared in 1986, after Syria had attempted to blow up an El-Al airliner on its way from London to Israel). Similarly, the European Council endorsed granting Israel special economic status in the EU.

36. Kissinger, *Years of Upheaval*, p. 740.

37. Barnet, *The Alliance*, p. 328.

38. Ole R. Holsti and James N. Rosenau, *American Leadership in World Affairs* (Boston: Allen & Unwin, 1984).

39. Nadav Safran, *Israel: The Embattled Ally* (Cambridge: Belknap Press, 1982), pp. 332–333.

40. Ibid., pp. 577–594.

41. As a strategic asset, Israel supplied to the United States valuable intelligence services and some useful technical advice on weapons remodeling. Duncan L. Clarke, "Entanglement: The Commitment to Israel," in Yehuda Lukacs and Abdalla M. Battah, eds., *The Arab-Israeli Conflict* (Boulder, Colo.: Westview Press), p. 230.

42. Shai Feldman, *U.S. Middle East Policy: The Domestic Setting* (Boulder, Colo.: Westview Press, 1988), p. 59.

43. Andrea Barron, "Jewish and Arab Diasporas in the United States and Their Impact on U.S. Middle East Policy," in Lukacs and Battah, *The Arab-Israeli Conflict*, pp. 239–247.

44. Clarke, "Entanglement: The Commitment to Israel," p. 218.

45. Steven Spiegel, *The Other Arab-Israeli Conflict* (Chicago: University of Chicago Press, 1985), p. 134.

46. At the beginning of 1968, Johnson agreed to sell Israel fifty Phantom fighter-bombers and other equipment. Clarke, "Entanglement: The Commitment to Israel," p. 218.

47. Safran, *Israel*, p. 431.

48. He thus refused an Israeli request, made in January 1970, for the purchase of military equipment to counter new massive Soviet arms shipments to Egypt. Ibid., pp. 436–437.

49. Spiegel, *The Other Arab-Israeli Conflict*, p. 195.

50. Safran, *Israel*, p. 461.

51. Clarke, "Entanglement: The Commitment to Israel," p. 219.

52. Spiegel, *The Other Arab-Israeli Conflict*, pp. 248, 257.

53. Clarke, "Entanglement: The Commitment to Israel," p. 219.

54. Ibid.

55. Ibid., pp. 223–224.

56. Ibid., pp. 226–227.

57. Ibid., pp. 228–229.

58. Deviating from its standard policy, Israel agreed not to retaliate against Iraq.

59. The full statement appears in Yehuda Lukacs, ed., *Documents on the Israeli-Palestinian Conflict, 1967–1983* (Cambridge: Cambridge University Press, 1984), pp. 8–9.

60. Ibid., pp. 13–14.

61. Seth Tillman, *The United States in the Middle East: Interests and Obstacles* (Bloomington: Indiana University Press, 1982), p. 58.

62. Perhaps Carter's most memorable endorsement of Palestinian self-determination appeared in his address to Notre Dame University in May 1977. For the text of that speech see *New York Times*, May 23, 1977, p. 12

64. Zbigniew Brzezinski, *Power and Principle* (New York: Farrar, Straus, Giroux, 1983), p. 102.

64. Jimmy Carter, *Keeping Faith* (Toronto: Bantam, 1982), p. 277.

PART TWO

Beyond Camp David

3

A New Beginning:
The Reagan Initiative

In 1982 Reagan set forth his own Middle East peace initiative. As its introduction coincided with the end of the Lebanon war and the defeat of the PLO, the United States assumed that Israel might accept the plan as a starting position to revive the stagnant Camp David peace process. But because it contained some elements that offended the Israeli Right—even though the plan did not deviate from existing U.S. guarantees to Israel— Prime Minister Begin rejected the Reagan initiative out of hand.

Political Background

On March 27, 1980, Egypt, Israel, and the United States agreed to extend the target date for the completion of the Camp David autonomy talks.

The talks had originally involved only Egypt, Israel, and the United States and had a twelve-month deadline from the May 1979 starting date. But it became clear that the target date was unattainable because of the Egyptians' and Israelis' opposing conceptions of autonomy and because of the differences between the United States and Israel over the issue of settlement activity in the occupied territories.[1] As part of the Camp David agreement, the autonomy talks—to be conducted among representatives of Egypt, Israel, Jordan, and the Palestinian people—were geared to determine the modalities by which a self-governing Palestinian authority would be elected and to define its powers and responsibilities. This Palestinian authority (called the administrative council) was to control civilian matters in the West Bank and Gaza for a five-year transitional period, during which the final status of the West Bank and Gaza would be determined.

Begin's concept of autonomy was shaped by his fervent opposition to the idea of an independent Palestinian state. To safeguard the prevention of the creation of such a state, his initial autonomy plan (December 27, 1977) limited Palestinian self-rule to administrative functions in social and educational affairs. Matters of security and public order remained under Israeli military control. Additionally, Israel insisted on control of water resources and the rights to acquire land and establish Jewish settlements in the West Bank and Gaza.[2] Egypt interpreted Palestinian self-rule to mean full autonomy in the West Bank and Gaza, as a first step toward independence and a transitional stage before full Palestinian self-determination.[3]

Disagreement over the issue of settlement activities derived from the U.S. belief that an increase in Jewish settlements in the West Bank and Gaza would jeopardize any progress in negotiations or destroy the prospect of negotiations altogether. In contrast, the Begin government held that the entire West Bank and Gaza were integral parts of Israel's sovereignty and that a sound Jewish presence should be established in those areas.

In view of these disparities, the negotiating parties agreed to relabel the original date as a "positive incentive" for the conclusion of negotiations and to extend negotiations to April 1982—the time designated in the Egyptian-Israeli peace treaty for Israeli withdrawal from the Sinai. But a series of events made a breakthrough by the new date just as improbable. In the July 1980 Israel passed legislation by which East Jerusalem became part of the "indivisible" capital of Israel. In April-March 1981 the Reagan administration closed a huge arms deal with Saudi Arabia and endorsed a Saudi peace plan Israel rejected. Sadat was assassinated in October 1981; Israel annexed the Golan Heights in December 1981 and invaded Lebanon in June 1982.

The Reagan administration sought to continue the autonomy talks. But the refusal of most Arab states to endorse the Camp David accords raised some difficulties for the new administration, especially since it looked for the cooperation of the moderate Arab states in its attempt to launch a regional defense strategy against Soviet expansionism.

Almost immediately upon entering office, the new administration decided to sell Saudi Arabia five Airborne Warning and Command System (AWACS) aircraft as well as 1,177 advanced Sidewinder air-to-air missiles and six K-135 aerial refueling aircraft and conformal fuel tanks to enhance the range of the sixty F-15 fighters sold to the Saudis in 1978. The deal—totaling $8.5 billion—was by far the largest up to that time.[4]

Not unexpectedly, the decision provoked fierce opposition from Israel and from the Jewish lobby in Washington. In fact, the sale became the most controversial arms deal in U.S. history, requiring the forceful intervention of President Reagan.[5] The controversy also required some reciprocal action from the Saudis. On August 8, 1981, the Saudi government—

while adhering to the Arab League boycott of the Camp David peace process—made public its own peace initiative. The plan, put forward by the Saudi crown-prince Ibn Abdul Aziz Fahd, came to be known as the Fahd proposal.

The Fahd plan implicitly recognized Israel's right to exist, deviating from the three famous nos adopted by the 1967 Khartoum summit—no recognition, no negotiation, no peace. At the same time, however, it contained elements unacceptable to Israel. Nevertheless, amid opposition in the Arab world to the plan's implicit "recognition" of Israel, on January 4, 1982, the Saudis withdrew their proposal. An important factor in the Saudis' decision was the internationally condemned Israeli annexation of the Golan Heights on December 14, 1981.[6]

The annexation of the Golan Heights also damaged U.S.-Israeli relations. While Prime Minister Begin, rebutting criticism, emphasized that no foreign power, including the United States, could dictate to the Israelis how to conduct their affairs, Washington, on December 18 announced its decision to suspend discussions with Israel on the implementation of a strategic cooperation agreement the two countries had signed a month earlier.[7] In the meantime the assassination of Sadat on October 6, 1981, froze the U.S.-Egyptian-Israeli autonomy talks until January 1982. Despite the U.S. administration's vigorous diplomatic steps, no progress in negotiations was made by April 1982.

On April 6, 1982, during a conference of the nonaligned countries held in Kuwait, a new Egyptian Middle East peace plan was made public. The plan had strong similarities to the Saudi proposal but, unlike the latter, it explicitly recognized Israel's right to exist within secure and recognized borders. Still, the Egyptians deliberately excluded from their plan any reference to the Camp David agreements, which Israel regarded as the only legitimate basis for further negotiations.[8]

As a result both Prime Minister Begin and Defense Minister Ariel Sharon declared that on completion of the Israeli withdrawal from Sinai on April 25, Israel would make no more territorial concessions to the Arabs in a quest for peace. And on May 3 Begin announced to the Israeli Knesset that at the end of the five-year transitional period designated under the Camp David accords, Israel would affirm its sovereignty over the West Bank.[9] On June 6 Israel launched its "peace for Galilee" military operation in Lebanon, a deathblow to the already impaired autonomy talks—the only remnant of the negotiation process.

The Reagan Administration's Motivation

On September 2, 1982, two days after PLO chairman Yasir Arafat had fled from Beirut, Reagan announced his new Middle East peace plan. The plan can be seen as evidence of Reagan's anxiety about the Soviet threat in the region (the Soviet invasion of Afghanistan coupled with the Iran-Iraq war) and his broader concerns about the global decline of U.S. power in the 1970s. But it was the Lebanon war and the impact that war had on the peace process that provided the dramatic setting for the Reagan initiative.

Within this context, four factors inspired the plan.[10] First, President Hosni Mubarak and King Hussein, along with other moderate Arab leaders such as King Fahd of Saudi Arabia and King Hassan of Morocco, had been urging the United States to resume leadership in the Arab-Israeli peace process. The Arabs persuaded Washington to demonstrate not only that it disapproved of the Israeli invasion of Lebanon but that it remained serious about the peace process.

Indeed, three years after the Egyptian-Israeli peace treaty was concluded, the Arab side questioned Washington's intent to advance and broaden the peace and to deal with the Palestinian issue. Egypt in particular was anxious to see the Camp David arrangement extended, and it encouraged the United States to do so. King Hussein, too, expressed his support of the accords. This was particularly important in view of his failure to join the Camp David process, which, along with the Palestinians' refusal to join, made the autonomy negotiations fail. The administration believed that if it could persuade King Hussein to take part in the peace process—preferably together with the Palestinians—the United States could force the Begin government to soften its position. Moreover, despite the collapse of the autonomy talks, Washington saw some progress in the negotiations and claimed the Reagan plan provided an opening for a new start under a different guise.

Second, unlike other Arab-Israeli wars, the Lebanon war aroused in many Americans distinct anti-Israeli feelings. Indeed, the Reagan plan was initiated at a moment when the U.S. government was under enormous domestic pressure for its apparent association with Israel in an unpopular act of aggression against Lebanon. It was perceived that unless the United States could quickly regain the image that it was in favor of peace—not just in favor of tacitly opposing the bombing of innocent Lebanese and Palestinian civilians—U.S. relations with the region would be seriously harmed.

Third, the Lebanon war convinced the United States that the lack of a solution to the Palestinian problem was a formula for continued violence and regional instability. Fourth, because the PLO seemed to be badly damaged, there was a sense of a moment of opportunity in which the PLO was not in a position to torpedo negotiations (as it had effectively done in 1978 after Camp David, with regard to the West Bank). Moreover, at the time the plan was initiated, the expectation was that Bashir Jumayyil was about to take office in Lebanon, that a friendly relationship was going to evolve between Lebanon and Israel, and that the PLO was out of the game.

The announcement of the Reagan plan alongside the completion of the forced evacuation of the PLO forces from Beirut was certainly no coincidence. As one observer pointed out, the United States felt the need to present its proposal as close as possible to the time of the PLO's defeat in Lebanon because of fear that members of the Israeli cabinet would downplay the urgency of the Palestinian problem.[11] The losses the PLO suffered, combined with its lack of aid from the Arab world in the war in Lebanon, convinced Washington that the PLO was more inclined to compromise.[12]

Aside from that, the Reagan administration was encouraged by an enduring bureaucratic tendency—usually centered in the Near East Bureau of the State Department—to do something about Arab-Israeli peace because of the assumptions that the conflict could not be contained indefinitely, that it could have regional or even global implications if it continued to escalate, and that diplomatic activity would give moderate forces in the region the reassurance they needed.[13]

Further, the administration expected the Western allies to demand that Washington get involved in the peace process. Washington's ability to orchestrate the election of a pro-Western president in Lebanon, engineer a cease-fire agreement in the Lebanon war, and arrange for the evacuation of PLO forces from Beirut were added encouragements.[14]

Finally, to use Secretary of State George Shultz's own words, the plan was an "opening position," to be followed by "quiet diplomacy to pursue the President's initiative and bring it to fruition."[15] According to Shultz, in view of the events that preceded the announcement of the plan, the administration believed that it had a special responsibility to help bring peace to the area and that no other country had the credibility—and therefore the ability—to provide the crucial link to all sides.[16]

The Reagan Plan

Against this background, on September 1, 1982, Reagan made public his new Middle East peace initiative. Calling for a "fresh start" in the peace process, the president invited "all those directly concerned to get involved—or lend their support—to a workable basis for peace."[17] The bases for the Reagan initiative were Security Council Resolutions 242 and 338 and the Camp David agreement. As a framework for an Arab-Israeli peace, it contained no new principles: It followed the land-for-peace formula and upheld previous U.S. commitments to Israel's security.

But in order to reignite a process that had died down with the breakup of the autonomy talks and gone out completely during the Lebanon war,

Reagan introduced what he regarded as procedural changes, going a little beyond the Camp David accords.[18] He objected to permanent Israeli control over the West Bank and Gaza; called for a freeze on Jewish settlements in these areas and the realization of Security Council Resolution 242 to be applied on all fronts; and declared that while Jerusalem must remain undivided, its final status should be decided through negotiations. Still, in a statement before the Senate Foreign Relations Committee on September 10, 1982, Shultz reaffirmed the administration's opposition to the dismantlement of existing settlements.[19]

Calling upon Israel to negotiate with Jordan and the Palestinians, in line with the Camp David autonomy talks, the plan shifted the role of representation of the Palestinians from Egypt to Jordan, a shift that was acceptable to Israel.[20] But the issue of Palestinian representation was a major obstacle. The key question regarding Palestinian representation in peace talks is threefold: Who in the Palestinian camp has the authority to negotiate? Who in the Palestinian camp would both Israel and the mediator (i.e., the United States) accept as a party to negotiation? And who in the Palestinian camp has the power to carry through a negotiated agreement?

Throughout the 1980s, for the Arabs in general and the Palestinians in particular, no legitimate Palestinian representative other than the PLO existed. Indeed, as Herbert Kelman pointed out, the PLO's function was no different from the function of any legitimate government of a sovereign state. For the Palestinians in the territories as well as those in the diaspora, the PLO was certainly not just an organization but the symbol and embodiment of Palestinian nationhood. This was true even for those Palestinians who were less enthusiastic than others about the PLO leadership.[21]

But Israel refused to talk with the PLO or any Palestinian representative connected, however loosely, to it, calling it a terrorist organization whose true aim was the destruction of Israel, an organization incapable of any meaningful transformation. But this conviction did not rule out negotiations with Palestinian Arabs not linked to the PLO. In any Arab-Israeli peace talks, Israel favored the inclusion of a Palestinian representation within a Jordanian delegation, in accordance with the Camp David agreements.

As for the United States, it refused to recognize the PLO as a legitimate party for negotiation until the organization accepted Israel's right to exist and renounced terrorism. The concept of U.S. recognition of the PLO in return for the PLO's recognition of Israel goes back to 1975; as part of Kissinger's interim agreements, the United States promised Israel that Washington would not recognize the PLO or negotiate with it until the organization recognized Israel and accepted Security Council Resolutions

242 and 338.[22] Yet the Reagan plan confirmed that the Palestinian question was more than a question of refugees. Nevertheless, the plan kept the realization of Palestinians' rights within the framework of the Camp David accords, thereby rejecting the idea of the creation of an independent Palestinian state and instead endorsing the principle of full autonomy under some form of Jordanian administration—preferably a federation.

Accordingly, the Palestinian inhabitants of the West Bank and Gaza, including East Jerusalem, were to be granted full autonomy over their own affairs over a five-year transitional period, beginning with free elections for a self-governing authority in association with Jordan. The purpose of the transitional period was to ensure a peaceful and orderly transfer of authority from Israeli hands to the hands of the Palestinian inhabitants of the West Bank and Gaza, providing that it would not interfere with Israel's security needs. Within the Arab world reaction to the Reagan plan was unusually optimistic. Although most of the Arab states did acknowledge some of the plan's positive aspects, the lack of Arab consensus prevented any Arab state from endorsing the plan outright.

Israeli Reaction

The Likud government reacted to the Reagan initiative with apprehension and outrage, not only because the Reagan administration did not consult with Begin prior to the announcement of the plan but also because the plan challenged Begin's commitment to the permanent control of the West Bank—including East Jerusalem—and Gaza.[23] In an emergency session of September 2, the Israeli government unanimously rejected the Reagan proposal on the grounds that it seriously deviated from the Camp David agreement. The most sensitive points for the Begin government were Reagan's call to apply Resolution 242 on all fronts and to decide the final status of Jerusalem through negotiations.

Begin, like many other Likud members, believed Resolution 242 (and 338, for that matter) did not exist in an abstract way but was relevant only within the context of the Camp David agreements. He feared that any deviation from Camp David would permit reinterpretation of the resolutions. With the introduction of a plan based on these resolutions yet involving a number of changes, Begin was convinced that his fears were realized in the most sinister terms.[24]

As for East Jerusalem, afraid that any reference to the city could eventually lead to its repartition, the Israeli cabinet claimed that Jerusalem was not mentioned in the Camp David agreements but that Begin had declared its status in a letter to President Carter, stating, "Jerusalem is one city indivisible, the capital of Israel."[25] The government also strongly objected to the participation of Arabs from East Jerusalem in the elections for the autonomy council of Judea, Samaria, and Gaza, insisting that there was no mention in the Camp David agreements of such voting rights. Such rights, according to a formal cabinet statement, meant placing Jerusalem under two separate authorities, the State of Israel and the administrative council of the autonomy. This was unacceptable.

Reagan's call for the total freeze on the establishment of Jewish settlements in the West Bank and Gaza was equally disturbing to Begin. On this issue the cabinet argued once again that there was no mention of such a freeze in the Camp David accords. Rather, at Camp David the prime minister agreed that although no new settlements would be established, inhabitants would be added to the existing settlements during the three-month negotiation period for the signing of the Egyptian-Israeli peace treaty. This commitment had been fully met, as the period had ended on December 7, 1978. Moreover, the government claimed, in addition to Israel's national security concerns, settlement in Judea, Samaria, and Gaza was a legitimate Jewish right.

As the Reagan plan was made public, the Israeli government and its hawkish supporters in the Knesset used the occasion to justify and bolster settlement activity in the occupied territories. It was no accident that at the inauguration ceremony of Ma'ale Adumim, a new settlement near Jerusalem, Deputy Prime Minister David Levy vowed to continue to resettle Judea and Samaria and never to allow the creation of a Palestinian state there. Deputy Foreign Minister Yehuda Ben-Meir added that the inauguration of Ma'ale Adumim was the answer "not only to the [Reagan] message, but the best proof to the world that no force and no one will be able to uproot us from our homeland."[26] On September 5, 1982, a ministerial committee approved the establishment of five new settlements in Judea and Samaria and one settlement in Gaza for the Yamit evacuees (Yamit was one of the Sinai settlements demolished with the return of the Sinai to Egypt). The cabinet further decided to continue a vigorous program of Jewish settlement in the territories—the first move in what became a clear pattern of action following every new peace initiative.

Other sensitive issues included the control of local security in the territories; the definition of autonomy; ties with Jordan; Israeli sovereignty over Judea, Samaria, and Gaza; and the notion of a Palestinian state. On Palestinian participation in domestic security, the cabinet claimed that the Camp David accords did not include any distinction between domestic and external security, and it argued that if domestic security did not remain in the hands of the Israelis, the PLO would cause continual bloodshed among Jews and Arabs alike. On the issue of autonomy, the government cited its Camp David arguments: It opposed granting the

Palestinians territorial autonomy because it believed autonomy did not concern territory but inhabitants only. On ties with Jordan, the cabinet insisted that no mention of the economic, commercial, and social and cultural links that Reagan called for was made in the Camp David agreements. On sovereignty, the government maintained that nothing in the Camp David agreements prevented the application of Israeli sovereignty over Judea, Samaria, and Gaza at the end of the transitional period.

On a Palestinian state, the government asserted that despite U.S. objection to the creation of a Palestinian state in Judea, Samaria, and Gaza, the implementation of the Reagan plan could help the PLO to establish a state in these territories and create a united front with Jordan. This concern was repeated in a strongly worded letter from Begin to Reagan in which the Israeli prime minister warned that the Reagan proposal would lead to a Palestinian state and a Soviet base in the heart of the Middle East, endangering Israel's very existence.

In the Knesset debate, the prime minister revealed his deep resentment of outside influence, especially on the issue of peace and security:

> I state that they [the Americans] will have to permit it [the Reagan plan] to drop out of sight, vanish. Nobody will negotiate it. They made one mistake when they thought they could formulate a "plan" and submit it to Israel and that we would then conduct negotiations on it. ... This the United States must realize: With all its power, it does not lay down the rules. It will not dictate to us whether the border will be the Jordan River or the Qishon. ... They can now shuttle between Riyadh and Amman—we will not budge from our position.[27]

He accused the United States of "gross intervention in Israel's domestic affairs," reminding Washington that "Israel is not Chile and I am not Allende."[28]

Defense Minister Sharon said the U.S. proposal constituted a threat to Israel's existence and accused Washington not only of attempting to drive a wedge between U.S. Jewry and Israel but also of trying to create a rift within the Israeli government.[29]

Statements by Foreign Minister Yitzhak Shamir added to Israel's anti-U.S. campaign. In an interview with the German *Badisches Tagblatt*, Shamir said he no longer viewed the United States as an honest mediator, nor did he regard the United States as a representative of Israel's interest. Counting Israel among those countries forsaken by their U.S. ally, Shamir later accused Washington of abandoning Israel "while showing maximum consideration for the Arabs," adding that the U.S. stance toward Israel had become uncertain and that he "would not want to enter the club of Korea, Taiwan, South Africa or Vietnam."[30] In another interview, asked whether it would not have been preferable to reject only the negative clauses of the plan, the foreign minister answered that even though some points in the plan might seem agreeable, the government had to respond in a drastic way because the plan's principles were dangerous to Israel's security.[31] Many of the right-wing Knesset members echoed similar sentiments, accusing Washington of violating the Camp David accords and calling for the application of Israeli law to the territories.

On the opposite side of the political spectrum—the reaction to the Reagan plan symbolized the internal dispute between the Likud and the Labor Alignment—Labor approved the Reagan plan. In fact, a number of Labor MKs identified similarities between the Reagan initiative and the Allon plan. Although not an official plan for the West Bank, the Allon plan, formulated in July 1967, represented the Labor government's idea of defensible borders. The central principle of that plan was the preservation of both the Jewish and democratic characters of the state, promoting a limit on Israel's territorial jurisdiction and a reduction in the number of Palestinian Arabs under Israeli control.

Believing that settlements in the Jordan Rift Valley and the border areas were essential for Israel's security, Labor leader Shimon Peres was at odds with Reagan's call for a total freeze on Israeli settlement in the occupied territories.[32] But few others in the party objected either to a total freeze on settlements or to the inclusion of East Jerusalem Arabs in the elections for an autonomy council—neither of which was part of the Camp David autonomy plan. Viewing the plan as an opportunity to resolve the Arab-Israeli conflict, the Labor Alignment condemned the cabinet's outright rejection of the Reagan plan.

For his part, Begin used the Likud-Labor disagreement over the Reagan plan as an opportunity to delegitimate Labor. In his concluding address to the Knesset during its session on the Reagan plan, Begin, in his familiar theatrical style, asked,

> Why is it that since September 1, since bits and pieces of information on the new U.S. administration report were leaked, has there been glee in the Alignment, frenzy in the opposition's domain? ... Apparently they ought to have been worried. ... Why? Because ... there will be participation of the Palestinian inhabitants of East Jerusalem in the elections to the authority of Judea, Samaria and Gaza. ... This is the division of Israel. ... Is this good timing? Should it lead to joy or even to rejoicing in your adversary's fall?[33]

He answered, "I assume that all the Alignment members, being patriotic and lovers of Zion and Jerusalem like myself—not more or less—think this is not a good suggestion, a negative one, one that should be fought against and opposed and removed from the agenda."[34]

Begin accused Labor of betraying the security of the state of Israel and orchestrating his downfall. Proposing early elections and cultivating the notion of disparity between the two political camps over the future of Eretz Yisrael (the land stretching from the Mediterranean to the Jordan River, also referred to as Greater Israel), Begin warned the Israeli public against the political realism of his adversaries. The Knesset, at least, was convinced: Begin won parliamentary approval for his tough stand on limited autonomy for the Palestinians and his commitment not to surrender control over the West Bank and Gaza.[35]

■ ■ ■

Although the Reagan initiative was both timely and feasible as a starting point to revitalize a stagnant peace process, Prime Minister Begin dismissed the plan in its entirety. He did so to secure Israel's hold over the West Bank and Gaza—areas of great ideological and religious value to the Israeli Right.

Notes

1. The terms *occupied land, occupied territories,* the *West Bank* and *Gaza* (or simply *the territories*) often denote international usage; the names *Judea, Samaria,* and *the Gaza district* (or simply *Gaza*) denote Israeli usage. I use all these terms interchangeably.

2. Seth Tillman, *The United States in the Middle East: Interests and Obstacles* (Bloomington: Indiana University Press, 1982), p. 34.

3. Ibid.

4. Andrew J. Pierre, "Arms Sales: The New Diplomacy," *Foreign Affairs* 60, 2 (1981–1982): 278.

5. Steven Spiegel, *The Other Arab-Israeli Conflict* (Chicago: University of Chicago Press, 1985), pp. 398–411.

6. *Keesing's Contemporary Archives* 29 (1983): 31911–31912.

7. Ibid., p. 31913.

8. Ibid., pp. 31911–31912.

9. Ibid., p. 31911.

10. I base my conclusions on Mordechai Gazit, "The Middle East Peace Process," in Colin Legum, Haim Shaked and Daniel Dishon, eds., *Middle East Contemporary Survey,* vol. 7: 1982–1983 (New York: Holmes and Meier, 1985), p. 156; William Quandt, ed., "U.S. Policy Toward the Arab-Israeli Conflict," in William Quandt, ed., *The Middle East Ten Years After Camp David* (Washington, D.C.: Brookings Institution, 1988), p. 382; George Shultz, *Turmoil and Triumph* (New York: Charles Scribner's Sons, 1993), ch. 6; and on information received during private conversations with Ambassador Samuel W. Lewis, Washington, D.C., April 26, 1991; and with former assistant secretary for Near Eastern and African affairs Richard Murphy, New York, April 9, 1991.

42 *A New Beginning*

11. Gazit, "The Middle East Peace Process," p. 156.

12. Ibid. For additional reasons for the plan's announcement, see William Quandt, "American Proposals for Arab-Israeli Peace," in Willard Belling, ed., *Middle East Peace Plans* (New York: St. Martin's Press, 1986), p. 70.

13. Quandt, "U.S. Policy Toward the Arab-Israeli Conflict."

14. Ibid.

15. Statement by Secretary of State George P. Shultz before the Senate Foreign Relations Committee, September 10, 1982, U.S. Department of State *Bulletin* (Washington, D.C.: October 1982), pp. 5–7.

16. Ibid.

17. *New York Times*, September 2, 1982, p. 11.

18. This conclusion is based in part on a conversation with Ambassador Lewis, Washington, D.C., April 26, 1991.

19. Statement by Secretary of State George P. Shultz before the Senate Foreign Relations Committee, September 10, 1982. pp. 5–7.

20. Herman Fredrick Eilts, "The United States and Egypt," in Quandt, *The Middle East*, p. 120.

21. Herbert C. Kelman, "Creating the Conditions for Israeli-Palestinian Negotiations," *Journal of Conflict Resolution* 26, 1 (1982): 39–79.

22. "Memorandum of Agreement Between the Governments of Israel and the United States, September 1975," in Yehuda Lukacs, ed., *Documents on the Israeli-Palestinian Conflict, 1967–1983* (Cambridge: Cambridge University Press, 1984), pp. 23–24.

23. I drew these conclusions in part from information gathered during private conversations with former assistant secretary of state for Near Eastern and African affairs, Richard Murphy, New York, April 9, 1991; and with I. William Zartman, director of African studies and conflict management programs, Paul Nitze School of Advanced International Studies, Johns Hopkins University, New York, March 27, 1991.

24. Private conversation with the former health minister and current mayor of Jerusalem, Ehud Olmert, Jerusalem, June 28, 1991.

25. For the text of the letter, see Appendix C in Quandt, *The Middle East*, pp. 458–459.

26. Jerusalem Domestic Service, September 9, 1982 (Hebrew). For the English translation, see *Foreign Broadcast Information Service/Daily Report: Middle East and Africa, (FBIS/DR)* (Washington, D.C.: U.S. Department of Commerce/Technical Information Service), September 2, 1982, pp. 11–12.

27. Jerusalem Domestic Service, September 10, 1980 (Hebrew). Translated in *FBIS/DR*, September 10, 1982.

28. Ibid.

29. Interview with Israeli TV, September 22, 1982. Translated in *FBIS/DR*, September 22, 1982, p. 27.

30. Translated in *FBIS/DR*, September 9, 1982, p. 6.

31. *Ha'aretz* (international ed.), September 17, 1982.

32. Still, Peres firmly believed that Israel should have accepted the plan. Private conversation with Shimon Peres, Tel Aviv, July 3, 1991.

33. Jerusalem Domestic Service, September 8, 1982 (Hebrew). For the English translation, see *FBIS/DR*, September 9, 1982, p. 26.

34. Ibid.

35. *New York Times*, October 20, 1982, p. 8.

4

The First Alternative:
Secretary Shultz's Initiative

From the time the Begin government rejected the Reagan plan until December 1987—when the Palestinian *intifada* erupted in the West Bank and Gaza—a number of events created a political atmosphere that stimulated renewed diplomatic involvement in the region. In spring 1988 prevailing global and regional conditions prompted the United States to revive the Reagan plan, Secretary of State George Shultz calling for an international peace conference on the Middle East. By the time Shultz's idea became official U.S. policy, the United States and the Soviet Union had already improved their relations and decided to cooperate on seeking peace in the Middle East; Egypt and Morocco had become increasingly active promoting peace in the Arab world; Jordan was willing to hold direct and open discussions with Israel under the umbrella of an international conference; Foreign Minister Peres of Israel endorsed the idea as a first step toward direct talks between Israel and a Jordanian-Palestinian delegation; and PLO chairman Arafat had implicitly accepted a two-state solution and a confederation with Jordan. But in Israel the struggle between those who supported the conference and those who repudiated the idea nearly toppled the National Unity government. In the end, a powerful right-wing axis managed to foil the plan for fear that an international conference was but an instrument to push Israel back to its 1967 borders.

Political Background:
From the Reagan Plan to the *Intifada*

Between October 1982 and April 1983, King Hussein and Arafat held a series of talks in order to arrive at a consolidated position on the Reagan plan. On April 2–4, 1983, they agreed on a negotiating position based on a compromise between the Reagan plan and the Fez plan, formulated by the Arab League in September 1982.[1] Hussein and Arafat decided to establish a joint Jordanian-Palestinian delegation to negotiate with Egypt, Israel, and the United States on Palestinian self-rule as outlined in the Reagan plan. The Palestinian part of the delegation was to include non-PLO-affiliated Palestinians approved by the PLO.[2]

But the more militant factions of the PLO rejected the Palestinian-Jordanian federation idea on the grounds that it dissented from the PLO's commitment to a fully independent Palestinian state and reflected Washington's pro-Israel Middle East policy. Arafat backed away from his agreement with Hussein at the last minute, and the king terminated negotiations with the PLO chairman.

Reagan took steps to demonstrate his continued commitment to his plan: (1) He immediately announced his disappointment at the "impediment" in the search for Middle East peace caused by Hussein's decision but added that he remained "very hopeful" that progress could still be made in the search for Arab-Israeli peace; (2) he revealed that he had consulted King Hussein and King Fahd and that they had agreed not to abandon the peace efforts; (3) he confirmed that other moderate Arab leaders, including King Hassan and President Mubarak, encouraged him to preserve his position; (4) he called upon the Palestinian leadership to make a "bold and courageous move" to break the deadlock; and (5) he declared that he would not abandon his initiative despite the setback.[3]

But soon after, the Reagan administration formulated a new Middle East strategy, seeking closer ties with Israel and Jordan and stronger links between Israel and Jordan. This was part of a broader concept according to which the moderate countries would join in an Arab coalition against Syria and Iran and move toward accepting UN resolutions that acknowledged the existence of Israel. Because King Hussein was more vulnerable than Israel to Syrian threats, the new strategy banked on his consent more than on Israel's. Thus the administration promised Jordan it would urge Israel to freeze settlements in the West Bank. It also tried to convince Hussein that once he came to the negotiating table, pressure for compromise would develop within Israel.[4]

Between February 1984 and April 1985, following Arafat's expulsion from Lebanon, King Hussein and the PLO chairman held another round of talks, still attempting to form a joint approach to negotiations. But in mid-March 1984 Hussein rejected the Reagan plan altogether. Perhaps Hussein's disenchantment with the United States' Middle East policy was in part the result of a disclosure that for a period of nine months the Reagan administration had conducted secret talks with the PLO, despite its announced policy of nonrecognition. The purpose of the talks was to persuade the PLO to recognize Israel in return for U.S. recognition of the organization.

Still, at the end of November 1984, the seventeenth Palestine National Council session convened in Amman.[5] The choice of the session's location was significant: It symbolized Arafat's willingness to join Hussein in a future diplomatic drive and to defeat the veto power of dissenting PLO factions.[6] Indeed, on February 11, 1985, the Jordanian government disclosed that Hussein and Arafat had reached an agreement on a framework for a joint peace initiative, the so-called Amman accord. The initiative was based on the land-for-peace principle formulated by United Nations resolutions and on the establishment of a confederal affiliation between Jordan and an autonomous Palestinian entity.

The agreement gave the United States an incentive to rejuvenate the peace process, especially since Secretary of State Shultz believed that it indicated a change in Hussein's position after his rejection of the Reagan plan.[7] In Vienna on February 19, 1985, the United States and the Soviet Union held exploratory talks on the Middle East. Far more important for their symbolism than for their substance, the talks appeared to be the first attempt by the superpowers to find common ground on the Arab-Israeli conflict since their joint October 1977 statement on the Middle East.

On February 24 President Mubarak offered to host a preliminary meeting between the United States and a Jordanian-Palestinian delegation so they could lay the groundwork for direct peace talks between Israel and that delegation. On April 10 Hussein and Arafat approved Mubarak's idea. Encouraged, the Reagan administration began a fresh diplomatic endeavor in the Middle East. On April 14 it dispatched Richard Murphy to the area for a two-week tour to discuss the possibility of talks between the United States and a Jordanian-Palestinian delegation. This was followed by discussions between President Reagan and King Hassan of Morocco on the various proposals for bringing the Palestinians into future Middle East peace talks. It seemed as if the Reagan plan—modified by the Hussein-Arafat agreement and Mubarak's ideas—had come to life. But Murphy could not secure an agreement for direct talks between Israel and Jordan or a PLO endorsement of the U.S. approach. Still, the United States continued its efforts to encourage the parties to negotiate. On May 10–13 Shultz visited Israel, Jordan, and Egypt to discuss an acceptable Palestinian component of the joint delegation. The United States was reportedly ready to accept members of the PNC as part of the delegation, provided that they were not declared members of the PLO.

On May 29–31, during talks with Reagan in Washington, King Hussein for the first time indicated his willingness to hold direct talks with Israel. He proposed a four-stage process by which the PLO would recognize Israel's right to exist in return for U.S. recognition of the Palestinians' right to self-determination. This was to be followed by preparatory talks between a joint Jordanian-PLO delegation and U.S. officials, leading to an international conference that was to pave the way for direct talks between Israel and the Jordanian-PLO delegation.[8]

Although Hussein's proposal was praised in Washington, the Israeli government initially rejected the conference idea as a device to evade direct negotiations.[9] But the prime minister of Israel's National Unity government, Shimon Peres, later endorsed it as an initial step toward direct Israeli-Jordanian talks.

In a speech to the Knesset on June 10, Peres called for direct negotiations with Jordan within the framework of a five-stage timetable, according to which (1) U.S., Egyptian, Jordanian, and non-PLO officials would meet informally in Washington; (2) a joint Jordanian-Palestinian-Israeli preparatory committee would be established; (3) the five permanent members of the Security Council would confirm their support for direct negotiations; (4) "authentic" Palestinian representatives from the occupied territories who would represent the inhabitants and who would be acceptable to all sides would be nominated; (5) an international peace conference, which would include direct talks between Israel and a Jordanian delegation containing Palestinian representatives and Jordanian officials, would be convened within three months.[10]

Despite some unresolved problems (which included the issues of the joint delegation, PLO recognition of Israel, and linkage between the steps Hussein endorsed and direct negotiations),[11] the State Department approved the Peres proposal. In mid-July the PLO submitted to Jordan a list of twenty-two candidates for the Palestinian component of the joint delegation. The Jordanian government submitted to the United States the names of seven of the proposed delegates. The United States in turn passed on the list to the Israeli government, which at first rejected all of the names but subsequently accepted two candidates: Hanna Seniora, the editor in chief of the Palestinian paper *Al Fajr*, and Faez Abu Rahme, chairman of the Gaza Chamber of Advocates. Meanwhile, in a much-publicized interview with *Der Spiegel*, Arafat reaffirmed his support for the confederation idea and implicitly accepted UN Resolution 181 of 1947, which endorsed a two-state solution.[12]

Determined to generate progress, the United States tried to break the impasse over Palestinian representation. In reply to the Israeli rejection of the Jordanian list, the administration insisted that Israel could not veto U.S. talks with a joint Jordanian-Palestinian delegations. In addition, prior to the opening of the August 1985 Arab summit in Casablanca, Washington urged the Arab leaders to endorse Hussein's plan and later dispatched Murphy back to the Middle East.

On September 14 King Hussein met in Cairo with President Mubarak to discuss ways to renew the peace process. Reagan and Mubarak met on September 23 in Washington. A few days later, in a speech before the UN General Assembly, the king invited Israel to negotiate under the auspices of an international conference to be sponsored by the UN Secretary General.[13]

Between the end of September and mid-October, President Reagan met with King Hussein and Prime Minister Peres in Washington. To accommodate Hussein, the Israeli leader announced before the UN General Assembly his readiness to negotiate with Jordanian officials without preconditions and to make territorial compromises. Peres also publicly endorsed Hussein's approach to peace and called for negotiations with a Jordanian-Palestinian delegation within the framework of an international conference under the auspices of the Security Council.[14]

Soon after, reports circulated in Israel, Western Europe, and the United States that Peres and Hussein had held secret talks in which the Israeli prime minister had urged the king to agree to direct negotiations on the basis of territorial compromise. On October 29 *Ha'aretz* reported that Hussein and the Israeli government had drawn up a secret plan for an Israeli-Jordanian condominium arrangement for the West Bank, pending a final settlement. According to the report, the plan—apparently approved by the United States—provided for Palestinian autonomy and for joint Israeli-Jordanian military patrols in the Jordan Valley to prevent guerrilla infiltration, leaving the responsibility for internal security in the West Bank in the hands of the Israeli Defense Forces (IDF).[15]

This was followed by an agreement between Hussein and Arafat to establish a permanent joint Jordanian-Palestinian committee to coordinate their peace efforts and by Arafat's Cairo Declaration, in which the PLO chairman denounced all forms of terrorism outside of territories occupied by Israel.[16] The Cairo Declaration was intended to reassure Hussein after the internationally condemned *Achille Lauro* episode. The incident occurred on October 7, 1985, when four Palestinian terrorists hijacked the Italian cruise ship *Achille Lauro* in the Mediterranean. They demanded the release of fifty Palestinians from Israeli jails and murdered a handicapped American tourist.

King Hussein invited the PLO leader to renounce all violence and publicly to accept Resolutions 242 and 338. But Arafat was unable to do so because the Fatah central committee and the PLO executive committee continued to reject the resolutions as a basis for a settlement.[17] Consequently, on February 19, 1986, Hussein announced that Jordan was "unable to continue to co-ordinate politically with the PLO leadership until their words become bonds, characterized by commitment, credibility and consistency."[18]

The failure of Hussein and Arafat to agree on a coordinated strategy in the peace process did not stop Washington's attempts to mediate between the parties. Immediately after King Hussein delivered his famous speech, Washington again dispatched diplomat Richard Murphy to the region to discuss the need for direct Israeli-Jordanian-Palestinian talks and the makeup of a Palestinian delegation to such talks.

In late July 1986, Vice President Bush arrived in the Middle East for talks with regional leaders, including West Bank Palestinians, and King Hassan of Morocco. This trip came after the Moroccan king had held a much-publicized meeting with Prime Minister Peres, a meeting described as bold and historic, though it failed to produce any real results.[19]

Peres and Mubarak met with Reagan in fall 1986 in Washington, pressing the administration to accept the international conference idea. With the exception of Israel, by mid-1987 all the major parties involved in the Arab-Israeli conflict endorsed the idea. The only disagreement centered on the question of the authority the conference should have over the parties. For example, the PLO, which reserved for itself a major role in the deliberations, favored a conference with full powers to impose a solution on the parties. Many Arab states supported this view, but the United States and some other Western powers strongly opposed it.

Yet the conference idea seemed to ripen as Arafat dropped his insistence on direct PLO representation.[20] On April 11, 1987, a secret meeting between Hussein and Peres in London produced a document of understanding. Subject to the approval of the governments of Israel and Jordan and the blessing of the United States, the document constituted a procedural agreement on direct Israeli-Jordanian negotiations under the auspices of an international conference, with the participation of all the parties involved, including Palestinian representation as part of a Jordanian-Palestinian delegation and the five permanent members of the Security Council.[21] On April 23, while briefing the Knesset Foreign Affairs and Defense Committee, Peres clarified his ideas of a conference: All sides, including the two superpowers, agreed that the conference would not have the power to force any decision on the parties; that after the opening, negotiations would be held in the framework of bilateral committees; and that the PLO would not be included in the Palestinian representation to the conference. Foreign Minister Shamir's office asked for further clarifications on a number of points, including questions such as whether the conference would be an opening only, what the Soviets' role would be, and whether there were any inclinations to include the PLO.

By May Washington agreed that if a conference were convened and Israel decided to withdraw from it because the conditions for its convocation had not been met, the United States would do the same. Syria was apparently also ready to participate in a conference under terms that would be acceptable to both Jordan and the United States. And in the meantime Jordan and the Soviet Union had reached a detailed understanding on the idea of an international conference.[22]

On May 21 U.S. ambassador to Israel Thomas Pickering announced that Jordan, Egypt, and the United States had reached an agreement on the framework of the conference: The conference would not have the power to impose a solution on the parties involved nor to veto agreements reached bilaterally. There would be face to face negotiations in which Palestinian representatives would participate as part of a Jordanian-Palestinian delegation. Participants in the conference were expected to endorse UN Resolutions 242 and 338 and to renounce terrorism.[23]

Meanwhile, in the United States Peres held unofficial talks with the Soviet ambassador to the United Nations, Uri Dubinin, regarding Soviet participation in the conference. In June Peres held talks with West European leaders, and in July he met in Geneva with President Mubarak, UN Secretary General Javier Perez de Cuéllar, and U.S. negotiator Richard Murphy. Further discussion on the international conference took place between the Egyptian foreign minister, Ahmed Esmat Abdel Meguid, and Prime Minister Margaret Thatcher of Britain and between Thatcher and King Hussein. In addition, PLO officials held talks with the Egyptian foreign minister and with the Jordanian prime minister.[24]

By July 1987, then, most barriers to holding the conference were removed, and in mid-October Shultz advanced the idea in a new peace proposal. Stressing that improved U.S.-Soviet relations presented new opportunities for Middle East negotiations—and proposing marginal Soviet participation in the conference— Shultz suggested that the next phase of negotiations would focus on interim arrangements. Careful not to mention the PLO by name, Shultz insisted that the Palestinians take part in the international conference, but he conditioned such participation on Palestinian consent to end terrorism and on Palestinian recognition of Israel.

Initially, Shamir, who had replaced Peres as prime minister in October 1986 (Peres became Israel's foreign minister), decided neither to accept nor reject Shultz's initiative until he learned whether Jordan and the Soviet Union had accepted the proposal. It was soon disclosed, however, that Shamir agreed to the conference as long as it took place after a peace agreement between the warring parties had already been achieved, so as to allow international support for such an agreement. He also accepted the limited involvement of the two superpowers.

But the international conference never materialized. Pressed by strong opposition not only from the Tehiya party and Gush Emunim, but also within his own party, Shamir effectively undermined the idea. For its part, with little more than a year left in its first term in office and with heated debate going on in Israel, the Reagan administration did not feel pressed to continue the peace process.

On the Arab side, King Hussein decided to reject the conference idea because of skepticism about Shamir's intentions, and no other Arab leaders insisted on sustaining the peace process. Indeed, an emergency Arab League summit on November 8–11 in Amman gave low priority to the Arab-Israeli conflict altogether. Instead, discussions centered on threats posed to the Arab world by Iran and the Islamic revolution there. This was the first time since the creation of the Arab League in 1944 that the primary focus of such a meeting was not the Arab-Israeli conflict or the plight of the Palestinians.

Such disregard convinced the Palestinians that neither the Arab countries nor the PLO leadership would solve the Palestinian problem. With no prospect for movement in the peace process, the Palestinians of the West Bank and Gaza launched a violent popular uprising known as the *intifada*. The *intifada* began in the Gaza Strip on December 9, 1987, ignited by the deaths of four Palestinians the day before in a crash involving a car driven by an Israeli. Earlier incidents had already provoked Palestinian frustration.

The Reagan Administration's Motivation[25]

The Shultz initiative was driven by developments that had occurred in the region between the Reagan initiative and the *intifada*. Events such as the Palestine National Council meeting in Amman in November 1984, Hussein's and Arafat's agreement, Prime Minister Peres's reiteration that he would not place any preconditions on Jordan's entry to the peace process, and President Mubarak's efforts to revitalize the peace process were indeed promising.[26] Moreover, the Shultz proposal was launched at a time when leaders of the countries involved in the conflict encouraged the United States to become more engaged in the peace process and showed "a clear willingness to consider new ideas and to look afresh at old ones." The mood surrounding discussions in the region was certainly "one of seriousness and of an honest desire to find a way to move forward."[27]

Peres's becoming prime minister added to the optimistic mood in Washington, inspiring the United States to begin a period of close consultations with Peres about tactics in the peace process.[28]

Yet the Reagan administration was initially opposed to an international conference involving the Soviet Union out of fear that the Soviets would reenter the Middle East peace process after having been effectively removed from it by Kissinger and Carter. But it was not long before

Washington agreed that an international conference was one way of getting to direct negotiations.[29]

Moreover, in 1987 the United States entertained the idea that the summit between Reagan and Mikhail Gorbachev—planned for the end of the year—might be used as a preliminary step in negotiations involving other parties to the Middle East peace process.[30] In this regard, Shultz believed that the "atmosphere of genuine change in Moscow" was amenable to an international conference.[31] He had great faith in bilateral talks on issues critical to national survival, and he might have accepted the view (shared by former foreign minister Abba Eban) that direct negotiations could best be accomplished with mediation.[32]

Since the Gorbachev-Reagan summit did not bring together the Arab and Israeli parties, Shultz saw in the *intifada* another opportunity to begin direct negotiations. The *intifada* created uncertainties and self-doubt in Israel; it also revived questions about the future of Israeli-Palestinian relationships with a sense of urgency that had not existed for years. On top of this, Shultz was encouraged by Shamir, who was anxious to engage the United States in the peace process, and he was persuaded by Mubarak, Peres, and King Hussein to increase U.S. diplomatic pressure in the area. Thus, having exhausted all other options, the United States by the end of 1987 believed that the international conference was the only workable idea and the only framework acceptable to the Arab side. Indeed, it is quite certain that had it not been for the *intifada* and the encouragement he received from local leaders, Shultz would not have rushed into a new initiative, even though the technicalities of the conference had already been worked out in the London document.[33]

The Shultz Initiative, March 4, 1988

Unlike the Reagan plan, the Shultz initiative came after a period of quiet diplomacy carried out by Richard Murphy and Philip Habib. Among the options for the renewal of the peace process that Shultz and other State Department officials discussed with Egyptian, Jordanian, and Israeli leaders prior to Shultz's initiative were the extension of the Camp David accords, the international conference idea, and interim autonomy for the Palestinians. Of these the administration favored the autonomy principle, with a central role allotted to King Hussein.[34]

The plan was basically a perfected version of Shultz's October 1987 initiative—one more in line with the autonomy plan of the Camp David accords. But to avoid outright Arab opposition to his new proposal, Shultz declined to associate his plan with the Camp David accords and refrained from using the term autonomy. Instead, he referred to a "transitional period" in which the parties could adjust to the conditions created under the negotiated agreement.[35]

Based on Resolutions 242 and 338, the plan called for a three-stage timetable, beginning with an international conference in mid-April 1988. The conference was meant to ease the entry of the parties into direct negotiations and was to involve the five permanent members of the Security Council and the parties directly involved in the conflict, including a Jordanian-Palestinian delegation.[36]

On May 1, 1988, the second stage was to open negotiations between Israel and each of its neighbors, including the Jordanian-Palestinian delegation. The purpose of these negotiations was to frame a three-year interim arrangement for the West Bank and Gaza, to be followed—beginning December 1—by direct negotiations to reach a permanent settlement.

The United States depicted the plan as fair and reasonable, realistic and workable, balanced to address the fundamental concerns of all parties, and able to lead quickly to negotiations. It specifically excluded the kind of authoritative international conference that would threaten the parties' participation; instead, it was a carefully structured conference that had a limited role. Although it was not intended to replace direct negotiations, the international conference provided, according to the United States, the only channel for direct talks between Arabs and Israelis.[37]

The reaction in the Arab world was once again a mixture of guarded optimism and criticism. King Hussein expressed doubt about the United States' ability to win Israeli compliance, but he stopped short of rejecting the initiative. After initially accepting the plan, the Jordanian government was unwilling to press the PLO on the issue of a joint Jordanian-Palestinian delegation. Instead, the Jordanians, including King Hussein, advocated direct participation of the PLO in the international conference.[38]

Arafat, who instructed Palestinian leaders from the occupied territories to boycott a mutual meeting planned by Shultz, rejected the plan on the grounds that it did not address the most fundamental concerns of the Palestinians and did not involve direct PLO participation in negotiations. He therefore insisted that he would not settle for a joint Jordanian-Palestinian delegation.

The Syrian government criticized the plan for falling short of Arab objectives as a whole. But isolated as it was because of its support of Iran in the Iran-Iraq war, Damascus could hardly afford to reject the plan outright. Instead, the Syrians left room for further contacts with the United States.[39]

Not unexpectedly, the only Arab leader fully to support the plan was the one least affected by it, namely, Egypt's Mubarak.

The International Conferences Idea

One of the main ideas behind international conferences is to provide an umbrella of international legitimacy to collective peace efforts. As a rule, international conferences are held for specific purposes and are quickly dissolved after reaching these goals. Conference negotiations fall into two categories. In the first, the parties maintain their decisionmaking power. The United Nations Security Council is perhaps the closest and most familiar example of such a conference. In the second category the parties surrender considerable decisionmaking power. The Laos conference of 1961–1962, in which the parties agreed to abide by the conference's decisions, is an example.[40]

Each conference determines its own rules, such as how decisions should be reached—by simple majority, absolute majority, or unanimity.[41] And because the parties involved in negotiations must agree on details such as the participating states, the location, the timing, and the agenda, the convening of international conferences requires a great deal of cooperation.[42]

International conferences typically bring together the parties that are directly involved in a conflict along with other parties who have a direct or indirect interest in solving the conflict. International organizations may be represented as well, though usually they serve as hosts for such meetings. Of course, no state can be compelled to participate in an international conference. But because of the increased acceptance in the global community of this framework of negotiation, rival states may voluntarily seek to solve their disputes within the framework of such a conference.

The idea of convening international conferences for the purpose of solving the Arab-Israeli dispute is relatively new. The first Middle East peace conference met in Geneva in December 1973, after the Yom-Kippur War. It assembled under the auspices of the United Nations Secretary General, and the Soviet Union and the United States co-chaired. But seeking to become the sole power behind Middle East diplomacy, the United States, under the leadership of Kissinger, managed to substitute for the conference idea step-by-step U.S. diplomacy.

In 1977 the Carter administration proposed another international Middle East peace conference, but Egypt and Israel were opposed both to an increased Soviet role in the area and to the participation of radical Arabs.[43] In the end President Sadat's dramatic trip to Jerusalem effectively killed the idea of that conference. But King Hussein rekindled the idea, and discussions about another international Middle East peace conference reached full force. Finally, in October 1991, a Middle East peace conference almost identical to what Peres and Shultz had envisioned did convene in Madrid.

Israeli Reaction

The idea of an international conference split Israel between Peres and Shamir and their followers. While Peres enthusiastically pushed the idea, Shamir (who initially welcomed the renewed U.S. involvement in the peace process) was vehemently opposed to it. Like the United States, Peres viewed the conference as an opening to direct talks between Arabs and Israelis. Shamir, in contrast, viewed it as an unqualified forum to address the essence of Israel's security and thus a dangerous trap for Israel. Indeed, Shamir regarded an international conference as a Soviet-Arab plot to include the PLO in a dialogue and to force Israel to return to its 1967 borders.

Shamir ultimately objected to the most fundamental elements of the plan: He rejected the concept of an international conference as a framework for negotiation and the idea of giving up any part of the occupied territories in exchange for peace. He also rejected the new time frame Shultz proposed, insisting on the original five-year autonomy period provided under the Camp David accords. Using the *intifada* as a pretext to lengthen rather than shorten the interim period, he demanded that negotiations on a permanent settlement begin no sooner than at the end of the first three years of autonomy.

In mid-March Shamir presented his own alternative to the Shultz plan. His outline, which was based on a three-part plan, included the following principles: (1) Israel was prepared to accept the token presence of the two superpowers in the opening of direct negotiations between the two sides, in accordance with Shultz's proposal of October 1987. However, negotiations would be conducted between Israel and a Jordanian-Palestinian delegation without outside interference in the content of the negotiations. (2) The Palestinian members of the delegation had to be acceptable to the parties involved in negotiations. Israel would not negotiate with the PLO, either directly or indirectly. (3) The purpose of negotiations would be to reach a peace treaty with Jordan and find a solution to the problem of the Arabs of Eretz Yisrael. Israel's position would be based on the Camp David accords, namely, on the agreement to establish autonomy in Judea, Samaria, and Gaza as an interim stage, followed by negotiations on the permanent status of these areas. (4) Israel would submit a proposal for the rehabilitation of the Arab refugees of Judea, Samaria, and Gaza, which would be financed by an international fund set up specifically for that purpose.[44]

In reaction to the Shamir plan, President Reagan made it unequivocally clear that Washington had grown impatient with the status quo and that the administration was serious about the Shultz initiative in its original form. The dispute between Shamir and Washington intensified when on March 26 Shultz met with two Palestinian American members of the Palestine National Council, Edward Said and Ibrahim Abu Lughod, to discuss a future Palestinian role in Middle East peace negotiations. It worsened still further when Shultz returned to the Middle East at the beginning of April to prepare for the international conference, hoping that the conference would be open at the foreign minister level on April 15, 1988. During his visit Shultz pledged to give Israel the necessary guarantees, assuring that the international conference would not impose any policy on Israel. But Shamir refused such guarantees, though he did accept the idea of a onetime meeting under the auspices of the superpowers.

Disillusioned by the United States' inability to influence Israel and seeking to force the United States and Israel to negotiate directly with the PLO as the sole legitimate representative of the Palestinian people, King Hussein announced on July 31 his decision to sever Jordan's administrative and legal ties to the West Bank. Hussein asserted, however, that he was still ready to participate in the peace process.

■ ■ ■

Shultz's idea to convene an international peace conference began after encouraging developments, including the establishment of a common Jordanian-Palestinian framework for negotiations; the secret agreement between Peres and Hussein that set the basis for the conference; Middle Eastern leaders urging the United States to become more absorbed in the peace process; the beginning of U.S.-Soviet cooperation; and the endorsement by the major players involved. Most important, by the beginning of 1988 the *intifada* created a great demand to revive the peace process. Yet in Israel a powerful political Right, concerned that an international conference might pressure Israel into making territorial concessions in the West Bank and Gaza, forced Shamir to renounce the plan.

Notes

1. The Fez plan called for the withdrawal of Israeli forces from all Arab territory occupied in 1967; the removal of Jewish settlements there; freedom of worship for all religions at the holy places; Palestinian self-determination under the leadership of the PLO; placing the West Bank and Gaza under temporary UN supervision; the creation of a Palestinian state with Jerusalem its capital; and guarantees for peace for all the states of the region, including an independent Palestinian state.

2. *Keesing's Contemporary Archives* 29 (1983): 32232; *New York Times*, March 25, 1983, p. 12, and April 11, 1983, p. 1.

3. *New York Times*, April 11, 1983, p. 1.

4. Ibid., March 8, 1984, p. 1.

5. The Palestine National Council is a 350-member parliament that has the supreme power to determine PLO policy. It meets annually and in emergency sessions; its members include representatives of guerilla groups, students, workers, women's unions, etc.

6. Dankwart A. Rustow, "Realignment in the Middle East," *Foreign Affairs* 63, 3 (1984): 592.

7. Mordechai Gazit, "The Middle East Peace Process," in Itamar Rabinovich and Haim Shaked, eds., *Middle East Contemporary Survey,* vol. 9: 1984–85 (Tel Aviv: Moshe Dayan Center for Middle Eastern and African Studies/Shiloah Institute, Tel Aviv University, 1987), p. 60.

8. *New York Times*, May 30, 1985, p. 1.

9. *Keesing's Contemporary Archives* 31 (1985): 34075–34076.

10. Ibid., p. 34076.

11. Barry Rubin, "The United States' Middle East Policy in 1987," in Itamar Rabinovich and Haim Shaked, eds., *Middle East Contemporary Survey,* vol. 11: 1987 (Tel Aviv: Moshe Dayan Center for Middle Eastern and African Studies/Shiloah Institute, Tel Aviv University, 1989), p. 38.

12. *New York Times*, July 18, 1985, p. 1.

13. Ibid., September 28, 1985, p. 5.

14. Ibid.

15. *Keesing's Contemporary Archives* 31 (1985): 34079.

16. Ibid.

17. Ibid.

18. Ibid., 33 (1987): 34898–34899.

19. House Committee on Foreign Affairs, *Development in the Middle East: Hearing Before the Subcommittee on Europe and the Middle East,* 99th Cong., 2d sess., August 14, 1986.

20. *Keesing's Contemporary Archives* 33 (1987): 35411.

21. Contesting Peres on July 18, 1987, Prime Minister Yitzhak Shamir also met secretly with King Hussein in London. Apparently, the two leaders did not get along. George Shultz, *Turmoil and Triumph* (New York: Charles Scribner's Sons, 1993), pp. 942–943.

22. *Keesing's Contemporary Archives* 33 (1987): 35411; Shultz, *Turmoil and Triumph*, p. 937.

23. *Keesing's Contemporary Archives* 33 (1987): 35411–35412.

24. Ibid., p. 35412.

25. Many of the following conclusions are based on a private conversation with Richard Murphy, former assistant secretary of state for Near Eastern and African Affairs, New York, April 9, 1991.

26. House Committee on Foreign Affairs, Development in the Middle East: *Hearing Before the Subcommittee on Europe and the Middle East*, 99th Cong., 1st sess., April 4, 1985.

27. Ibid., March 15, 1988; Richard Murphy, "An American Vision of Peace in the Middle East," address before the Washington Institute on Near East Policy, Washington, D.C., April 18, 1988.

28. Private conversation with Ambassador Samuel Lewis, Washington, D.C., April 26, 1991.

29. House Committee on Foreign Affairs, *Development in the Middle East: Hearing Before the Subcommittee on Europe and the Middle East,* 100th Cong., 1st sess., September 15, 1987

30. Private conversation with former assistant secretary for Near Eastern and African affairs, Richard Murphy, New York, April 9, 1991.

31. Shultz, *Turmoil and Triumph,* p. 939.

32. Private conversation with Murphy, New York, April 9, 1991.

33. Private conversations with Murphy, New York, April 9, 1991; and Ambassador Lewis, Washington, D.C., April 26, 1991.

34. Rubin, "The United States' Middle East Policy in 1987," p. 40.

35. George Shultz, "The Administration's Approach to Middle East Peacemaking," address before the Washington Institute for Near East Policy, Wye Plantation, Queenstown, Maryland, September 16, 1988.

36. Ibid.

37. *Development in the Middle East,* March 15, 1988; Murphy, "An American Vision."

38. *Ha'aretz* (international ed.), February 4–5, 1988.

39. *New York Times,* February 29, 1988, p. 1; March 1, 1988, p. 8.

40. Arthur Lall, *Modern International Negotiation* (New York: Columbia University Press, 1966), p. 101.

41. William L. Tung, *International Law in an Organizing World* (New York: Queens College Press, 1977), p. 282.

42. Ibid.

43. Louis Kriesberg, *Social Conflict* (Englewood Cliffs, N.J.: Prentice-Hall, 1982), p. 258.

44. Jerusalem Domestic Service (Hebrew). For the English translation of Shamir's speech, see *Foreign Broadcast Information Service/Daily Report: Near East and South Asia* (Washington, D.C.: U.S. Department of Commerce/Technical Information Service), March, 28, 1988, pp. 28–31.

5

Another Approach:
The Baker Peace Initiative

The rejection of the idea of convening an international conference did not deter the Bush administration from proceeding with the peace process, especially in view of a number of promising regional events. These included King Hussein's decision to surrender Jordan's claim to the West Bank, the PLO's acceptance of Israel and its denouncement of terrorism, and the opening of a U.S.-PLO dialogue. Thus in 1989 the United States introduced still another peace plan—the Baker initiative, which called for a dialogue between Israel and West Bank Palestinians. But in spite of favorable external conditions, the Israeli Right once again undermined the plan for fear that its acceptance would challenge Israel's claim to sovereignty over East Jerusalem and would involve indirect negotiations with the PLO. After Likud rejected a number of reasonable compromises, the Israeli National Unity government collapsed, along with the Baker proposals.

The U.S.-PLO Dialogue

An unprecedented development that could have marked a new chapter in Middle East diplomacy did occur at the Arab summit in Algiers on June 7–9, 1988. During the summit a senior PLO official and a personal aide to Yasir Arafat, Bassam Abu Sharif, submitted a statement entitled "PLO View: Prospect of a Palestinian-Israeli Settlement." The statement called upon the PLO and Israel to attend UN-sponsored negotiations for a "two-state solution."[1]

Although the statement represented a dramatic shift in PLO politics, a closer look shows that the organization had actually started a process of moderation with the aftermath of the 1973 Arab-Israeli war. At the twelfth Palestine National Council in June 1974, the PLO abandoned the goal of creating a democratic secular state in all of Palestine, calling instead for the creation of "a Palestinian national authority in any Palestinian areas liberated from Israeli control." This was the first expression of the two-state idea.[2]

At the thirteenth PNC in March 1977, the PLO formally declared its willingness to participate in negotiations for a political settlement. In July 1981 the organization accepted a cease-fire agreement mediated by Philip Habib, which it carefully observed until the Israeli invasion of Lebanon in 1982.[3] In summer 1985 Arafat implicitly accepted the two-state solution.[4] In September 1986, addressing a summit of the nonaligned movement in Harare, Zimbabwe, Arafat tacitly accepted Resolution 242.[5]

In another shift from his demand for a "single democratic" Palestinian state, on May 4, 1987, Arafat expressed willingness to meet with Shamir or any other Israeli leader under United Nations auspices to discuss the possibility of establishing a dual-nationality Israeli-Palestinian state.[6] On September 7, 1987, in a meeting with left-wing Israeli politicians, Arafat proposed a plan for direct talks between the PLO and Israel on the basis of UN Resolutions 242 and 338, to be preceded by a cease-fire, a freeze on Israeli settlement activities in the West Bank and Gaza, and mutual recognition.

The extraordinary statement by Abu Sharif was followed by a statement from Arafat himself, in a speech before the European Parliament in Strasbourg on September 13, 1988. Arafat publicly declared for the first time that the PLO was ready to negotiate with Israel on the basis of all relevant United Nations resolutions, including Resolutions 242 and 338. He said the PLO would accept the right to security of all states, including Israel, in return for Israeli recognition of an independent Palestinian state and the legitimate rights of the Palestinian people. Until such arrangements could be achieved, Arafat endorsed two options: the declaration of Palestinian independence, including the formation of a provisional government, or the placement of the occupied territories under UN trusteeship.[7] That intention was formalized during the PNC's nineteenth session, held in Algiers on November 12–15; the council voted to endorse Resolution 242, thereby implicitly recognizing Israel. The PNC also published a "political statement" that repeated the call for an international conference based on Resolutions 242 and 338, under United Nations auspices, with the participation of the five permanent members of the Security Council and the parties involved, including the PLO. It also denounced all forms of terrorism.[8]

The next climactic development occurred December 6–7, when Arafat met with an American Jewish delegation in Stockholm. At the conclusion of the meeting, Arafat reaffirmed the PNC's Algiers resolution and announced his acceptance of the Jewish State of Israel alongside a Palestinian state. In reply the U.S. delegation confirmed its satisfaction that the PLO had indeed recognized Israel and renounced terrorism, thereby establishing the conditions for a U.S.-PLO dialogue.

Both Shamir and Peres rejected Arafat's statement. Even so, while addressing the UN General Assembly on December 13, Arafat called on Israel to open peace negotiations with the PLO. He presented a three-point peace initiative that called for an international conference under United Nations auspices, a UN peacekeeping force to supervise Israeli withdrawal from the occupied territories, and a comprehensive settlement based on UN Resolutions 242 and 338. Like the PNC at Algiers, he denounced terrorism "in all its forms."[9]

Although Israel dismissed Arafat's speech, the United States requested that Arafat clarify a number of points. On December 14 Arafat acknowledged "the rights of all parties concerned in the Middle East conflict to exist in peace and security and this included the states of Palestine, Israel, and other neighbors, according to resolutions 242 and 338." On terrorism, he said, "I repeat for the record that we totally and absolutely renounce all forms of terrorism."[10] During a visit to France in early May, Arafat declared null and void the Palestinian National Charter, long a source of anxiety for Israelis, who frequently cited it as evidence of the PLO's intentions to liquidate Israel. On May 5 Arafat condemned Iranian leader Ali Akbar Hashemi Rafsanjani's suggestion that citizens of Western countries be killed in revenge for Palestinian casualties of the *intifada*.[11]

Both President Reagan and President-elect Bush were convinced that the PLO had finally met U.S. conditions for direct U.S.-PLO talks. As a result, Reagan authorized the State Department to enter into a substantive dialogue with the organization.

Coincidental with the White House statement, Secretary of State Shultz designated the U.S. ambassador to Tunisia, Robert H. Pelletreau Jr., as a go-between for the dialogue with the PLO. Both sides described the first formal meeting between Pelletreau and PLO representatives, which took place in Tunis on December 16, as "practical and constructive."[12]

The Shamir-Rabin Peace Plan

The reaction in Israel was one of shock and alarm. But Washington did not try to appease Israel. Safeguarding its broader diplomatic capacity in the Middle East by opening a dialogue with the PLO and less worried about Soviet intervention in the area, the United States intended to create a more balanced Middle East policy.

With Washington's fresh approach to the Middle East under a newly elected administration,[13] another National Unity government at home, a changed PLO, and the continuation of the *intifada*, Shamir faced a dilemma: He could not remain intractable, but he was aware of the restrictions that were imposed on him by fellow hard-liners. He thus came up with the best he could offer: a new version of the autonomy plan.

Careful not to antagonize his critics on the right, Shamir did not disclose his plan immediately but revealed it piecemeal. By adopting a gradual approach, he could pacify those at home and abroad who were pressing to revitalize the peace process, and at the same time he could reconcile those who opposed any changes in Israel's policy. Most of all, he was able to test the reactions in Israel to a potential shift in his policy.

Immediately after the new National Unity government was approved by the Knesset on December 22, 1988, Shamir relayed a message to President Mubarak that he was ready to launch a peace initiative between Israel and a Palestinian delegation. At the same time Foreign Minister Moshe Arens sent a message to King Hussein in which he encouraged the king to reenter the peace process. Shamir's new peace initiative then began to unfold: The prime minister was preparing to invite the superpowers to jointly mediate direct talks with a Jordanian-Palestinian delegation, with Egyptian assistance. The plan was based on the Camp David accords, but it left open the timetable for the establishment of autonomy in the territories until negotiations were held to determine their final status.

On January 7, 1989, while attending an international conference on chemical weapons in Paris, Arens submitted the plan to Secretary of State Baker. Under the plan Shamir was ready to reduce the period of Palestinian autonomy from five to three years and to open negotiations on the permanent status of the territories sooner than the period allowed in the Camp David agreements. He was also prepared to accept a limited confederative link (in the economic sphere only) between Jordan and Israel.

The plan included the following points: (1) The superpowers would host a Middle East peace conference; (2) Israel would negotiate directly with Palestinians who had been elected in the territories; (3) in the post-autonomy negotiations with Jordan, Israel would accept a Jordanian-Palestinian confederation; (4) Jordan and the autonomous Palestinians would have access to Israeli ports; (5) the economies of the three entities would be tied together in a common market covering items such as trade, currencies, and transportation; (6) a special governing body would be established to deal with water and land rights.

Shortly after the Paris conference, Shamir agreed to accept formal UN participation in the peace process in order to start direct negotiations with the Arabs, as long as the organization would not be involved in the content of negotiations.

On January 20—the day the new U.S. administration was entering office—Labor Party Defense Minister Rabin presented to the Israeli public his own four-stage plan for the occupied territories. Based on the Camp David agreements, the plan called for free elections in the West Bank and Gaza (preferably to be held under Israeli supervision) for the purpose of choosing a delegation that would represent the Palestinians in negotiations with Israel. These negotiations would aim at the establishment of a transitional period of Palestinian self-rule. During this period the Jewish settlements in the territories would remain in place, and security matters would stay in Israeli hands. Negotiations on the final status of the territories would follow.

Within hours, Prime Minister Shamir's office issued a statement that characterized the plan as Rabin's private view. Furthermore, at a session of the Knesset Foreign Affairs and Defense Committee, Shamir said Rabin's proposal was "impractical" and announced that his own plan was being consolidated.

The Soviets could not remain publicly indifferent to Washington's potential gains from the U.S.-PLO dialogue. On February 17–27 the foreign minister, Eduard Shevardnadze, toured the Middle East and outlined a three-point peace plan based on an international conference and United Nations mediation. More significant than the plan itself was Shevardnadze's speech, "The Middle East: A Chance for a Historic Compromise," in which he declared that the Soviet Union favored the elimination of superpower rivalry in the Middle East and its replacement by constructive cooperation.[14]

The Soviet plan was received with apathy by the major players in the conflict. But it induced Washington to reveal the United States' intentions. According to its new scheme, Israel was to reduce its troop presence in heavily Palestinian-populated areas, free Palestinians detained in the *intifada*, and reopen schools in the occupied territories. Palestinians were requested to stop violent demonstrations in the territories, stop distributing anti-Israeli literature, and end raids into Israel from Lebanon.

But Israel was soon baffled by remarks Baker made before the Senate Appropriations Subcommittee. Baker stated that Israel might at some point in the future be required to negotiate with the PLO if no other Palestinian representatives could be found. Arens promised that his government would study the U.S. proposal but insisted that Israel would never negotiate with the PLO.

In the midst of these developments, some Israeli military and political analysts concluded that the cost of continuous Israeli domination over a hostile population in all of the territories would exceed any Israeli gains, thus a continued occupation would not serve Israel's interests. They also believed that there was no chance of settling the Arab-Israeli conflict without direct talks with the PLO or its authorized representative.[15] Shortly afterward, an intelligence report presented to members of the Israeli cabinet confirmed some of these conclusions.[16]

On March 22 the United States held a second round of talks with the PLO in Tunis. But basic procedural and political differences continued to characterize the discussions. For example, disagreement surfaced over the very framework of negotiations and over the question of what constituted terrorist activities against Israel. But on April 1–5, in a meeting with Mubarak, President Bush acknowledged that Egypt and the United States shared certain goals: security for Israel, the end of occupation, and the achievement of Palestinian political rights. He also said that "a properly structured international conference could play a useful role at an appropriate time."[17] Bush's reference to occupation and to an international conference did not escape Prime Minister Shamir's attention. On April 6 Shamir presented to the United States a four-point Middle East peace plan.[18]

The plan—a restricted version of the autonomy plan of the Camp David agreements—called for elections in the West Bank and Gaza to form a non-PLO Palestinian delegation to participate in negotiations on an interim settlement. The interim settlement would provide for a self-governing period to be followed by negotiations on the permanent settlement in which Israel would be prepared to discuss "any option."[19]

Shamir also proposed (1) that Israel, Egypt, and the United States reconfirm their commitment to the Camp David agreements; (2) that the United States lead an international effort to solve the "humanitarian problem" of Arab "refugees" in the West Bank and Gaza; and (3) that the United States and Egypt call on Arab countries to cease hostilities toward Israel and to "replace belligerency and boycott with negotiation and cooperation."[20]

On May 14 the Israeli cabinet approved the plan, but not without debate. While the political Right claimed that the plan gave too much ground to the Palestinians and that the *intifada* had to be quelled before any negotiations could start, the Left claimed that talks with Palestinians by necessity depended on the approval of the PLO, thus Israel should negotiate with the PLO directly. The Knesset approved the plan on May 18.

Initially, the PLO, leading Palestinians from the occupied territories, and Arab leaders rejected Shamir's plan. But the PLO executive committee subsequently outlined a conditional acceptance of elections, provided that they were part of a comprehensive settlement. The executive committee called for elections supervised by the United Nations, to be followed by an Israeli withdrawal from the territories. It demanded that

PNC members be eligible for election and that those elected join PLO leaders in negotiations in an international conference. The PLO soon demanded that Palestinian detainees held in Israel be included in the Palestinian delegation to the talks with Israel and Egypt.

Meanwhile, in late April the UN Secretary General announced in Vienna that the United Nations would be willing to supervise free and democratic elections that would lead to peace in the occupied territories if the organization were commissioned to do so. But Israel rejected unequivocally any PLO involvement in the peace process or any linkage between interim and final settlements. Moreover, Israel reaffirmed its opposition to the establishment of a Palestinian state, claiming the purpose of the peace process was to reach an agreement between it and Jordan.[21]

Hence, the Palestinians dismissed the new Israeli outline as a "warmed-over Camp David." Whether they were ignoring the dynamics that might have been stimulated if they were to respond positively—as Mark Heller has suggested[22]—or whether they deliberately rejected the new outline precisely because they were aware of the effects a positive response might have had is an open question.

Mubarak's Peace Initiative

In an attempt to end the impasse, on September 15, 1989, President Mubarak presented his own ten-point peace plan. Mubarak, who was more reserved toward Israel than was his predecessor, had only intermittently participated in the peace process since he succeeded Sadat, despite a fruitful meeting with Arafat in December 1983 (shortly after the second evacuation of PLO forces from Beirut).

For Mubarak, as for the United States, the continuation of the Camp David peace process was not a matter of altruism. First, he was bound to the autonomy talks as part of his commitment to the Camp David agreements; second, Egypt had been receiving attractive sums of economic assistance from the United States as part of the Camp David agreements and the 1979 Egyptian-Israeli peace treaty; third, Egypt is obligated to the Arab collective defense treaty, and breaking the stalemate would mean avoiding the dilemma of joining Arab forces in case of another Arab-Israeli war; fourth, progress in the peace process could bring Mubarak greater stability at home if he wanted to continue to honor the Egyptian-Israeli treaty; last, if other Arabs made peace with Israel, there would be less effective pressure on Mubarak from Islamic radicals.

But in fact peace with Israel brought Mubarak's government serious domestic challenges after the 1982 Israeli invasion of Lebanon. Many Egyptians demanded that the government freeze the normalization process with Israel and return to the Arab fold. The more militant even called for the total abrogation of the peace treaty and helping the PLO in Lebanon, especially by the third month of the war, when the Israeli bombing of Beirut reached an all-time high. After the October 1985 Israeli bombing of PLO headquarters in Tunisia, the faith of the Egyptians in the peace treaty further deteriorated.[23] Moreover, the harsh manner in which Israel repressed the *intifada* only added to the Egyptians' doubt about the legitimacy of the peace treaty with Israel.[24] Mubarak's aspiration to get out from under Nasser's shadow and to end the spread of Islamic fundamentalism in Egypt added to his desire to see the peace process enhanced.[25]

Based in part on Shamir's election plan for the Palestinians, the heart of Mubarak's plan was for elections in the occupied territories to choose a delegation to represent the Palestinians in negotiations with Israel. His plan demanded the following: (1) the right of every person in the West Bank—including East Jerusalem—and the Gaza Strip to vote and to stand as a candidate; (2) freedom to campaign before and during the elections; (3) the acceptance of international supervision of the election process; (4) a prior commitment by the Israeli government to accept the election results; (5) a commitment by the Israeli government that election would lead not only to an interim phase (of Palestinian self- government) but also to a final settlement based on Security Council Resolutions 242 and 338 and on the principle of land-for-peace; (6) the withdrawal of the Israeli army from voting areas prior to elections; (7) a ban on Israelis entering territories on election day (except for those who worked or lived there); (8) preparations for elections by a joint Israeli-Palestinian committee over a period not exceeding two months; (9) a U.S. guarantee on all the above provisions; and (10) the imposition of a freeze on Israeli settlement activity.[26]

Not unexpectedly, the Israeli coalition government was divided on the Mubarak plan. The leaders of the Labor Party were in favor of the plan, while the hawks in Likud, including Shamir, were strongly opposed to it, insisting that the only legitimate peace plan was the Israeli plan of May 14. Shamir objected to the absence of an interim period after the proposed elections, relinquishing parts of the West Bank and Gaza, imposing a freeze on Jewish settlement activity in the occupied territories, and accepting Palestinian residents of East Jerusalem as part of a Palestinian delegation. The latter point became a sensitive issue, as Likud interpreted the inclusion of candidates from East Jerusalem in the delegation as a challenge to Israel's sovereign claims over East Jerusalem.

The United States, however, did not view Mubarak's ten points as an alternative to the Israeli plan but as Egypt's acceptance of Shamir's proposal and a way to start tripartite negotiations. Thus, on his return to Egypt on October 4, Mubarak produced a list of twelve Palestinians, including exiled and prominent West Bank residents, to negotiate with an Israeli delegation. But on October 5–6 the Likud ministers in the twelve-member inner cabinet rejected Labor's proposal to accept Mubarak's invitation to attend preliminary talks, Shamir proclaiming that it would "lead to the participation of the PLO in the peace process."[27]

The Baker Plan

In spite of Shamir's resistance, Washington was determined to move ahead with Mubarak's initiative. At the beginning of October, the administration released a series of informal propositions put forward by Secretary of State Baker. By October 10, 1989, the final form of these proposals (which came to be known as Baker's five-point plan) reached Israel. Built upon the Reagan and Shultz initiatives, the plan called for a dialogue between Israel and West Bank Palestinians whose names would be approved by Israel in advance. The basis of the dialogue, which was to be held in Cairo, was the Israeli government's initiative of May 14, 1989. Finally, to facilitate the dialogue the foreign ministers of Israel, Egypt, and the United States were to meet in Washington within two weeks from the time Baker's proposals were made public.

The PLO initially rejected the plan on the grounds that it failed to meet a basic requirement—namely, the PLO's representation in any peace talks in the region. But by fall Egypt and the PLO publicly approved Baker's five points, though the PLO insisted on the right to name the delegates and to determine policies, causing a rift with Egypt.

Israeli Reaction

Whereas Labor immediately accepted Baker's proposals, Likud officials demanded a modified version of the plan to include assurances that the PLO would not participate in any talks and that elections would not be linked to any future settlement.[28] In reply Washington offered to conclude a binding bilateral understanding with Israel. The memorandum of understanding was to include U.S. guarantees pertaining to Shamir's two main concerns: the noninclusion of the PLO and the possibility that the dialogue would digress to topics other than elections in the territories. It would have fulfilled the same function as Kissinger's 1975 memorandum, in which Washington agreed not to negotiate with the PLO until the organization recognized Israel's right to exist and renounce terrorism.

But Shamir and Arens rejected the U.S. guarantees, insisting that they be incorporated into the five points. Moreover, they asked Washington for an advance commitment to support Israel if it decided to walk out of any dialogue with the Palestinians, in the event the dialogue deviated from discussions on the election process. In April 1987 the United States had committed itself to join Israel in walking out from an intended international conference if any of the procedural agreements were violated. This time, however, Israel was asking for open-ended support from Washington in case of any break-down in the proposed dialogue.

But Baker was willing only to provide assurances that the PLO would not participate in the dialogue and to make "cosmetic changes" in his five-point plan. In reply Shamir reiterated Israel's rejection of the plan as it stood. His objections centered on the composition of the Palestinian delegation and the agenda of the intended meeting. He insisted that until elections to determine negotiating partners could take place, any talks with the Palestinians could only be on procedural matters regarding the continuation of the peace process.

Thus, by November 1 Baker limited the scope of discussion to the electoral process. He also pledged that the United States would reveal to the Israelis beforehand the composition of the Palestinian delegation; that Israel would not be forced to negotiate with the PLO; and that the United States would insist that there be no deviation from the fixed agenda for negotiations, which would concentrate on the election process itself.

The Israeli inner cabinet finally endorsed the plan but requested six guarantees: (1) Israel would only negotiate with residents of Judea, Samaria, and Gaza after approving the Palestinian delegation; (2) Israel would not negotiate with the PLO; (3) the Cairo talks would focus on the Israeli election proposal only; (4) the United States would publicly support Israel's position and would stand by Israel should another party deviate from an approved agenda; (5) the United States and Egypt would declare their support for the Camp David accords; (6) one meeting would take place in Cairo, its results to determine if the talks would continue.

For fear of jeopardizing the entire peace process, the United States refused to provide all the guarantees Israel sought. Washington instead urged Shamir to demonstrate more flexibility, particularly on the issue regarding the composition of the Palestinian delegation. By mid-February 1990 Washington had become thoroughly irritated with Israel's demands that the United States stop its dialogue with the PLO. Moreover, the administration had become suspicious that Israel was deliberately making it difficult for Arafat to include non-PLO figures in negotiations, and it believed that Shamir's misgivings on the issue of the agenda for the talks was the only obstacle for progress toward negotiations. Bush and Baker therefore intimated to the Israeli government that unless it moved forward with its own peace plan, the United States might abandon its efforts to persuade the Palestinians to accept the Israeli plan.[29]

Baker stressed that "the time to move is now" and that he expected a "quick—very quick" response from the Israeli government because the United States believed matters should not be dragged on any longer.[30] In a later announcement Baker disclosed that the United States would condition loan guarantees to Israel for settling Soviet immigrants on a cessation of Israeli settlement activities in the occupied territories. His remark was made in response to Shamir's declaration that a "big Israel" was needed to accommodate the new wave of immigration by Soviet Jews, a remark that created an uproar in the Arab world.[31]

In itself, Baker's announcement was not a deviation from past policy, since the United States had always demanded that its aid not be spent in the occupied territories. However, the context of the announcement made it more difficult for Shamir to face the opposition to the Baker plan within his own party. Indeed, if Shamir wanted to find a way out of accepting Baker's proposals, the timing of Baker's announcement could not have been better. But if Shamir hoped to convince his Likud colleagues that conditions were ripe for the first step toward negotiations, the timing of the announcement could not have been worse.

Ultimately, after a heated debate over the Baker plan, Shamir and other Likud ministers agreed to participate in talks with Palestinians in Cairo on two conditions: First, Arabs from East Jerusalem would not be allowed to participate in the Cairo negotiations or in the election that the talks intended to produce; second, Israel would reserve the right to walk out of the meeting if there were any connotation that the PLO was participating even in the background.

The Israeli Labor Party rejected Shamir's terms for the talks and gave the Likud one day to change its mind if it expected to prevent the fall of the government. Labor decided to submit the issue to a cabinet vote the next day. If the cabinet refused to approve the plan, Labor would vote on whether to remain in the government. When the cabinet failed to reach a decision on the designated day, the vote was postponed for four more days.

During this crucial time, in what seemed to be a breach of Washington's standard policy toward Israel, President Bush rebuffed the creation of new Jewish settlements "in the West Bank or in East Jerusalem." By publicly questioning Israel's claim to sovereignty over East Jerusalem, Bush created a furor in Israel at the time when the country was debating whether or not to enter the U.S.-sponsored peace process. Bush had clearly deviated from the principle of ambiguity, a tenet mediators are bound to uphold. Such a sensitive question as the status of East Jerusalem should have remained vague enough to permit the beginning of negotiations.[32] Although none of the previous administrations officially recognized the Israeli annexation of East Jerusalem after it was captured in the Six-Day War, they unofficially disassociated East Jerusalem from the rest of the occupied territories by their reluctance to criticize Israel for settlement activities there—although they did voice disapproval of Israeli settlement activities in the rest of the West Bank and Gaza. Indeed, the typical comment of previous administrations about East Jerusalem had been that Jerusalem must be a united city, that it must never be divided again, and that the city's final status should be determined through negotiations. The administration denied that the president had intended to question the status of East Jerusalem. But the damage his remarks made could not be easily undone.

Yet it was Baker who was the focus of Shamir's distrust. In contrast to the personal trust Shamir had in Shultz, Shamir felt betrayed by Baker—primarily because Shamir thought Baker distorted the Israeli plan of May 14, 1989. But he also regarded Baker as manipulative, believing that he leaked information against the Israelis and slandered Shamir and Arens.[33] Shamir resented the United States' complaint that he was not ready to endorse his own plan and perceived that the Americans had altered the Israeli plan to such an extent that it had lost its original content. For example, the U.S. plan demanded that Cairo be included in negotiations and that Israel negotiate with representatives of the Palestinian diaspora. This raised doubts in Israel about Washington's integrity and evenhandedness. If the United States understood very well the casus belli on the Arab side, it seemed less willing to understand those on the Israeli side and was even constantly trying to break through with the points that were most sensitive to Israel. This, according to Shamir, caused antagonism that destroyed the whole basis for negotiations.[34] As for the inclusion of residents from East Jerusalem who had dual residency in the negotiations, perhaps these issues could have been discussed at a later stage in the process. But for the moment the point was too disturbing to Shamir.[35]

On March 11 the Israeli cabinet was due to vote on Baker's plan. But after Shamir and his Likud Party refused to put the plan to a vote, Labor ministers stormed out of the meeting. On March 15 the Israeli Knesset dissolved the government in a vote of no confidence over Shamir's refusal to accept the terms for starting the Cairo peace talks. This was the first time in Israel's history that a government was toppled by a vote of no confidence.

■ ■ ■

Unlike the Reagan plan, which was motivated by the aftermath of the Lebanon war, or the Shultz plan, which was motivated by the *intifada*, the Baker plan was the result of various diplomatic developments, beginning with the PLO's recognition of Israel and ending with Mubarak's peace plan. Thus Baker's peace proposals were introduced under international or regional conditions more favorable than the conditions that existed when either the Reagan or Shultz initiatives were launched. Yet because of the Israeli Right's exaggerated fear that the acceptance of Baker's proposals (which were based largely on Israel's own peace initiative) would jeopardize Israel's claim of sovereignty over East Jerusalem and would result in an indirect dialogue with the PLO, the Likud preferred to dissolve the Israeli government rather than to compromise on these issues.

Notes

1. *New York Times*, June 10, 1988, p. 6.
2. Cheryl A. Rubenberg, "The Structural and Political Context of the PLO's Changing Objectives in the Post-1967 Period," in Yehuda Lukacs and Abdalla Battah, eds., *The Arab-Israeli Conflict* (Boulder, Colo.: Westview Press, 1988), p. 96.
3. Ibid.
4. A July 1985 interview with Arafat in *Der Spiegel* was translated by *Foreign Broadcast Information Service/Daily Report: Middle East and Africa* (Washington, D.C.: United States Department of Commerce/Technical Information Service), July 16, 1985, p. 1.
5. Rubenberg, "Structural and Political Context," p. 96.
6. *Keesing's Contemporary Archives* 34 (1988): p. 35411.
7. Ibid.
8. Yet the council reaffirmed previous resolutions in this regard, including the 1985 Cairo Declaration, which confined terrorist activities to Israel and the occupied territories. It also proclaimed an independent Palestinian state with Jerusalem its capital. Ibid., p. 36438.
9. Ibid.
10. Ibid.
11. Ibid, p. 36670.
12. *New York Times*, December 15, 1988, pp. 1, 18; *Keesing's Contemporary Archives* 34 (1988): 36670.
13. The new administration was committed to the promotion of a comprehensive peace, based on Resolutions 242 and 338; direct negotiations within the framework of an international conference; a transitional Palestinian self-rule in the West Bank and Gaza; opposition to a permanent Israeli control of the West Bank and Gaza or the creation of a Palestinian state. James Baker, "Principles and Pragmatism: American Policy Toward the Arab-Israeli Conflict," address before

the American-Israel Public Affairs Committee (AIPAC), Washington, D.C., May 22, 1989.

14. For the plan's details, see *Keesing's Contemporary Archives* 35 (1989): 36475.

15. For details of one such study conducted by the Center for Strategic Studies at Tel Aviv University in March 1989, see Jerusalem Domestic Service (Hebrew), translated in *FBIS/DR*, March 9, 1989, p. 27.

16. Ibid., March 21, 1989, p. 28.

17. *Keesing's Contemporary Archives* 35 (1989): 36599.

18. The initiative was originated by the Labor Party at the end of the 1988 election campaign. This conclusion is drawn in part from a private conversation with Shimon Peres, Tel Aviv, July 3, 1991.

19. *Keesing's Contemporary Archives* 35 (1989): 36670.

20. Ibid.

21. Mark Heller, "The Middle East: Out of Step with History," *Foreign Affairs* 69, 1 (1989–1990): 153–171.

22. Ibid.

23. Saad Eddin Ibrahim, "Domestic Developments in Egypt," in William Quandt, ed., *The Middle East Ten Years After Camp David* (Washington, D.C.: The Brookings Institution, 1988), pp. 30–36.

24. Ibid., p. 37.

25. Abdel Monem Said Aly, "Egypt: A Decade After Damp David," in Ibid., pp. 63–93.

26. *Keesing's Contemporary Archives* 35 (1989): 36904.

27. Ibid., pp. 36986–36987

28. Ibid., p. 36987. Baker reportedly claimed that anything short of acceptance of all five points amounted to rejection of the plan.

29. *Ha'aretz* (international ed.), February 21, 1990.

30. *New York Times*, February 24, 1990, p. 4.

31. *New York Times*, March 3, 1990, p. 1.

32. This conclusion was based in part on a private conversation with I. William Zartman, New York, March 27, 1991.

33. Private conversation with former health minister Ehud Olmert, Jerusalem, June 28, 1991.

34. Ibid.

35. Ibid., and private conversation with Zartman, New York, March 27, 1991.

6

The Final Building Block:
The Madrid Conference

The collapse of the Israeli National Unity government in March 1990 over the Baker initiatives and the ultraright coalition that Prime Minister Shamir subsequently put together appeared to undermine the peace process. That changed with the outbreak of the Gulf war and the exceptional global and regional conditions that prevailed soon after. These conditions left Shamir with no choice but to join the Madrid conference. This ultimately caused two ultraright parties to leave the government, depriving Shamir of a parliamentary majority in the Knesset. That in turn produced early elections and the return of Labor to power. Thus not until the sixth round of negotiations, which corresponded with the return of the Labor Party to power in June 1992, did Israel begin to make special efforts to foster the peace process. Indeed, the Israeli negotiating teams arrived at the sixth round with a double mandate—continuity with regard to framework and innovation concerning substantial matters.

Background and Motivation

On October 30, 1991, after intensive diplomatic maneuvering by Secretary of State Baker, the Middle East peace conference opened in Madrid under the cosponsorship of the United States and the Soviet Union. This was the first time that representatives from all the major parties to the Arab-Israeli conflict—Israel, Egypt, Syria, Lebanon, and a joint Jordanian-Palestinian delegation—faced one another to discuss peace.

Although the Madrid conference should be viewed as part of the Reagan-Bush Middle East peace efforts, the immediate catalyst behind the conference was the Gulf war. The willingness of the major powers and prominent Arab states to cooperate and collectively punish Saddam

Hussein for the invasion of Kuwait and the sense of renewed hope in the aftermath epitomized Bush's idea of a "new world order"—a term not clearly defined yet signifying the president's view of a more harmonious international system made possible by the termination of the Cold War and the defeat of aggression in the Persian Gulf.

Whatever Bush's twist on the term involved, *world order* has usually been understood as the practices that allow for the restraint of parties in international disputes that threaten relative security and stability.[1] It is perhaps ironic that from the end of World War II until the end of the Cold War, world order was preserved by the two superpowers, in spite of their fierce global competition. The rest of the world had come to expect each superpower to manage disputes in its own sphere of influence, as neither wanted the eruption of total conflict between themselves or among their client states. And so the Soviets did not directly intervene in the Korean War or the war in Vietnam, and the United States did not directly intervene when the Soviet Union invaded Hungary in 1956 and Czechoslovakia in 1968 or sent troops into Afghanistan in 1979.

But with the end of the Cold War and the collapse of the Soviet state, the maintenance of world order was left in the hands of the only remaining superpower—the United States—even if that required the cooperation of friends and allies and the help of a more potent United Nations. This was most evident during the Gulf crisis, when President Bush skillfully put together an effective political and military coalition against Saddam Hussein, with the help of the Unites States' Western allies, the Soviet Union, China, and a number of Arab states.

In global terms, certainly, the demise of the Soviet Union, the skill with which the U.S. president built a near global coalition to fight Iraqi aggression, and the military victory this coalition scored in the Gulf war awarded the United States the role of single most influential global actor. In the Middle East, too, the United States emerged as the dominant power: In spite of many obstacles, it successfully preserved the coalition it had built to fight Saddam Hussein; it won over the most powerful leader of the Arab confrontationist front (Assad of Syria); it defeated a hostile oppressor, liberated Kuwait, and protected other allies in the region; and it secured the free flow of oil from the Persian Gulf to the industrial world at moderate prices. Indeed, no power other than the United States could tackle the postwar regional problems caused by Saddam Hussein's invasion of Kuwait.

What were these problems? In attacking Kuwait, Saddam Hussein (1) invoked prevalent grievances in poor Arab countries over inequality in the Arab world; (2) evoked democratic sentiments in the Arab world, challenging the legitimacy of Arab leaders; (3) offered the Palestinians a military solution against Israel and rekindled existing anti-Western sentiments in the region; and (4) reminded all spectators that the Middle East remained one of the most unstable regions in the world.[2]

To confront these apprehensions and to stabilize the region, a number of acclaimed Middle East specialists suggested that the United States, as the dominant postwar power, develop a new Middle East strategy involving four key areas: regional security, arms control, the Arab-Israeli peace process, and economic development and political change.[3] And so four days after the UN Security Council set the terms to oversee the end of hostilities in the Gulf, on March 6, 1991, President Bush told a joint session of Congress that he was committed to peace in the Middle East. Bush outlined four main foreign policy goals, including: (1) the creation of shared security arrangements in the region; (2) the control of the proliferation of weapons of mass destruction and the missiles used to deliver them; (3) the creation of new opportunities for peace and stability in the Middle East; (4) the fostering of economic development for the sake of peace and progress.[4] This outline inaugurated the peace initiative that resulted in the Madrid conference.

The Madrid Initiative

Bush initially believed that because Arabs and Israelis faced a common enemy during the Gulf war, the prospect of an Arab-Israeli peace at the end of that war was better than ever. But he offered no new ideas on how to achieve peace. Instead, Bush reiterated long-standing U.S. positions, maintaining that a comprehensive Arab-Israeli peace must be based on: (1) UN Resolutions 242 and 338, and the principle of territory for peace; (2) the preservation of Israel's security and the recognition of Israel by the Arab states; (3) the granting of legitimate political rights to the Palestinians.[5]

The day after Bush delivered his speech, Baker arrived in the region for a weeklong visit—the first of eight exploratory trips geared to promote the idea of convening an international conference. According to Baker, the Gulf war created unique opportunities for renewed U.S. mediation in the Arab-Israeli conflict: The Iraqi invasion of Kuwait had brought about a "historic" international coalition, with the United Nations playing its intended original role, and the defeat of Saddam Hussein had created new hope for diplomacy and negotiations.[6]

Ostensibly, Baker's views were well received among the major Arab leaders. During his first trip to Israel since assuming the position of secretary of state, Baker was thus able to convey to the Israeli government his impression of a prevailing new thinking in the Arab world. The Israelis agreed to a two-track approach to a Middle East settlement, involving the opening of peace talks between Israel and Arab countries on the one hand

and between Israel and Palestinians on the other hand, under the auspices of a limited regional conference. But the Israeli government conditioned participation in the conference on the seclusion of Palestinians
from East Jerusalem and Palestinian supporters of the PLO from the talks.
It also refused to permit the United Nations to sponsor the conference or
to empower the conference with any authority to impose a solution on
the parties.

Baker's second visit to Israel (April 8–10, 1991) was marked by an
attempt to begin the "confidence-building measures"—steps Baker had
previously suggested the Israelis and Arabs should take in order to ease
the path toward negotiations. These attempts, symbolized by the release
of 1,300 Palestinian detainees, were thwarted by Housing Minister
Sharon's commitment to increase the number of Jewish settlements in the
occupied territories, as signaled by the establishment of two new settlements in the West Bank—Revava and Talmon.

The settlements issue turned into a stumbling block with the unfold-
ing of the loan guarantees controversy in May. At issue were Israel's
refusal to agree to suspend the building of Jewish settlements in the occupied territories for the duration of the peace process and the United
States' concern that discussions regarding the approval of loan guarantees to Israel at that time would jeopardize Baker's diplomatic efforts. The
controversy eventually became a power struggle between Shamir and
Bush.

The dispute over the loan guarantees dates to the beginning of 1991.
On February 21 of that year, after months of bitter negotiations, the
United States approved $400 million in a loan guarantee to Israel for the
housing of new Soviet immigrants. But the Bush administration agreed to
guarantee the loan only after the Israeli government had assured Washington that it would not use the loan for settlements in the territories. In
March, however, Sharon announced that his ministry planned to build
13,000 new homes in the West Bank over two successive years. He denied
that Soviet immigrants would be directed to the new homes.

Upon Baker's protest, Prime Minister Shamir assured the U.S. secretary of state on April 9 that Sharon's plan would not receive the full
cabinet approval it needed in order to be implemented. But a day later
Sharon refuted Shamir, declaring that his plan had already been
approved by the government. As if to accredit Sharon's claim, Israeli settlers began moving into the settlement of Revava on April 16.

The controversy intensified in May, when the U.S. appealed to Israel
to delay its formal request for $10 billion in loan guarantees until after the
proposed peace conference was under way. But aware that resentment
over the linkage between the loan guarantees and concessions in the
peace talks could push Israel to submit the request anyway, Baker on Sep-

tember 4 asked Congress to delay any consideration of the matter until the conference had begun. Two days later, threatening to use his presidential veto if necessary, Bush demanded that Congress delay for 120 days any discussions on loan guarantees to Israel, on the grounds that its approval could harm the peace process. Disregarding the president's appeal to Congress, the Israeli ambassador to Washington, Zalman Shoval, presented to the United States a formal request for the $10 billion in loan guarantees. On September 8 Bush told congressional leaders that if they postponed discussions on the Israeli request until January, he would not seek further delays. Moreover, he pledged to pay for any additional costs Israel incurred as a result of the four-month delay, but he refused to give assurances that he would support the request when it came up for discussion before Congress in January 1992. To further cool the dispute, in his address to the United Nations General Assembly on September 23, Bush called upon the assembly to repeal its 1975 resolution equating Zionism with racism (Resolution 3379). On October 1 the U.S. Senate formally agreed to postpone for 120 days any consideration of Israel's request for the loan guarantees.

The loan guarantees dispute notwithstanding, by mid-May the main points of contention between Israel and its neighbors—Syria in particular—remained the conference format and the role the United Nations would play, Syria demanding an extensive conference and a "significant" UN role in it and Israel objecting to both.

To break the deadlock, on June 1 President Bush sent letters to key regional leaders, including Prime Minister Shamir, President Assad, President Mubarak, and King Fahd, in which he offered that (1) the United States and the Soviet Union would preside over the conference, to be attended by Israel, Syria, Egypt, Lebanon, and a joint Jordanian-Palestinian delegation; (2) the United Nations and the European Community would attend the conference as "silent observers"; (3) the conference would dissolve into a series of bilateral negotiations but would be periodically reconvened.[7]

On June 6 Shamir rejected Bush's compromise, ruling out any UN role in the conference. Since it voted for partition in 1947 the UN has steadily acquired an anti-Israeli and pro-Arab character. This was especially evident since 1973 when the Arabs began to use oil and money as political weapons against Israel. As a result, all attempts to solve the Arab-Israeli conflict have been made outside UN auspices.[8] On July 14 Assad dropped his insistence on a major UN role in the conference. On July 18–21, during Baker's fifth trip to the region, Syria, together with Jordan and Lebanon, formally accepted the U.S. proposals for the convening of the conference.

But when Baker visited Israel on July 21–22, he was unable to obtain from Shamir an explicit response to the Syrian move because Shamir still saw sharp differences between the Israeli and U.S. positions on Palestinian representation, insisting on Israel's right to veto the participation of any member of the joint Jordanian-Palestinian delegation. What irritated Shamir and his government was Bush's call on Israel to curb settlement building and Baker's reaffirmation of the U.S. position that East Jerusalem was part of the occupied territories and that the Palestinians alone had the right to determine who would represent them in peace talks. It was thus no accident that during this time the Israeli Housing Ministry approved the construction of 380 new apartments in the Golan Heights and announced that work had begun on what Sharon himself hoped would be the largest Jewish settlement in the West Bank, Avneh Hafetz.[9]

Shamir's apprehension notwithstanding, on July 31, during the first post-Cold War summit in Moscow, Bush and his Soviet counterpart, Gorbachev, issued a joint statement in which they called for a jointly sponsored Middle East peace conference, to be held in October at an undetermined site. With practically all of the other major parties in agreement, on August 1, during Baker's sixth Middle East trip, Shamir announced that Israel would participate in the talks, provided that his conditions on the composition of the Palestinian delegation to the conference were met.

By August 7, Israeli and U.S. officials began to clarify the procedure of the Madrid conference and the terms of the parties' participation. These terms were set in the letters of assurance Washington sent to each of the participants in mid-October (Appendix B). Among other things, Israel was reassured that the opening conference would have no power to make decisions, hold votes, or impose positions; that negotiations would be direct only; that the United States would not support linkage between the various bilateral negotiations; that no party would have to negotiate with another party against its will; that the United States would not insist on an Israeli-PLO dialogue; that only Palestinian residents of the West Bank or Gaza who accepted phased direct negotiations in two tracks and who were ready to live at peace with Israel could take part in negotiations; that the United States would not support the creation of an independent Palestinian state; that Israel could retain its own interpretation of Security Council Resolution 242; that the United States still honored the written commitment of September 1975 regarding the importance of the Golan Heights to Israel's security and that the United States was prepared to guarantee any border agreed upon between Israel and Syria; and that the United States was committed to Israel's security and to the maintenance of Israel's qualitative military balance.

The Madrid conference was modeled after the 1987 London document and Shultz's international conference idea of 1988—which Shamir had zealously rejected. Yet the essential requirements that the Likud government had asked of Baker in 1989–1990 were also met at Madrid. The London document determined that the international conference would not have the power to impose a solution or to veto any agreement reached by the sides; that negotiations would be conducted by bilateral committees in a direct manner; that the Palestinian representatives to the conference would be part of a Jordanian-Palestinian delegation; that participation in the conference would be based on the acceptance of UN Resolutions 242 and 338; and that each committee would conduct negotiations independently. These principles were incorporated in Shultz's international conference concept, which was eventually reduced to a mere "international event" in the form of a symbolic opening ceremony leading to direct negotiations, sponsored by the two superpowers. As to Israel's demands of 1989–1990, the Likud government would agree to participate in talks with Palestinians in Cairo only on two conditions: Arabs from East Jerusalem were not to be allowed to participate in the Cairo negotiations or in the election that the talks intended to produce, and Israel would reserve the right to walk out of the meeting if there were any connotation that the PLO was participating behind the scene.[10]

On October 18 Secretary Baker and the Soviet foreign minister, Boris Pankin, announced in Jerusalem that their governments had invited Israel, Egypt, Lebanon, Syria, Jordan, and Palestinian representatives to attend a Middle East peace conference to be held on October 30 in Madrid. Earlier that day the USSR and Israel resumed full diplomatic relations, restoring ties that had been severed by Moscow in 1967. On October 20, in a vote of sixteen to three, the Israeli cabinet approved Prime Minister Shamir's recommendation to attend the Madrid conference.

Israeli Reaction to the Gulf War and to the Postwar U.S. Peace Initiative

The endorsement of the Madrid conference by Shamir's right-wing coalition, however reluctant, can only be understood within the context of events that began with the Gulf war. The war and the Iraqi Scud attacks on Israeli cities produced two immediate internal developments in the Israeli polity. Initially, the country rallied around the Likud government. This occurred not only because of the basic social impulse to unite against a common enemy but also because the majority of Israelis supported Shamir's difficult decision to accede to Washington's plea not to retaliate against the Iraqi attacks so as not to risk the continued participation of the Arab members in the coalition against Saddam Hussein.

Second but related, the anxiety and anger the Scud attacks generated in Israel hardened the attitude of many Israelis who otherwise favored a compromise solution with the Arabs.[11] In fact, faced with the images of Palestinians cheering the raids, many of Israel's best-known doves, such as Yael Dayan, Amos Oz, A. B. Yehoshua, and a considerable number of other members of Peace Now (the best known peace movement in Israel), publicly supported the war efforts against Saddam Hussein. And while some politicians believed that Israel should have joined the war, 74 percent of the Israeli public supported Shamir's policy of nonretaliation.[12]

In this context Ehud Sprinzak identified two syndromes that developed among the Israelis as a direct result of the Scud attacks: the Qadaffi-Saddam syndrome and the Scud syndrome. Sprinzak described the first syndrome as the feeling that somewhere, sometime, with no direct relation to either the occupied territories or the Palestinian problem, another Saddam would emerge in the Arab world, ready and able to destroy Israel. The second syndrome is the sense of vulnerability to new kinds of attacks,[13] as for the first time in Israel's war-fighting history, the civilian centers of the country were defenseless against a weapon (which was introduced to the region only during the Gulf war). The frustration caused by this new sense of helplessness was especially strong among Israeli reservists, who remained in the rear for the first time, unable to defend their loved ones.

In the period immediately following the Gulf war, Sprinzak, like most political scientists, predicted that the Likud would overwhelmingly win the ensuing elections in Israel.[14] But the general solidarity the government enjoyed during the war collapsed once the debate over the postwar peace began. While Labor leaders welcomed the Bush administration's postwar peace efforts, the Israeli Right was alarmed by Bush's reference to the land-for-peace formula and to Palestinian political rights.

Baker's eight exploratory trips to the region were often met with acrimonious demonstrations by Jewish settlers who were opposed to any discussions on Palestinian autonomy in the West Bank and Gaza. As noted, Baker's visits also frequently coincided with public appearances of the hawkish housing minister Sharon, who routinely pledged to bolster the settlement drive.

Inevitably, the more ardent members of the government—Science Minister Yuval Ne'eman of Tehiya (a right-wing party established by two former Likud members who rejected the Camp David agreements, joined the opposition, and became very vocal on the issue of the occupied territories), Minister Without Portfolio Rehavam Ze'evi of Moledet (the ultra-nationalist party formed prior to the 1988 elections by former army General Rehavam Ze'evi, who called for the transfer of the Arabs from the territories to Arab countries), Agriculture Minister Rafael Eitan, and Housing Minister Ariel Sharon—demanded the renunciation of the Israeli peace initiative of May 1989, a plan the Israeli government still endorsed. Instead, they demanded the formulation of a new Israeli peace plan that would denounce altogether the concepts of election in the West Bank and Palestinian autonomy. To replace the Israeli initiative, Sharon proposed a two-stage plan of his own. First, before any negotiations could take place, Sharon offered to create an appropriate background by conducting discussions with Saudi Arabia and Iraq on the question of peace or the cessation of warfare. A second stage included a process of democratization in the Middle East.[15]

By contrast, Labor promoted the idea of an international conference, as Peres introduced a new peace plan calling for the establishment of a Jordanian-Palestinian federation (or confederation) to be negotiated under the auspices of an international peace conference. The Likud criticized Peres's plan as harmful to Israel's image. For their part, Labor's doves, who recognized the menace behind the Palestinians' growing frustration, criticized the plan because it did not provide for Palestinian self-determination. With the backing of a cabinet majority, Shamir managed to uphold the 1989 Israeli peace plan.

Although politically and diplomatically Shamir had little choice but to join the conference (if he wanted continued U.S. aid), the period between the initial discussions on the post-Gulf war peace process and the decision to participate in the Madrid conference was not free of government crises. The first dispute erupted when on March 17 Health Minister Olmert suggested at an AIPAC gathering in Washington that Israel was ready to negotiate all issues, including all territorial demands of the Syrians.[16]

As if to make matters worse, on March 21 Israel's army chief of staff, Lieutenant General Dan Shomron, announced that Israel might safely give up some of the occupied territories if it obtained satisfactory peace agreements with Arab neighbors. In response some members of the Knesset called for Shomron's immediate resignation, even though he was scheduled to retire in a month.

Shamir's announcement that he would conditionally accept Baker's invitation to attend the proposed conference generated another upheaval in the government at the beginning of August. This time the possibility arose that the prime minister might fire Sharon for his blunt criticism of Shamir's decision. In addition, some in Tehiya demanded that the party leave the government. But the party's central committee decided to remain in the cabinet until the actual convening of the conference.[17]

The Madrid Conference: Ten Rounds of Futile Negotiations

The Madrid conference opened on October 30, 1991, as scheduled, marking the start of bilateral Arab-Israeli peace negotiations and multilateral talks on regional issues.

As could be expected, the opening speeches at the conference ranged from shrill partisan attacks to plain cordiality. Still, the opening session—which lasted from October 30 to November 3—constituted the first time all major parties to the Arab-Israeli conflict faced one another to discuss peace. Eventually, five rounds of bilateral negotiations took place before Labor returned to power in Israel and before some progress in negotiations could be noted.

The second round of bilateral talks opened in Washington on December 10 after a six-day delay. During this round the Israeli and the Jordanian-Palestinian delegations could not agree on the meaning of two-track negotiations. The Palestinians demanded that Israel hold separate talks with the Jordanian and the Palestinian segments of the joint delegation—each having only a symbolic representation from the other section. Israel said it would negotiate with the joint delegation only, but it allowed the joint Jordanian-Palestinian delegation to be divided into subcommittees to discuss specific issues. As a result, daily discussions were held in a State Department corridor.

In the third round of bilateral talks in Washington on January 13–16, 1992, Israel offered the Palestinians limited self-rule, under an interim self-governing authority. But Israel ruled out the possibilities that it would withdraw its forces from the territories or that it would place Jewish settlers in these areas under Palestinian jurisdiction. Still, discussion on Palestinian autonomy caused the two right-wing parties, Tehiya and Moledet, to resign from the government. Coupled with the resignation in December of Agriculture Minister Eitan of Tzomet (an ultranationalistic list formed in 1984 and merged with Tehiya on the eve of the 1984 elections) over Shamir's opposition to electoral reforms, the departure of the two ultraright parties deprived Shamir of a parliamentary majority in the Knesset. Rather than toppling the Shamir government with a no-confidence motion, Labor cooperated with Likud on moving up the impending national elections from November to June 1992.

The multilateral talks, which constitute an integral part of the peace process, started on January 28–29, 1992, at the Moscow conference. The participants broke into five working groups corresponding to the regional issues under discussions: regional and economic cooperation, the environment, water resources, arms control, and refugees. Sessions were held in Brussels, Geneva, The Hague, Ottawa, Paris, Rome, Tokyo, Vienna, and Washington. Syria and Lebanon decided not to participate in the multilateral talks until progress was made on the bilateral talks; Israel refused to attend some talks if Palestinians from outside the territories participated in them.

The fourth round of bilateral Middle East peace talks involving Israeli, Syrian, Lebanese, and Jordanian-Palestinian delegations opened in Washington on February 24, 1992. During this round Israel presented to the Palestinians a detailed document on Palestinian self-rule. The offer, which sought to maintain Jewish settlements in the West Bank and Gaza, did not contain provisions for the withdrawal of Israeli forces from these areas, nor did it mention an elected Palestinian authority to oversee Palestinian self-rule in the territories. But it proposed that residents of the West Bank and Gaza be allowed to manage their own affairs in twelve areas, including industry and commerce, civil services, municipal government, education, taxation, agriculture, justice, tourism, social security, and labor.

The Palestinian delegation denounced the Israeli plan as an attempt to legitimize the Israeli annexation of the territories. To supplant the offer, the Palestinian delegation presented its own plan for holding elections by September 29, 1992, to choose a 180-seat parliament that would assume control over most matters in the territories during a period of interim self-rule. The plan also called for the creation of a Palestinian executive and judiciary.

Palestinian self-rule was also the major theme during the fifth round of bilateral discussions on April 27–30 in Washington, the last round of bilateral talks before the Israeli elections of June 23, 1992. In this round, Israel proposed a "pilot municipal election plan" by which Palestinians would hold municipal elections in the West Bank and Gaza. Israel also suggested that the Palestinians control all local health services in these areas. While not rejecting the Israeli plan outright, the Palestinian delegates said it fell short of their demands for broader self-rule.

It was not until the sixth round of talks, which resumed on August 24, 1992, that negotiations became substantive. The new Labor government contributed to the progress, making a conscious effort to ameliorate the atmosphere surrounding the peace process. To this end Prime Minister Rabin pledged to stop construction of "political settlements" in the West Bank and Gaza and to bring about Palestinian self-rule in these areas within nine months after his government took power. Rabin further called for the repeal of an existing law that prohibited Israelis from communicating with PLO members. He also loosened some restrictions on Palestinians in the West Bank and Gaza, released 800 Arab prisoners, and revoked existing expulsion orders against eleven Palestinians who were accused of provoking terrorist activity in the territories. But the most encouraging step—at least from an Arab perspective—was the announcement that Israel was prepared to apply UN Resolution 242 to the Syrian front.[18] On September 9 Rabin explicitly accepted the notion that in return for peace with Syria, Israel would have to make territorial concessions in the Golan Heights. Although Rabin made it clear that he would not return all of the Golan to Syria under any circumstances, this was a direct departure from Likud's position that Israel should accept only "peace for peace."[19]

In response the Syrian foreign minister, Faruk al-Sharaa, disclosed that Syria was "ready for a total peace" with Israel in return for a "total Israeli withdrawal from the occupied Arab territories."[20] Although neither side offered further details regarding its intentions, this was the first time that an Israeli prime minister accepted the idea of any withdrawal from the Golan Heights or that a Syrian official publicly accepted the principle of "total" peace with Israel.

There was progress in the Israeli-Jordanian negotiations as well. The spokesman for the Jordanian delegation, Maruan Maasar, conveyed to reporters that the Israeli draft proposal to his delegation contained essential positive changes, including a statement that the Israeli government was committed to a "comprehensive peace" between Israel and all its neighbors. This formulation, according to Maasar, had been a bone of contention between the Israeli and Jordanian delegations during previous rounds of bilateral talks.[21]

As for the Israeli-Palestinian negotiations, the Israeli offer to the Palestinian delegation envisioned the creation of a Palestinian administrative council to administer the proposed Interim Self-Government Agreements. The council—which would be freely elected by the Palestinians in the territories from among the Palestinians in the territories—would be assigned agreed powers and responsibilities to administer the daily affairs of the Palestinians. The offer included a phrase stating that the territorial/geographical aspects would be reserved for future permanent-status negotiations, insinuating that Israel did not intend to view the interim agreements as a permanent solution for the territories. Still, issues relating to security, foreign relations, Israeli settlers, and unspecified vital Israel needs in the territories were to remain in Israel's hands in the framework of "residual powers."[22]

In reply the Palestinian delegation insisted that only general elections carrying a "political tone" could bestow the Palestinian leadership with wide popular support and legitimacy. The Palestinians also demanded that East Jerusalem be included in the debates over a final settlement and that Resolution 242 be applied to the occupied territories, including East Jerusalem—something no Israeli government could agree to.

The seventh round of bilateral talks, which resumed on October 21, 1992, in Washington, marked one year since the Madrid conference was convened. The only noteworthy progress in this round was an Israeli-Jordanian agreement on a joint agenda, formulating the structure of the talks, the principles governing the negotiations, and the issues to be negotiated. The agenda was divided into three major subheadings. The first contained an outline of the general goal of the Israeli-Jordanian negotiations: the achievement of a lasting and comprehensive peace between Israel and the Arab states and the Palestinians. The second segment comprised the components of negotiations, including the issues of borders, water, security, refugees, and the essence of future relations between Israel and Jordan. The third section stated that negotiations would culminate in a peace treaty (Israel was pleased that Jordan agreed to the term treaty, which is more formal than a mere agreement).[23]

Likewise, some Israelis saw improvements in the Israeli-Palestinian talks: Even though the gap between the two sides remained wide, they began discussing core issues regarding the concept of the interim arrangements, including the composition of the body that would administer the arrangements and its structure, jurisdiction, authority, powers, and responsibility.[24] In contrast, no progress, however obscure, could be acknowledged in the Israeli-Syrian or the Israeli-Lebanese talks.

The eighth round of peace talks opened on December 7 in Washington. This round was overshadowed by an outbreak of violence on the ground and the Israeli expulsion of 415 Palestinians linked to militant Islamic groups. And with only six weeks left until a new administration assumed power in Washington, no meaningful negotiations occurred.

It was not until April 27, 1993, that the new secretary of state, Warren Christopher, opened the ninth round of peace negotiations. As was the case in previous rounds, the Palestinian track attracted the most attention. But the gap between the Israeli and Palestinian delegations was still unbridgeable: First, the Palestinian delegation demanded legislative, executive, and judicial powers for the future Palestinian Interim Self-Government Authority and full territorial control over the occupied territories (including East Jerusalem)—both to be granted immediately after the elections of the interim authority. The Palestinians thus tied negotiations on the permanent status of the territories to the establishment of an independent Palestinian state, a move the Israelis formally objected to, and took a hard line on the issue of Jerusalem. Furthermore, the Palestinians demanded that negotiations on the permanent status begin no later than October 1994, after a year and a half of self-rule rather than the three years the Israelis proposed.[25] To break the impasse, the United States offered its own draft proposal, but it left open the timetable of negotiations on the permanent status of the territories.[26] The PLO (and hence the Palestinian delegation to Washington) rejected the U.S. proposal because of its resemblance to the Israeli position.The two delegations did agree, however, to set up a committee on human rights and to establish three official working groups to discuss interim government arrangements and land and water issues. But before the working groups had a chance to achieve sufficient results, they were suspended.

On the Jordanian track, reports disclosed that negotiations ended with calls for the establishment of three formal working groups to discuss a range of issues, including water, energy and environment; security, borders, and the elements of peace; refugees; economic issues; and bilateral cooperation. In addition Foreign Minister Peres publicly announced that Israel and Jordan were on the verge of signing an agreement, though he did not offer details.[27] Talks with the Syrian delegation produced no results, as the Syrians still refrained from spelling out what kind of peace Syria had in mind. Nor was there progress in the Israeli-Lebanon talks.[28]

The tenth round of negotiations opened in Washington on June 15, 1993. This time the gap between the Israeli and Palestinian positions widened. The Palestinian delegation had pushed the issue of East Jerusalem to the top of the agenda, though the Israeli position on Jerusalem had not changed. The Palestinians also demanded from the United States the reestablishment of a direct dialogue with the PLO and a more balanced draft proposal.[29] Still another issue of contention was the idea of "early empowerment," which the Israelis tried to advance, their attempts to do so during the previous round having failed. Early empowerment meant granting immediate authorization to a Palestinian civil administration to run the Palestinians' own affairs in spheres such as health, education labor, welfare, and tourism—not as a substitute for interim agreements, but to inject momentum into the peace process. But the Palestinians rejected the idea on the ground that early empowerment was but a fragmentation of the process itself.[30]

As the gap between the Israeli and Palestinian positions grew, an Israeli-Jordanian agreement seemed less likely, if only because of the Jordanians' reluctance to sign a separate agreement with Israel.

On the Syrian track, both sides attempted not to repeat the standoff of previous rounds. They thus delayed negotiations on the more substantial issues of Israel's withdrawal in the Golan Heights and Syria's interpretation of peace and instead began to discuss the security needs of both countries in the event of a future peace agreement. But without Syrian clarification on the nature of peace or Israeli explanation on the extent of a future withdrawal in the Golan, the Israeli-Syrian talks remained at a standstill.[31]

By midsummer 1993 the future of the negotiation process seemed increasingly bleak because of Israel's massive assault on South Lebanon. A retaliation for a series of attacks by pro-Iranian Hezbollah guerrillas on northern Israeli towns and on Israeli soldiers stationed in southern Lebanon, the assault was the heaviest since the 1982 invasion of Lebanon. But with the intervention of Syria, which blocked new arms shipments to the Shiite guerrillas and forced them to stop shelling Israeli territory; the Lebanese army's disarming of some guerrillas; the cease-fire brokered by Secretary of State Christopher and his active mediation efforts; and the decision by the Arabs to return to the negotiation table, the eleventh round of negotiations started up in August. It was during the discussions leading to this round that the agreement on the Gaza-Jericho plan became public. But it was not until January 24, 1994, that negotiations among Israel, Syria, Lebanon, and Jordan resumed in Washington—the first since the signing of the Israeli-PLO agreement on September 13, 1993.

■ ■ ■

A number of international and regional circumstances created exceptionally favorable conditions that helped Baker's efforts to convene the Madrid peace conference: Bush's unprecedented popularity as a result of his performance in the Gulf war; the collapse of the Soviet Union and the cessation of Soviet influence in the Middle East and Moscow's willingness to collaborate with the United States in the region; Syria's need to cooperate with the West as a result of its loss of Soviet patronage; the drastic deterioration of the PLO's status in the Arab world as a result of Arafat's support for Saddam Hussein during the Gulf war and the shifting of the balance of power from Tunis to the Palestinians of the West Bank and Gaza; Israel's shocking trauma as a result of the Iraqi Scud attacks during that war and the country's need for loan guarantees to help settle the influx of Soviet immigrants; and the Arab world's great sense of expectation that the United States, as the only remaining superpower, could influence the peace process.

These conditions left Shamir with little choice but to join the Madrid conference. Indeed, as former ambassador Alfred Leroy Atherton pointed out, once it became clear that all the Arab parties were prepared to accept the invitation to Madrid, the Israelis realized that they had to accept as well. Moreover, Israel could not ignore the changed international scene any more than could the Arabs. A refusal by Shamir to attend the conference would have resulted in a domestic political crisis in Israel and would have strained relations between Israel and the United States and between Israel and important elements of the American Jewish community.[32] If Shamir's reluctant consent to attend the conference did not accelerate the peace process, the Labor Party made conscious efforts to hasten it. Likud had never been ready to discuss any idea that permitted anything more than personal autonomy for the Palestinians, enabling them to run only the most elemental aspects of their daily life. After Labor replaced Likud, the Israeli government for the first time raised the territorial or geographic aspects of Palestinian self-rule.

Notes

1. Stanley Hoffman, *Primacy or World Order* (New York: McGraw-Hill, 1980), pp. 5, 188.

2. For further details on U.S. concerns in the postwar Middle East, see the testimonies of Martin Indyk, Judith Kipper, and Shibley Telhami in *Post War Policy Issues in the Persian Gulf. Hearings Before the Subcommittees on Arms Control, International Security and Science, and on Europe and the Middle East, of the Committee on Foreign Affairs*. House of Representatives, 102d Cong., 1st sess., January 31, February 28, and April 11, 1991.

3. Ibid.

4. George Bush, "The World After the Persian Gulf," address before a joint session of Congress, March 6, 1991, U.S. Department of State *Dispatch* 2, 1 (March 18, 1991).

5. Ibid.

6. *Foreign Operations, Export Financing, and Related Programs Appropriation for Fiscal Year 1992. Hearing Before the Subcommittee of the Committee on Appropriation,* United States Senate, 102nd Cong. 1st sess.

7. Bush promised Shamir that the United States would exclude the PLO from the peace process and called on Israel to freeze settlement activity in the territories. Bush promised Assad not to recognize Israel's annexation of the Golan Heights (1981) and to include the area as subject to UN Resolution 242. Document D2, *Journal of Palestine Studies* 21, 1 (autumn 1991): 184–185.

8. Alvin Rubinstein, "Transformation: External Determinants," in Alvin Rubinstein, ed., *The Arab-Israeli Conflict* (New York: HarperCollins, 1991), pp. 79–84.

9. *Keesing's Contemporary Archives* 37 (1991): 38359.

10. In order to give a formal role to some Palestinians whose participation in Madrid was rejected by Israel, a steering committee of seven members was set up. Four of its members were from East Jerusalem, three others were from the Palestinian diaspora.

11. Don Peretz, "The Impact of the Gulf War on Israeli and Palestinian Political Attitudes," *Journal of Palestine Studies* 21, 1 (autumn 1991): 17–35.

12. Ibid.

13. *Post War Policy Issues in the Persian Gulf. Hearings Before the Subcommittees on Arms Control, International Security and Science, and on Europe and the Middle East, of the Committee on Foreign Affairs,* House of Representatives, 102d Cong., 1st sess., January 31, February 28, and April 11, 1991.

14. Ibid.

15. Jerusalem Domestic Service (Hebrew). For the English text of Sharon's interview, see *Foreign Broadcast Information Service/Daily Report: Near East and South Asia* (Washington, D.C.: United States Department of Commerce/Technical Infor-

mation Service), March 8, 1991, pp. 25–26; see also Peretz, "The Impact of the Gulf War."

16. Sharon responded with an announcement of a plan to increase the Israeli population in the Golan Heights from 11,000 to 20,000. *Keesing's Contemporary Archives* 37 (1991): 38117.

17. A public opinion poll commissioned by *Ma'ariv* found that some 86 percent of the Israeli public supported the government's decision to accept Baker's invitation.

18. *Ha'aretz* (international ed.), August 20, 1992. Focusing on the establishment of a just and lasting peace in the Middle East, UN Resolution 242 (November 22, 1967) requested the withdrawal of Israeli armed forces from territories captured in the Six-Day War and the mutual recognition of the sovereignty, territorial integrity, and political independence of every state in the area and their right to live in peace within secure and recognized boundaries.

19. *New York Times*, September 10, 1992, p. 8.

20. *Ha'aretz* (international ed.), September 25, 1992.

21. Ibid.

22. The Israeli offer depicted the council as a single administrative-functional body composed of fifteen members in accordance with the fifteen spheres of operation it would administer: justice; personnel matters; agriculture; ecology; education and culture; finance, budget, and taxation; health; industry and commerce; labor; local police; local transportation and communication; municipal affairs; religious affairs; social welfare; and tourism. *Israel's Interim Self Government Proposal to the Palestinians* (Washington, D.C.: Embassy of Israel), September 17, 1992.

23. "Talking Points: The Israeli-Arab Peace Negotiations, an Update Following the First Half of the Seventh Round, October 21–29, 1992" (New York: Information Department, Consulate of Israel), November 3, 1992.

24. Ibid.

25. *Palestinian Delegation to the Peace Talks, 'Draft Proposal for a Declaration of Principles,'* Tunis, May 9, 1993; and *Israeli Delegation to the Peace Talks with the Palestinians, Draft of 'Agreed Statement of Principles,'* Washington, D.C., May 6, 1993, Documents B5 and C4, Journal of Palestine Studies, 22, 4 (Summer 1993).

26. *U.S. Draft of 'Israeli-Palestinian Joint Statement,'* Washington, D.C., May 12, 1993, Document D5, ibid.

27. *Ha'aretz* (international ed.), June 7, 1993; *New York Times*, June 7, 1993, p. 6.

28. Israeli delegation press conference, May 6, 1993 (released by Israel Press Center, Washington, D.C.).

29. *Ha'aretz* (international ed.), July 4, 1993.

30. Press briefing with the Israeli delegation to the Middle East peace talks, Washington, D.C., June 30, 1993.

31. Ibid.

32. Alfred Leroy Atherton Jr., "The Shifting Sands of Middle East Peace," *Foreign Policy* 86 (spring 1992): 114–133.

7

The Breakthrough:
The Oslo Connection

The secret negotiations in Oslo that produced the breakthrough in the Arab-Israeli peace process demonstrated that the true fate of a peace process rests in the hands of the protagonists rather than in the hands of the intermediaries. At the same time, the domestic changes that had occurred in Israel—and in the PLO, for that matter—and the regional and global conditions that prevailed at the time of negotiations revealed that the ability of the protagonists to conclude peace with one another depended as much on the internal environment in which they operated as it did on the external milieu. Certainly, if Labor had not won the 1992 election in Israel, the regional and global situation would not have been enough to produce a breakthrough. The Labor government was more receptive than its predecessor to making the concessions necessary for meaningful negotiations, and (as the 1992 election results showed) the government enjoyed sufficient domestic support to take such action.

Background and Motivation

The fourteen months of clandestine negotiations between Israel and the PLO that began in July 1992 and culminated in September 1993 fostered their reciprocal recognition and led to the agreement both signed on September 13, 1993, in Washington. The secrecy of the Oslo talks provided the parties with the confidentiality and freedom of movement necessary for mutual cooperation. As Abba Eban observed, there has hardly been a success in international conciliation without the use of secrecy at a crucial stage in the negotiating process. Without Moshe Dayan's disguised visit to Morocco in 1977 and the seclusion and secrecy of the Camp David negotiations in 1978, the Egyptian-Israeli peace treaty might not have been possible.[1] Similarly, as disclosed by Nabil Shaath, the chief

PLO diplomat negotiating the Israeli-PLO agreement, the PLO had concluded that it could not reach an agreement with the Israelis in the spotlight of the media.[2]

One of the primary benefits of secret diplomacy is reducing the chance that negative public opinion at home will undermine the success of talks. Undoubtedly, had the opposition in Israel been aware of the official contacts between Israel and the PLO, let alone the government's intention to recognize the PLO and to make concessions on Gaza and Jericho, it would have zealously and perhaps successfully campaigned against the deal. As for the PLO, because of its frailty at the time of the secret negotiations, its very survival might have been threatened had Hamas—the Islamic resistance movement that sprung up in the territories during the *intifada*—and the more radical PLO factions based in Damascus known about the talks. As the Norwegian foreign Minister stated, "Secrecy was absolutely essential for the talks to succeed because talking together was in and of itself controversial and probably could have been torpedoed unless one was in a position to demonstrate success, and that meant that the talks might have been completed by the time we went public."[3] Secret contacts are also necessary to avoid potential conflict by assuring that each side correctly understands the other's intentions, enabling the parties to gauge each other better.[4] In this respect the informal and intimate setting of the Oslo rounds were critical.[5]

But secret diplomacy would have been as futile as open diplomatic channels if the protagonists themselves had not been determined to put an end to their long strife. To understand their decision and its timing, one must examine the factors that brought the Israeli-PLO agreement into being. On the international level these included the collapse of the Soviet Union and the end of the Cold War, the failure of the talks in Washington, President Clinton's pro-Israeli sentiment, and European involvement. On the regional level the combined elements working in favor of an agreement included the defeat of Saddam Hussein, the cutoff of funds to the PLO by the Arabs, the inability of the Palestinians from the territories to commit to peace, and the unrest in the territories. Finally, in Israel the return of the Labor Party to power, the survival of Rabin's coalition government in spite of a number of crises, Israeli self-confidence, and the close collaboration between two old rivals—Prime Minister Rabin and Foreign Minister Peres—all helped to bring about the Gaza-Jericho agreement.

The Collapse of the Soviet Union and the End of the Cold War

Just as these two events facilitated the opening of the Madrid conference, so they encouraged the mutual recognition of Israel and the PLO, as both the Israeli and PLO leadership saw that conflict in the Middle East would no longer be subsidized by two competing superpowers. In fact, in Israel both Rabin and Peres had long been aware that peace in the Middle East depended to a large extent on cooperation between the superpowers: In 1978 Peres acknowledged that the conditions set by the superpowers were crucial to peace in the Middle East.[6] A decade late Rabin predicted that with the continuous improvement of U.S.-Soviet relations—culminating in Gorbachev's announcement in December 1988 of a unilateral reduction of forces in Europe—the superpowers would become increasingly interested in eliminating conflict as an obstacle to their rapport. The superpowers would therefore continue to cooperate in order to reduce hostilities in many areas of the globe (they did so in the Iran-Iraq conflict and in Afghanistan, Nicaragua, Angola, and Namibia), including the Arab-Israeli conflict or parts of it.[7]

Furthermore, when the Cold War ended, Israel understood that Washington might not be able to continue its high level of foreign aid to Israel ($3 billion per year) as public concerns turned to domestic problems. As for the Palestinians, the end of the Cold War and the collapse of the Soviet Union meant the discontinuation of political, economic, and military aid from their traditional supporter. Israeli and PLO leaders thus realized that the future of the Middle East depended on regional economic development that could not be achieved without a political settlement.[8] More than that, they realized that by creating peace they might create friends out of former enemies.[9]

Shortcomings of the Washington Talks

The failure of the Washington talks and the lack of authority of the Palestinian delegation there to negotiate on its own were the most important reasons behind the Israeli decision to recognize the PLO. The Rabin government of 1992 was ready to negotiate a broader Palestinian autonomy than any Likud government was ever willing to discuss. Indeed, whereas Prime Ministers Begin and Shamir kept narrowing their interpretation of the Camp David autonomy, Rabin long believed that Israel had to offer to the Palestinian inhabitants of the West Bank and Gaza new ideas that surpassed the Camp David definitions.[10] But the Palestinian delegation to the Washington rounds made demands that even the Labor government was not yet able to negotiate. For example, it insisted on full territorial autonomy as well as legislative, executive, and judiciary powers, and it demanded that UN Resolution 242 be applied to East Jerusalem. In fact, when Arafat instructed the Palestinian delegation to adhere to more realistic demands, three prominent members of the delegation threatened to resign.

Finally, as Johan Holst, Norway's foreign minister, asserted, after they had concluded that the Washington negotiations would not generate an alternative Palestinian political leadership in the territories, the Israelis preferred to deal with the PLO directly. The organization's authority was enhanced, not weakened by the earlier negotiations, and further talks directly with the PLO would reinforce the legitimacy of the agreement and the commitment to its implementation.[11]

In fact, on July 4, 1993, the stalemate in the Israeli-Palestinian talks prompted a cabinet debate, as a number of ministers from Labor and Meretz (Labor's left-wing coalition partner) demanded that Israel reexamine its position on recognizing the PLO. They cited the following reasons: (1) By directly negotiating with the PLO, Israel would demonstrate its willingness to break the deadlock in the negotiations; (2) to foster negotiations, Israel needed to elevate discussions to a ministerial level (on the Palestinian side only senior PLO officials were equivalent to ministers); (3) because the Palestinians had recognized the PLO as their sole legitimate leadership, the PLO was the only body that possessed the authority to make decisions; thus, (4) the Palestinian delegation to the peace talks would not make a move without approval from the PLO; hence, (5) Arafat was the sole decisionmaker on the Palestinian side of the negotiations.[12]

Rabin and Peres formally (and undoubtedly to maintain secrecy) rejected these demands on the grounds that a changed course in negotiations would undermine discussions over substantive issues, perhaps paralyzing the peace process. But Rabin and Peres later said they believed that Israel could not make any progress in negotiations with a Palestinian delegation that lacked decisionmaking authority and in any case received its orders from the PLO.[13] Indeed, as Rabin himself admitted, since the opening of the Madrid conference, Israel had in essence negotiated with the PLO whenever the Palestinian delegation to the talks sought the advice of the Tunis leadership.[14]

But the Israelis were becoming impatient with the other Arab delegations to the Washington talks as well: In January 1993 President Clinton entered the White House, and in February Secretary of State Christopher arrived in the Middle East to resume the negotiations that had ended in December 1992 after eight rounds of fruitless talks. But it was not until April that the ninth round of negotiations opened in Washington. By that time the Israeli government had already decided to become involved in the talks that had begun secretly in July 1992 between private Israeli citizens and PLO members. In the meantime two additional rounds of talks in Washington had produced no results. Indeed, aside from the impasse on the Israeli-Palestinian track, the Syrians refused to spell out their intentions, the Lebanese were hostage to the Syrians, and the Jordanians were all but ready to conclude an agreement with Israel but would not go it alone. Hence the Oslo alternative.

Still, rather than replacing the Washington talks, the Oslo negotiations provided a back channel that expedited the process. Indeed, even though the implementation of the Israeli-PLO agreement was expected to be a difficult procedure in itself, the Oslo breakthrough is the key to a much more promising future for the entire peace process. King Hussein, who throughout much of the peace process was to negotiate with the Israelis on behalf of Jordan and the Palestinians (who form about 50 to 60 percent of the Jordanian population), became free to negotiate peace with Israel on his own. Hussein's new freedom quickly produced results: the Israeli-Jordanian agreement on a mutual agenda of negotiation, signed in Washington on September 14, 1993; the agreement between Foreign Minister Peres and Crown Prince Hassan to normalize relations before concluding full peace, signed in Washington on October 1, 1993; and most significantly, the Washington declaration signed by King Hussein, Prime Minister Rabin, and President Clinton on July 25, 1994. In that declaration the leaders of the Hashemite Kingdom of Jordan and the State of Israel proclaimed that they had ended the state of belligerency and agreed to continue vigorous negotiations to produce a peace treaty based on Security Council Resolutions 242 and 338. Furthermore, Hussein and Rabin expressed their readiness to meet as often as necessary personally to direct those negotiations. On July 26, 1994, before a joint meeting of both houses of Congress, King Hussein announced that the state of war between Israel and Jordan was over, and Prime Minister Rabin thanked the king in the name of the entire Israeli nation for accepting Israel's offer of peace.

The Syrians, who since the early 1950s made themselves hostage to the Palestinian cause and for whom the first stage of Palestinian self-government was essential, could now move forward with their own negotiations as well. And even though the Syrians might have manipulated the Palestinian issue to strengthen their own bargaining position, they did not go ahead with the peace process immediately after the Israeli-PLO agreement mainly because of their discontentment at being left out of the agreement rather than any substantial matter. Moreover, King Hussein's decision to make peace with Israel independently left Assad little choice but to join the peace process ultimately. As Assad must have realized, not doing so would bring Damascus back to the position of isolation it was in on the eve of the Gulf crisis. And once Syria agreed to negotiate with Israel earnestly, so could Lebanon.[15]

The Clinton Administration's Pro-Israeli Stand

President Clinton's stand on Israel is another reason for the Oslo breakthrough. As a candidate, Clinton criticized the Bush administration for linking peace talks to humanitarian efforts to settle Soviet immigrants;

praised Rabin for the steps he had taken as prime minister to revive the peace process and called upon the Arab side to reciprocate; repeatedly asked the Arabs to end their boycott against Israel; and promised to help Israel maintain its qualitative military balance in the Middle East.[16] As president-elect, Clinton publicly disclosed that he would end the policy of pressuring Israel to make unilateral concessions to its Arab opponents, adding that "a Clinton Administration will treat the Arab-Israeli conflict as one in which the survival of Israel is at stake."[17] In March 1993, in his first meeting with the Israeli prime minister, President Clinton promised that he would prevent any measure to cut U.S. military and economic aid to Israel.[18] This affirmation came amid warnings by the U.S. ambassador to Israel, William Harrop, that the United States might not be able to continue its level of foreign aid to Israel, and in view of criticism by some members of Congress of the level of aid to Israel and Egypt (Israel, the largest recipient of U.S. foreign aid, receives about $3 billion annually, Egypt about two-thirds that, or $2.1 billion). Moreover, during that meeting, Clinton did not discuss with the Israeli prime minister the issue of the 400 or so Palestinians exiled to Lebanon, for which Israel was widely criticized. But Clinton's affection for the Jewish state was perhaps best expressed in an interview recorded by the *New York Times* the day before the Israeli-PLO agreement was signed in Washington: "The only time I went to Israel was with my pastor, who told me after I got back that he thought one day I would be president. ... And he said 'Just remember, God will never forgive you if you turn your back on Israel.'"[19]

The warmth with which the president approached his relations with Israel, a contrast to the frosty manner of his predecessor, could not have escaped the PLO leadership. Neither did this reassurance escape Israel.

European Involvement

The choice of a European site for negotiations was another element that advanced the process, especially for the PLO. Since the outbreak of the *intifada* in December 1987, the EC had attempted to become more involved in the peace process and repeatedly called for a greater UN role in negotiations, something Arafat had insisted on for some time. The EC finally got its wish with the multilateral negotiations that began under the Madrid formula. But more important, most EC member states long interpreted Resolution 242 to mean total Israeli withdrawal to the 1967 boundaries, and a majority of them supported the idea of Palestinian self-determination through the creation of an independent Palestinian state in the West Bank and Gaza. In 1980 the EC recognized the PLO as the sole legitimate representative of the Palestinian people, and it has since been a strong supporter of the inclusion of the PLO in peace negotiations.

By contrast, until 1988 the United States had refused to recognize the PLO and for the most part sided with Israel on the interpretation on UN Resolutions 242 and 338. Moreover, formal relations between the United States and the PLO ceased to exist after Washington discontinued its dialogue with the PLO because Arafat had refused to denounce the May 1990 seaborne guerrilla attack on Tel Aviv. It was only after Israel had recognized the PLO that the Clinton administration resumed formal ties with the organization. Thus, for the PLO, the European connection was a comforting element. As for Israel, it has been no secret that throughout his political career, Foreign Minister Peres had, through the Second Socialist International, warmer relationships with European leaders than with their U.S. counterparts.

The particular choice of Norway as a channel to negotiation was also significant. Norwegian forces had participated in all of the peacekeeping operations in the Middle East since the 1950s, and its forces cohabited with the PLO as part of UNIFIL (UN Interim Forces in Lebanon) since the end of the 1970s. Moreover, Norway was a disinterested party with a reputation for evenhandedness, and its role would be based not on leverage but on trust.[20] Last, Norwegian foreign minister Holst's involvement in the negotiations must have reassured Israel and the PLO alike. An acclaimed expert on international security and defense issues, Holst understood Israel's security dilemma all too well.[21] His wife, Marianne Heiberg, had done a great deal of research on the conditions of the Palestinians in the territories and was the author of a study for the Norwegian Institute for Applied Social Sciences, which got the talks started.

The Defeat of Saddam Hussein

With the weakening of Saddam Hussein, its most militant supporter, and the disappearance of the Iraqi threat from Israel's security concerns, the PLO found itself isolated in the Arab world and weaker than ever before. Moreover, Arafat's support of Saddam during the Gulf war combined with Saddam's defeat not only delegitimized the PLO's role in the peace process but also reduced overall Arab support for the Palestinian cause.[22]

The PLO's decision to accept a minimalist solution, however temporary it might be, was simplified by the organization's financial bankruptcy, the result of the termination of foreign aid from the former Soviet Union and East Europe and the cutoff of funds from the Gulf states in retaliation for Arafat's support of Saddam. Members of his own organization even accused Arafat of mismanaging the PLO's financial resources and of poor leadership altogether. By the time the Israeli-PLO agreement became imminent, the PLO seemed on the verge of total collapse. Thus, securing a formal role in the peace process through the reconciliation with Israel meant for the PLO rejuvenated leadership and renewed financial aid that would help resuscitate the organization. Indeed, on October 1, 1993, delegates from forty-three nations who gathered in Washington promised close to $2 billion in aid for the West Bank and Gaza over the ensuing five years, including a $25 million grant from Israel and a loan of $50 million. For Arafat, an agreement with the Israelis, signed in Washington under the sponsorship of the United States and Russia, also meant his acceptance as an equal in the community of international leaders. Palestinians are not likely soon to forget the scenes of Arafat standing next to President Clinton and Prime Minister Rabin against the backdrop of the White House during the signing ceremony, and his warm reception by congressional leaders on Capitol Hill.

Conditions in the Territories

The state of affairs in the territories was still another factor that prompted the mutual recognition between Israel and the PLO and their subsequent agreement on limited autonomy. A new wave of intensified anti-Israeli violence in the West Bank and Gaza forced Prime Minister Rabin to cut short his trip to Washington in March 1993.[23] The Israeli government eventually sealed the territories until October 22, 1993, when it eased travel restrictions on the Palestinians in order to help the PLO bolster its position and ease the way toward the implementation of the Israeli-Palestinian Declaration of Principles. But residents of the territories, Gaza in particular, reached the point of desperation, as most of the 120,000 Palestinian day laborers whose livelihood depended on Israel were unable to cross into that country. The scarcity of funds from the PLO added to the plight of the Palestinians, many of whom began questioning the efficacy of PLO leadership. With the deterioration of conditions and weakening of the PLO, Hamas was able to elevate its authority in the territories. Its objection to the acceptance of the PLO as the sole representative of the Palestinian people, its rejection of the PLO's political program, its opposition to any negotiated solution with Israel, its endorsement of Islam as an alternative to the secular teachings of the PLO, and its increased popularity in the territories alarmed both the PLO and Israel: Each regards Hamas as a greater threat than the other.[24] And alongside the growing popularity of Hamas, a growing Palestinian middle class with a stake in maintaining stability in the territories raised its own expectations for a political solution.

For their part, the Israelis distinguished between an armed Palestinian minority motivated by *jihad* and devoted to killing Israelis and Palestinians—a minority that had become increasingly dangerous—and an unarmed Palestinian majority with an elected leadership, which they obviously chose to strengthen and legitimize.[25]

The Reemergence of Labor
as the Leading Party in Israel

Of course without the return of Labor to power in the 1992 elections, none of the global or regional conditions that permitted the Oslo negotiations in the first place would have brought these negotiations to life or to their successful conclusion. Foreign Minister Holst acknowledged that the Oslo process started to move only after the arrival of the Labor government in Israel; indeed, he insisted that had the Israelis not changed their government, the process would not have been completed.[26]

In fact, the Rabin government's recognition of the PLO should be less astonishing than the speed with which it was done. After all, members of the Labor Party had urged formal contacts with the PLO for the purpose of advancing the peace process for some time, but especially after the opening of the U.S.-PLO dialogue in December 1988, following Arafat's renunciation of terrorism and his acceptance of UN Resolutions 242 and 338.

Further, Rabin understood that without the PLO, direct negotiations between Israel and a representation of the inhabitants of the West Bank and Gaza were useless. In 1989 he thus tried to arrange for an indirect dialogue with the PLO leadership in Tunis so that the PLO could indirectly participate in the peace process (see Chapter 11). In 1991 the Labor Party adopted as part of its platform a document of principles issued by the party's doves that recognized the need for Israel to begin a dialogue with the PLO.

Thus, from July 1992, when Labor returned to power, the shift in Israel's policy toward the PLO was becoming increasingly evident. To begin with, the "Basic Policy Guideline of the Rabin Government" deviated from earlier comparable documents: It did not directly pledge to refrain from a formal or informal dialogue with the PLO. Neither did it directly reaffirm Israel's opposition to the creation of an independent Palestinian state on Israel's borders. Rather, paragraph 2.7 of the document only confirmed that the peace process would continue in accordance with the framework and the schedule formulated at the Madrid conference.[27]

In a symbolic gesture three months after taking office, the government withdrew its objection to the participation of Palestinians from outside the occupied territories in the multilateral talks. Furthermore, while insisting on negotiations only with the leaders of the Palestinians in the territories, Rabin openly acknowledged that those leaders could not do so on their own, in part because they were more fearful of the extremists who opposed the peace process than of the leadership in Tunis. Rabin's explanation of his insistence on a dialogue with Palestinian leaders from the territories rather than Tunis was notable in that it did not rest on the rationale that a dialogue with the PLO leadership might legitimate the organization but on a more prosaic issue: Unlike the leaders in Tunis, those in the territories were fully aware of the problems the Palestinians in the territories faced and therefore tended to be more pragmatic.[28]

On November 30, 1992, the Israeli government submitted a proposed amendment to the Knesset that would repeal a law banning contacts between Israelis and members of the PLO. On December 20, ministers from Meretz met with Rabin, urging him to open a dialogue with the PLO and ease restrictions in the occupied territories; on December 21 Foreign Minister Peres articulated his belief that Israel must enter a dialogue with any Palestinian organization that expresses a willingness to reach a peace agreement with Israel. On December 26 it was made public that thirty Labor MKs supported negotiations with the PLO.[29]

On January 19, 1993, the Knesset repealed the law forbidding contacts between Israelis and PLO members. On March 24 Meretz approved its own plan for withdrawal from the Gaza Strip, and on March 25 Peres reportedly called for a negotiated withdrawal from Gaza.[30] In line with this offer, on April 23 he suggested the establishment of a Palestinian police force in the territories, a proposal that outraged the Jewish settlers and their supporters.[31] On July 8 the chairman of the Committee for Knesset Affairs Hagai Marom of Labor, stunned his colleagues during a debate on the peace process, by identifying Labor ministers he believed had supported an open dialogue with the PLO and the "Gaza first" proposal. He then demanded that they "get out of hiding" and mobilize a government majority toward a breakthrough in negotiations.[32] Related or not, on July 13 Peres floated an idea before the State Department Middle East negotiations team headed by Dennis Ross; the modification of the basic approach of the talks and, simultaneous with the ongoing discussions on Palestinian autonomy, the opening of a dialogue on the permanent status of the territories, based on the concept of a confederation with Jordan. The PLO and Jordan were reportedly engaged in negotiations on the confederation idea at the same time.[33]

In the beginning of August, it became known that Environment Minister Yossi Sarid and MK Dedi Zuker, both members of Meretz, had met secretly in Cairo with Nabil Shaath, a high-ranking PLO official who was one of the senior PLO negotiators in Oslo. This was the first approved meeting of an Israeli cabinet member with any PLO official. On August 30 the cabinet accepted a draft statement of principles on Palestinian self-rule negotiated at secret Israeli-PLO talks in Norway and Tunis, with sixteen ministers endorsing it and two abstaining—Interior Minister Aryeh Deri and Police Minister Shimon Shitrit.

On September 23, 1993, after three days of bitter debate, the Knesset endorsed the Declaration of Principles by a vote of sixty-one to fifty. Of the affirmative votes forty-four came from the Labor Party, twelve from Meretz, and five from two small Arab parties. Shas (Sephardi Torah Guardians), the religious party that until September 12 was Labor's coalition partner, abstained. (Shas left the coalition not because of a conflict over the peace process but because Deri had been indicted for corruption.)

The Survival of Rabin's Coalition

The survival of Rabin's government—in spite of a number of coalition crises—was another factor that helped secure the Israeli-PLO agreement. The first test of Rabin's coalition occurred two weeks after its inception, when the Knesset defeated five no-confidence votes submitted by Likud, Tzomet, the National Religious Party (NRP), United Torah Jewry, and Moledet over the government's position on territorial compromise with Syria and its decision to freeze settlement activity in the territories. But a more serious crisis was averted in November 1992 when the government survived two no-confidence votes after the ultraorthodox Shas Party had threatened to leave the coalition unless Shulamit Aloni, the outspoken left-wing education minister from Meretz, resigned. At issue were remarks Aloni had made that affronted Orthodox Jewish leaders; the controversy was resolved after Aloni apologized. But a similar crisis emerged in May 1993, Shas leader and interior minister Deri resigning from Rabin's coalition to protest other offensive statements Aloni had made. To avert this crisis, Rabin assumed control over the education and interior ministries, thereby allowing Deri to withdraw his resignation, and the government was reformulated in June. Energy Minister Amnon Rubinstein of Meretz assumed the position of education minister, while Moshe Shahal of Labor assumed Rubinstein's post as energy minister and Deri was reconfirmed as interior minister.

The withdrawal of Shas from the coalition might not have brought down Rabin's coalition, which controlled sixty-two of the 120 Knesset seats. But it would have jeopardized the government's decisionmaking ability, as it meant that on policy issues that needed Knesset approval, Rabin would have had to rely on the support of the five votes of two small Arab parties that were not members of the government, thereby losing a Jewish majority. Rabin therefore recruited Shas to his coalition government even though Deri had been under investigation since 1990 and even though by June 1992 Deri's indictment on charges of bribery and fraud was imminent. And since it was politically too risky for Rabin to depend on the Arab vote on matters as vital as peace and security, Rabin insisted on retaining Deri in his government in spite of the controversy. For his part, Deri agreed that if charged in court, he would suspend himself from the government; thus on September 12, 1993, Deri handed in his resignation. By that time the government had already approved the Israeli-Palestinian agreement. To Rabin's satisfaction, when Shas abstained from the Knesset vote on the Israeli-PLO agreement, thus depriving the government of six affirmative votes, the government did not have to rely on a non-Jewish majority because of the defection of three Likud members who refused to join their party in condemning the agreement.

Finally, the cooperation between Rabin and Peres was another factor contributing to the success of the Oslo talks: These two political rivals had long been feuding over the leadership of the Labor Party, occasionally splitting the party into two camps. Their quarrels were settled through the first party primaries, which took place before the 1992 elections, a solution that many Israelis viewed as temporary at best. Nonetheless, during the Oslo negotiations the two old contenders put their rivalry behind them, coordinating their efforts and concentrating instead on what they believed to be their country's national interest.

Israel's Self-Confidence

The sense of security that Rabin had fostered in Israel was another reason he was able to conclude an agreement with the PLO. Between 1988 and 1990, as defense minister in the National Unity government, Rabin had utilized severe force to quell the *intifada*—and was often criticized by international observers for doing so. His announcement on January 19, 1988, of his new policy for dealing with the Palestinian uprising, to include "force, might, and beatings" in an effort to lessen deaths of rioters through security force use of live ammunition, drew protests not only from the State Department but also from tens of thousands of Israelis.[34]

In December 1992, after a wave of violence in the West Bank and Gaza, Rabin exiled to Lebanon 415 Palestinians linked to militant Islamic groups. Although the mass expulsion threatened the eighth round of the Washington talks and invited harsh criticism both in Israel and abroad, it nonetheless gave many Israelis the sense that under no circumstances would Rabin jeopardize the security of Israel or Israelis. In March 1993, amid intensified anti-Israeli violence in the West Bank and Gaza, Rabin sealed the area, knowing that the move would create unbearable conditions for the inhabitants in the territories. Finally, on the eve of the eleventh round of the Washington talks in summer 1993, Rabin retaliated for a series of attacks by Hezbollah guerrillas on Israeli soldiers stationed in Israel's security zone and on northern Israeli towns. He ordered a massive assault on south Lebanon, forcing hundreds of thousands of refugees to flee the area and thereby compelling the Lebanese government to appeal to Syria to control the guerrillas. While many international and Israeli spectators found Rabin's policy appalling, his tactics revealed once again that Rabin would not hesitate to use any means necessary to secure the safety of his citizens. With a stronger sense of self-confidence, fewer Israelis were opposed to the agreement with the PLO.

The Gaza-Jericho Plan

The plan that envisaged the implementation of Palestinian self-rule in the Gaza Strip and the West Bank town of Jericho went into effect at the signing ceremony on the White House lawn on September 13, 1993, when Israeli foreign minister Shimon Peres and the foreign policy spokesman for the PLO, Mahmoud Abbas, endorsed what was officially called The Declaration of Principles on Interim Self-Government Arrangements.

Basically, the declaration is a blueprint for a two-phased solution to the Israeli-Palestinian problem. The first phase consists of a five-year period of Palestinian self-rule. The second phase envisions the implementation of permanent arrangements, to be negotiated no later than the beginning of the third year of the interim period or two years after the conclusion of the Gaza-Jericho plan.

The declaration leaves open some uneasy questions—it does not spell out the consequences of its violation, nor does it provide for the possibility that the PLO would be incapable of controlling the territories or for the extradition to the Israeli authorities of a Palestinian who had harmed an Israeli citizen. But it does elaborate on the conduct of general elections in the territories in order to create a self-governing council whose function is to carry out the interim arrangements. It also outlines an array of responsibilities for each side. Under the plan the Palestinians will govern their own affairs in all spheres of daily life and will provide for their own internal security. Israel, for its part, will retain responsibility for external defense as well as the security of Jewish settlements and Israeli civilians. The status of Jerusalem is to be unchanged throughout the five-year period of interim self-rule but is to be raised in the course of negotiations on the permanent status of the territories. (However, the agreement leaves no doubt that Israel would not forsake its demand that Jerusalem remain its undivided capital under Israeli sovereignty.)

Much like the Camp David accords, the plan aims to establish an interim self government authority in the form of an elected council in the

West Bank and Gaza. The purpose of the council is to administer a transitional period not exceeding five years, leading to a permanent settlement based on Security Council Resolutions 242 and 338. But elements introduced in the Declaration of Principles differ significantly from any earlier approved Israeli document. For one, it includes the Gaza-Jericho plan as a first and immediate step toward implementation of Palestinian self-rule. This would enable Arafat to control the Gaza district—an impoverished and violent area that many in Israel have long wanted to vacate—and the tranquil town of Jericho, which is situated in the West Bank and is therefore politically important to Arafat.

Other new elements (elements similar to those opposed by the Likud government in previous initiatives) include international observation of the future election, the granting of legislative authority to the council, and permitting Palestinians who live in East Jerusalem to participate in the election process. Finally and most significant, the agreement sets forth a speedy timetable for Palestinian self-rule:

1. Elections are scheduled for no later than nine months from the time the agreement took effect.
2. Transfer of authority from the Israeli military government and its civil administration to the authorized Palestinians would begin upon the entry into force of the declaration and the Israeli withdrawal from Gaza and Jericho.
3. Within two months from that date of entry, the two sides would sign an agreement for the withdrawal of Israeli forces from Gaza and Jericho. Beginning immediately with the signing of the agreement Israel would implement an accelerated withdrawal, to be completed within a period not exceeding four months.
4. The five-year transitional period is scheduled to begin upon the withdrawal from Gaza and Jericho.
5. Negotiations on the permanent status of the territories are scheduled to begin as soon as possible but no later than the beginning of the third year of the interim period.

Israeli Reaction

As might have been expected, the opposition in Israel reacted strongly against the agreement. Aside from the antigovernment rhetoric and the stormy demonstrations organized by the political Right, the opposition called for the resignation of the government before the agreement could be approved in the Knesset. Binyamin Netanyahu, who on March 25, 1993, won the leadership of Likud in primary elections, accused the Labor government of treason and promised to use "all available legitimate means that exist in a democratic country" to prevent the agreement.[35] Others in the opposition, including MK Rehavam Ze'evi of Moledet—and leaders of the settlement movement—provoked the Israeli public and the military to defy the government. Knesset members such as Ariel Sharon and Uzi Landau of Likud and Rafael Eitan of Tzomet, equated the effects the Declaration of Principles would have with the Holocaust.

On the positive side polls showed that support for the agreement was on the increase: A *Yediot Aharonot*/Dahaf poll taken on September 10, 1993, showed that 57 percent of adult Jewish Israelis supported the Gaza-Jericho agreement, 41 percent were opposed to it, and 2 percent had no opinion. A poll taken on September 14—a day after the agreement was signed in Washington—showed that 61 percent of adult Jewish Israelis supported the agreement, 37 percent were opposed, and 2 percent had no opinion.[36]

On the Palestinian side news of the agreement met with mixed emotions. While many Palestinians supported the agreement, others believed that they got too little from the Israelis and that self-rule might not just begin in Gaza and Jericho but end there as well. As expected, the plan was condemned by the ten radical Palestinian groups based in Syria—some of which threatened Arafat's life—and by Islamic groups, including Hezbollah in Lebanon and Hamas in the territories.[37]

On October 13, 1993, the agreement between Israel and the PLO officially went into effect as both sides began negotiations in Taba, Egypt, on shifting authority in Gaza and Jericho from Israel to the Palestinians. On February 9, 1994, Foreign Minister Peres and Arafat signed the Cairo agreement, a partial agreement on security issues related to the Gaza-Jericho accord, such as border crossing and joint Israeli-Palestinian patrols. But the Hebron massacre of February 25, 1994—carried out by a fanatic Jewish settler from Kiryat Arba, who entered the Tomb of the Patriarchs in Hebron, killing twenty-nine Muslim worshipers and injuring a score of others— froze the ongoing negotiations until March 31, when Israel and the PLO signed an agreement regarding security arrangements in Hebron. They also decided to renew negotiations on the Gaza-Jericho agreement. Thus, on May 4, 1994, Rabin and Arafat signed in Cairo the Agreement on the Gaza Strip and the Jericho Area, a detailed document specifying terms concerning the implementation of the Declaration of Principles.[38]

While the original date for the beginning of the withdrawal of the Israeli military from Gaza and Jericho was December 13, 1994, Israeli troops began to retreat from these areas in mid-April.[39] The departure of Israel's military forces from Gaza and Jericho was completed the day the

Gaza-Jericho agreement was signed. One day later, on May 5, 1994, with an enormous display of local support, the Palestinian police began moving into the area.

On July 1–5, 1994, against strong protest from the Israeli Right and amid violent demonstrations orchestrated by Jewish settlers in the West Bank, Arafat visited Gaza and Jericho—reportedly his first visit to the occupied territories in twenty-seven years. In Jericho, he was sworn in as the head of a new Palestine National Autonomy. But with no improvement in the lives of the Palestinians, the enthusiasm with which Arafat was received by the inhabitants of Gaza and Jericho, confirming his position as the legitimate leader of the Palestinian Arabs, is steadily eroding.

On July 7, 1994, against the opposition of the Israeli Right, Prime Minister Rabin, Foreign Minister Peres and Chairman Arafat entered a new phase of talks in Paris, to discuss extending Palestinian autonomy to the rest of the West Bank. As noted, these developments encouraged King Hussein to begin open and direct negotiations with Israel, resulting in the peace agreement signed on October 26, 1994, in the border area between Eilat and Aqaba.

■ ■ ■

The agreement reached in Oslo between Israel and the PLO reveals that even though rivaling sides may need the assistance of third parties to help them negotiate, only the protagonists themselves can decide if and when they will enter negotiations. That decision is greatly influenced by existing international and regional conditions. But the Oslo negotiations and the progress that Israel and the PLO made in the negotiation process thereafter also show that unless there is domestic support for negotiations within the countries concerned, the prevailing external conditions alone will not produce a breakthrough.

Unlike its predecessor, the Labor government in Israel was long willing to adapt to existing global and regional conditions. But if the majority of Israelis had not become pragmatic during the 1992 elections, the mutual recognition between Israel and the PLO and the Gaza-Jericho agreement would not have been possible.

However, as part 2 shows, negotiations are a long and trying process. The conservative nature of the international systems can inhibit innovative ideas on vital issues such as peace and security. Similarly, the negotiating process itself is often restrained by domestic considerations, thus preventing diplomats from submitting imaginative proposals to their negotiating partners.

For example, from the time the Camp David agreements were concluded in 1978 until the end of the Cold War, no dramatic global changes prompted the Arabs and Israelis to negotiate peace with one another. But improved relations between the two superpowers in the late 1980s, the end of the Cold War in 1989, the Gulf war of 1991 and its aftermath, the collapse of the Soviet Union in December 1991, and the enduring economic recession in the United States in the early 1990s together created global conditions that forced Arabs and Israelis to modify their positions on an Arab-Israeli peace. But the negotiation process itself reacted to these global changes only after domestic conditions in Israel permitted that to occur.

Indeed, a negotiation process does have a life of its own. For example, it took the Arab-Israeli peace process fifteen years to incrementally construct the Gaza-Jericho plan: A close look at the peace process beginning with the Camp David agreements and ending with the Gaza-Jericho plan of September 1993 shows that new ideas were introduced throughout the process in a deliberately slow and careful manner. First, plans for an Arab-Israeli peace during that period were based on the Camp David accords, which were modeled after Prime Minister Begin's autonomy plan of December 1977. It envisioned the abolition of Israel's military authority in the West Bank and Gaza and its replacement by an administrative body, elected by and from the Palestinian inhabitants of the West Bank and Gaza. The purpose of this body was the management of the basic aspects of the daily lives of the Palestinian inhabitants of the West Bank and Gaza during a five-year transitional period of self-rule. Negotiations on the permanent status of the territories were to start no later than three years after the initiation of the transitional period.

Not surprisingly, the Gaza-Jericho agreement also envisioned a five-year period of Palestinian self-rule. But self-rule under this plan was to be implemented first in Gaza and Jericho only. It, too, called for a Palestinian self-governing council to carry out the interim arrangements during a five-year period of self-rule. Under this plan negotiations on the permanent status of the territories were scheduled to begin as soon as possible but no later than the start of the third year of the interim period. The difference between this and other plans is that the Gaza-Jericho agreement set forth a speedy timetable for the beginning of the Palestinian self-rule—not a very striking change considering the fifteen-year interval.

Certainly, variations in the peace plans that were introduced between 1978 and 1993 were small building blocks. The Reagan plan built onto the Camp David agreements the element of territorial autonomy and Palestinian control over water resources. Although Begin rejected the plan, in 1993 the Labor government agreed to territorial autonomy—a principle Labor had long adhered to. And the control of water resources is covered under the negotiation process that began on October 14, 1993, in Taba, over the implementation of the Gaza-Jericho plan, and is also discussed in the multilateral portion of the Madrid peace talks.

The Shultz plan shortened the interim stage of Palestinian self-rule to three years, but the Israeli proposal of May 14, 1989, kept the five-year period. Baker's plan focused only on elections in the West Bank and Gaza for Palestinian representatives to peace talks with the Israelis, but it raised the issue of far broader Palestinian representation than Likud would ever have permitted. The Madrid conference—or rather the Palestinian track of that conference—also focused on the creation of a Palestinian administrative council to administer the proposed Interim Self-Government Agreements. However, unlike previous peace plans, the Madrid conference was the first forum for face to face negotiations involving Arab states, the Palestinians, and Israel. Most important, it provided for indirect negotiations between Israel and the PLO when the latter was the only body capable of making decisions for the Palestinians. Madrid thus set the stage for the mutual recognition between Israel and the PLO. Rabin himself best described his decision:

> For a long time I believed that the Palestinian inhabitants in the territories would utilize their own authority. But after over a year of negotiations, I reached the conclusion that they do not have the power to do so. They did not arrive in Madrid without ready-made decisions from Tunis; they did not act without faxes and telephones from Tunis.[40]

Even so, the crucial element enabling Israel to recognize the PLO as the only authoritative Palestinian body and to conclude with that organization an agreement based on territorial compromise was the domestic change that had occurred in Israel during the 1992 elections there, a change that gave the Labor-led government the mandate it needed to break the impasse in peace negotiations.

Notes

1. Abba Eban, *The New Diplomacy* (New York: Random House, 1983) p. 353.

2. Nabil Shaath, interview with Charlie Rose (PBS), September 13, 1993.

3. Johan Holst, Norwegian foreign minister, speaking before the National Press Club, Washington, D.C., October 4, 1993.

4. Aharon Klienman, *Statecraft in the Dark: Israel's Practice of Quiet Diplomacy* (Tel Aviv: Jaffe Center for Strategic Studies, Tel Aviv University, 1988), p. 113.

5. *New York Times*, September 5, 1993, p. 1.

6. Shimon Peres, *Tomorrow Is Now* (Hebrew) (Jerusalem: Keter, 1978), p. 232.

7. Interview with Yitzhak Rabin of December 1988, "The Leon Charney Report," CCN LTD/JMS Productions, September 26, 1993.

8. Shimon Peres, "Let's Build a New Middle East," *Ha'aretz* (weekend supplement), July 7, 1993; interview with Bassam abu-Sharif, "This Week with David Brinkley" (ABC), September 5, 1993; interview with Yasir Arafat, "Larry King Live" (CNN), September 13, 1993.

9. Holst, speaking before the National Press Club, Washington, D.C., October 4, 1993.

10. Interview, "The Leon Charney Report," December 1988.

11. Holst, speaking before the National Press Club, Washington. D.C., October 4, 1993.

12. *Ha'aretz* (international ed.), July 5, 1993.

13 . Interview with Peres, "This Week with David Brinkley" (ABC), September 5, 1993; interview with Yitzhak Rabin, "MacNeil/Lehrer Newshour" (PBS), September 13, 1993.

14. Interview in *Yediot Aharonot* (weekend supplement), September 4, 1992.

15. Some of these conclusions were based in part on a private conversation with former assistant secretary of state for Near Eastern and Africa affairs Richard Murphy, New York, September 9, 1993.

16. Appendix A: "Compilation of Statements on the Middle East by Presidential Candidate Bill Clinton, March 31–November 2, 1992," in Raphael Danziger and Arthur Rubin, *The Clinton-Rabin Partnership in the Mideast Peace Process* (Washington, D.C.: AIPAC, 1993).

17. *Facts on File* 52, 2714 (November 26, 1992).

18. Ibid.

19. *New York Times*, September 12, 1993, p. 10.

20. Holst, speaking before the National Press Club, Washington, D.C., October 4, 1993.

21. Johan Holst wrote dozens of books and articles on the subject. Among his books are *A Nuclear Freeze Zone in the Nordic Area* (Oslo: Norsk Utenrikspolitisk Institute, 1983); *Civilian-based Defense in a New Era* (Cambridge: Albert Einstein Institution, 1990); *European Security and the Role of Arms Control* (Brussels: Center for European Policy Studies, 1948); *Exploring Europe* (Los Angeles, Calif.: Rand/ UCLA, 1990). His articles include "Arms Control in the Nineties: A European Perspective," *Daedalus* 120, 1 (winter 1991): 83–110; "Conventional Stability in Europe," *Scandinavian Review* 77, 2 (summer 1989): 7–18; "Norwegian Defense Policy for the 1990s: A Conceptual Framework," *Scandinavian Review* 76, 2 (summer 1988): 30–42; and "Perusing a Durable Peace in the Aftermath of the Cold War," *NATO Review* 40, 4 (August 1992): 9–13.

22. For a discussion on the Palestinians and the Gulf war, see Muhammad Hallaj, "Taking Sides: Palestinians and the Gulf Crisis," *Journal of Palestine Studies* 20, 3 (spring 1991): 41–47.

23. During this wave of violence, a *Yediot Aharonot* poll showed that 53 percent of Israeli Jews favored a unilateral withdrawal from Gaza; 34 percent opposed it. *Yediot Aharonot*, March 19, 1993.

24. For a discussion on the position of Hamas in the territories, see Ziad Abu-Amr, "Hamas: A Historical and Political Background," *Journal of Palestine Studies* 22, 4 (summer 1993): 5–19.

25. Interview with Peres, "This Week with David Brinkley" (ABC), September 5, 1993; interview with Rabin, "MacNeil/Lehrer Newshour" (PBS), September 13, 1993.

26. Holst, speaking before the National Press Club, Washington, D.C., October 4, 1993.

27. *Basic Policy Guideline of the Rabin Government* (Jerusalem: Israel Ministry of Foreign Affairs, July 13, 1992).

28. Interview with *Al-Hayat*, October 20, 1992.

29. At the same time a *Yediot Aharonot*/Dahaf Institute poll showed that nearly half of the Israeli Jews supported the participation of the PLO in the peace process. *Yediot Aharonot*, December 23, 1992, and January 1, 1993.

30. Israel Defense Forces Radio, March 25, 1993.

31. *Ha'aretz* (international ed.), April 24, 1993.

32. Ibid., July 8, 1993.

33. Ibid., July 14–15, 1993.

34. In January 24, amid criticism and reports of excessive brutality, the Israeli army repealed the beating policy.

35. A small number of Likud leaders, including MK Beni Begin, rejected the Holocaust analogy and the instigation to defy the government. Ronnie Milo (who was running for mayor of Tel Aviv and was courting the doves within the population) supported the government. *Ha'aretz* (international ed.), August 30, 1993; September 5, 14, 22, 1993.

36. *Yediot Aharonot*, September 15, 1993. A poll taken in September in the West Bank and Gaza showed that 66.4 percent of Palestinians favored the agreement while 29.3 percent were opposed. *New York Times*, October 16, 1993, p. 2.

37. Public support for the Gaza-Jericho agreement has declined sharply in Israeli and Palestinian communities alike since the agreement was signed in September 1993.

38. Three points remained unresolved: the designated area of Jericho, the stationing of a Palestinian police officers on each of the two bridges connecting Israel and Jericho, and the refugee question.

39. The Israeli withdrawal from Gaza and Jericho started about three weeks prior to the signing of the agreement in order to allow the relatively smooth entry of the Palestinian police into these areas.

40. *Yediot Aharonot*, August 31, 1993.

PART THREE

The Israeli Domestic Scene

8

The Domestic Debate over Peace, Security, and Territorial Rights

More than any other Arab-Israeli war, the 1967 Six-Day War produced a constant debate in Israel regarding not only the future of the territories the country had acquired during that war but also the future of the state as a Zionist entity. The descendants of the Labor Zionist establishment maintained that the survival of Israel as both a Jewish and a democratic state was incompatible with the control of a vast Arab population stripped of any political rights. On the opposite side of the political spectrum, the descendants of Revisionist Zionism refused to consider the repartition of the Land of Israel any time in the future. Taken to their extreme, these convictions also produced a call for a unilateral Israeli withdrawal from the occupied territories and a bid for the expulsion of all Arabs from Israel to neighboring Arab states. Together these conflicting ideas shaped the country's reactions to the peace process from 1967 to the 1993 agreement with the PLO and for some time will continue to shape the national debate over peace and security.

The System of Government and Factional Divisions

Israel is without doubt the most stable country in the Middle East. It is a functioning democracy with effective political institutions; it enjoys a high level of popular participation in political affairs, involving a relatively large number of political parties; and its political system is widely accepted by its citizens. It is a strong regional military power, capable of deterring any enemy and remaining in relative security.

These achievements, however, are not taken for granted by the Israelis. Not only were they hard to obtain but many Israelis believe that Israel's enemies—some of whom have never accepted Israel's boundaries—are relentlessly trying to destroy the Jewish state. Suspicion certainly runs deep in the Israeli political culture, rooted in the Jewish experience of exile and oppression, isolation and rejection, the Holocaust, and recurring war with the Arabs. Although Israelis may have an inherent distrust of Arabs, they are also skeptical about everyone else's intentions. More important, most Israelis believe that they can rely only upon themselves to guarantee their own security, by maintaining a powerful military; others believe that Israel's security depends on controlling large territories beyond the country's Green Line (the boundaries of the State of Israel).

It is not surprising, then, that the issues of peace, security, and territoriality have consistently been manipulated by all of Israel's political parties, as well as all of its governments.[1] Indeed, these issues not only influence voting behavior in Israel but often determine how much faith the Knesset has in the government. Since the government is accountable to the Knesset, the Knesset's approval is essential for its survival.

The Israeli government is a party government: The party that wins the national elections controls the government, and the party leader becomes the prime minister.[2] In Israel's proportional representation system, any list that receives a minimum of 1.5 percent of the national vote wins representation in the Knesset, which is composed of 120 seats. This low requirement, coupled with a relatively high number of lists competing in the Israeli elections, has invariably resulted in the absence of simple winning majority. Because no party has ever won a simple majority, coalition governments have always been formed.

Since they are often the groups with which the winning party strikes the coalition agreement, some of the fringe parties have the power to make or break a government. In Israel these have traditionally been the religious parties. Any important issue—and hardly any issue is more important in Israel than the Arab-Israeli conflict—can determine not only the makeup of a coalition but also its duration. Naturally, if one or more members of a coalition disagree with the government's policies, the coalition may collapse.

Until 1977 the Labor Alignment dominated every Israeli government (with the exception of the wall-to-wall National Unity coalition in the 1967 Arab-Israeli crisis). But in 1977 the traditional opposition party—Likud—stunned the nation when it unexpectedly emerged as the largest party. In the 1981 elections Likud remained the largest party, but in 1984 the Labor Alignment won forty-four Knesset seats and the Likud forty-one, the balance of thirty-five seats being divided among the remaining parties. In the 1988 elections the Likud won forty seats, Labor won thirty-nine seats, and the remaining forty-one went to other parties. Thus, from

September 1984 until the collapse of the government in March 1990 (over the peace process), Labor and Likud cogoverned the country under two National Unity coalitions.

The way in which the future of the Arab-Israeli struggle determines internal politics in Israel was best articulated by Asher Arian and Michal Shamir: Since reactions to the conflict are reflected in voting behavior and coalition negotiations, the ability of Israel's major political parties to manipulate the issue turns it into an asset or a drawback.[3] But perhaps the most cynical view regarding the manipulation of the issue of peace and security in Israel is expressed by Gad Barzilai and Bruce Russett, who infer that in Israel (1) the use of military action is a conscious effort by the government to gain voters' support; (2) the public is usually hawkish because of recurrent Arab attacks; and (3) members of the government tend to exaggerate the degree of external hostility when they are most vulnerable politically and thus react more vigorously at election time.[4]

Be that as it may, since the 1967 and the 1973 wars, almost all of Israel's political parties (the exception being the non-Zionist religious parties) have linked matters of peace and security to the future of the occupied territories. This is hardly surprising, as many Israelis connect Israeli control over the occupied territories and its inhabitants with their personal security. Indeed, the future of the occupied territories is the very issue on which the Israeli public is nearly evenly divided.[5] Those who are least open to compromise are those who feel the most threatened.[6]

Since 1967 a number of options have emerged in Israel concerning the West Bank and Gaza (or the resolution of the Israeli-Palestinian conflict): the territorial compromise, also known as the Jordanian option; the nonterritorial compromise, also known as the autonomy plan; and expulsion, also known as transfer. Few Israelis call for a unilateral Israeli withdrawal from the territories.

While the Labor Alignment and the parties on the left advocate the territorial compromise, Likud and other right-wing parties prefer the nonterritorial option. Some in Likud and the NRP, along with other right-wing parties (i.e., Tzomet), favor annexation, whereas others (i.e. Kach—the extreme right-wing movement formed in 1981 by the late Rabbi Meir Kahane; Moledet) favor expulsion. Because the heart of the debate is territory, before we turn to the different options concerning the future of the occupied territories, it is worth briefly discussing the concept of territoriality.

According to those who espouse territoriality, political power should be based on a specific piece of territory, and sovereignty should extend only to certain natural frontiers corresponding with historical or ethnic divisions.[7] Territorial claims are not a modern phenomenon, of course. But in earlier times territory was associated primarily with habitation and livelihood, whereas in modern times territory has been closely connected to nationbuilding. The institutional framework for the promotion and defense of territoriality is thus the territorial state.[8]

The very idea of nationalism and self-determination and the emergence of the nation-state are based on the premise that the universe is divided into specific groups of human beings, each uniquely distinguished by certain characteristics and each charged with the duty of cultivating these characteristics within a distinct territorial domain, to which the group has special rights. Until the French Revolution territorial claims were essentially based on legitimacy, which in turn was based on the principle of monarchical heredity. But with the rise of nationalism—prompted in Europe by the French Revolution and the industrial revolution—legitimacy was replaced by other claims, the most important of which were historic and ethnic.[9]

Historic claims are based on earlier ownership and usually involve the practice of citing selected facts of history to show how they logically point to the moral or legal rights of possession. Ethnic claims are a direct outgrowth of nationalism and are usually related to the principle of self-determination. In fact, the ethnic claim is based on the territorial requirements of the national state, asserting that the boundaries of states should correspond to the actual distribution of national groups.[10]

Territorial Compromise

Central to the option of territorial compromise is the notion that to preserve the Jewish character of the State of Israel, it is necessary to withdraw from parts of the West Bank and Gaza, so long as this would not lead to the establishment of an independent Palestinian state. It differs from the autonomy plan in that it encourages the end of Israeli control over most of the West Bank and Gaza and allows the Palestinians to determine their own affiliation.

This theory assumes that any Palestinian entity must by nature be hostile to Israel (the signing of the Israeli-PLO agreement in September 1993 still leaves this an open question). Thus the establishment of a future Palestinian state on Israel's border is too risky for Israeli security and must be prevented. Yet proponents of territorial compromise conceive an Arab-Israeli settlement as possible and view Jordan as the most logical partner for a negotiated solution to the Palestinian problem, without the inclusion of the PLO in negotiations. The acceptance of the PLO as a negotiating partner by the Labor government did not reverse the overwhelming rejection in Israel of a future independent Palestinian state. But it envisioned a federal or confederal arrangement between a Palestinian entity and Jordan or even Israel.[11]

Labor's initial policy was outlined and adopted in 1969 and served as a guide to the Labor government until 1977, when Likud took over. Since 1977 Labor's policy has been modified to accommodate domestic, regional, and global changes. These changes included the rise of Likud to power, the Camp David agreements, the outbreak of the *intifada*, the rise of militant Islam in the territories, the PLO's acceptance of Israel and its willingness to renounce terrorism, the opening of a U.S.-PLO dialogue, the demise of the USSR and the end of the Cold War, and the Gulf war.

Labor's policy is thus based on the various proposals put forward after the Six-Day War, formulated primarily by Yigal Allon, then deputy prime minister. The central principles of his plan were the preservation of both the Jewish and democratic characters of the state through limited Israeli territorial control over the West Bank and Gaza and a limit on the number of Palestinian Arabs under Israeli rule.

The most ardent opponent of the Allon plan was Moshe Dayan, defense minister at the time. Dayan, who objected to any partition of the area between the Jordan River and the Mediterranean, engineered the integration of the West Bank economy into the Israeli system. He also insisted that Israel undertake all governmental responsibilities in the occupied territories without formally annexing the area and without granting any rights to its inhabitants. In addition Dayan ordered the creation of "established facts" in the occupied territories through the creation of Jewish settlements in areas that were vital for Israel's security, a notion that guided Labor's settlement policy until its 1977 defeat.

Foreign Minister Abba Eban, who was mostly concerned with Israel's international status, introduced his own plan. It called for an Arab-Israeli peace treaty based on mutual recognition; secure and recognized borders between Israel and the individual Arab states; and the formation of a five-year plan for the solution of the refugee problem. The plan also suggested that Christian and Muslim inhabitants of the occupied territories be given control over their holy places in Jerusalem.[12]

Unlike the Allon plan, which the government neither adopted nor officially rejected, Eban's plan was approved by the Labor-controlled Israeli government on October 6, 1968, and became official government policy. Nonetheless, the 1969 Labor Party outline depicted Israel's security borders in conformity with the Allon plan. It stated that a peace settlement ought to be concluded with Jordan (the Jordanian-Palestinian state) and permitted that "the Jordanian delegation for peace negotiations include Palestinian representatives from Judea and Samaria."[13]

As occupation continued, some Labor Party members became increasingly concerned with economic and other consequences. Fearing Jewish dependency on Arab labor, the more dovish sector of the party called for withdrawal from all or most of the occupied territories as the only safe way to preserve the Zionist nature of the State of Israel. This view was incorporated into the 1973 party platform and remained the party's policy for the 1977 elections.

After Labor lost the elections in 1977, the party revised its platform. In 1981 it perceived a demilitarized Jordanian-Palestinian state extending over the territories of Jordan as well as over defined densely populated areas in Judea, Samaria, and Gaza, which would eventually be evacuated by the Israeli Defense Forces with the signing of a peace treaty with the Jordanian government. The platform accepted the Camp David autonomy as "one possibility in a transitional period." It stressed Labor's growing concern with what became known as the "demographic problem."[14]

As Tables 8.1 and 8.2 show, the occupation of the West Bank and Gaza resulted in a changed demographic balance between Jews and Arabs. Coupled with a birthrate that is much higher among Arabs than it is among Jews, the occupation will slowly decrease the population gap between the two groups. Indeed, population projections for the West Bank and Gaza show a significant increase for the Palestinian population by the year 2002.[15] And although over 400,000 Russian Jews emigrated to Israel between 1989–1992, the macrocosm of that population may not alter the Jewish-Arab ratio in the Israel in the long run.

Be that as it may, the 1984 Labor platform did not diverge dramatically from that of 1981 except to state that Likud's rigid territorial policy regarding the West Bank and Gaza created the danger of transforming Israel into a binational state, contradicting both Zionism and democratic principles. The Labor Alignment offered to transfer broad powers and responsibilities over civilian matters to local authorities of the occupied areas, leaving overall authority in the hands of Israel. It denounced the

TABLE 8.1   Jewish and Non-Jewish Population Ratio, in Israel and the Territories, 1967–1990 (in millions)

	Jews	Muslims	Christians	Druze/Others	Total
1967	2.40	0.30	0.07	0.03	2.8
1977	3.00	0.50	0.08	0.05	3.6
1987	3.60	0.60	0.10	0.08	4.4
1990	3.90	0.70	0.10	0.08	4.8

Note: As of 1967, the population includes the residents of East Jerusalem. After 1969, the population includes potential immigrants. In 1982 the Druze and Muslim population of the Golan was added.

Source: Statistical Abstract of Israel 1992 (Jerusalem: Central Bureau of Statistics, 1992).

TABLE 8.2   Non-Jewish Population Growth in Judea, Samaria, and Gaza, 1967–1990 (in thousands)

	Judea and Samaria	Gaza
1967	595.9	389.7
1977	683.3	437.4
1987	837.7	545.0
1990	916.0	610.4

Note: Because of the intifada, from the beginning of 1988 there were difficulties in collecting statistical data. As a result, the quality of the tables is poorer in a number of respects than in previous years. In statistical series, in which it was impossible to obtain data of the minimal acceptable standards, data appears only until the end of 1987. In addition, since April 1979, the tables do not include the population of El Arish—about 30,000—and since 1982 the other parts of North Sinai—about 7,000 inhabitants of Rafa.

Source: Statistical Abstract of Israel 1992 (Jerusalem: Central Bureau of Statistics, 1992).

rise of a Jewish underground terrorist group and pledged to outlaw their activity.

With some exceptions, Labor, like Likud, had viewed the PLO as a terrorist organization with whom no dialogue could be held. Like Likud, it vowed not to recognize the PLO, rejected the idea of establishing another Palestinian state east of the Jordan River, and reaffirmed the framework of a Jordanian-Palestinian solution based on United Nations Resolutions 242 and 338.[16]

The party's 1988 platform adhered to the Jordanian option. It also supported the Shultz initiative and advocated the opening of a dialogue with a Jordanian-Palestinian delegation as a first step toward negotiations, possibly within the framework of an international conference. It also validated the London document and professed its willingness to negotiate with Palestinian representatives who would recognize Israel, denounce terrorism, and accept Resolutions 242 and 338. But it still renounced the PLO as a negotiating partner and rejected the creation of a separate Palestinian state.[17]

The 1992 party platform called for negotiations with the Palestinians on the autonomy plan and affirmed that a permanent solution to the Arab-Israeli conflict would be based on territorial compromise—especially in areas of dense Palestinian population (it also stated that a territorial compromise was possible in the Golan Heights). But it assured the Israeli voters that there will be no return to Israel's 1967 borders.[18] Some members of the far Left, such as the parties of Rakakh (the Communist Party), the Progressive List for Peace, and some members of Ratz and Mapam—even some in Labor—advocate a total Israeli withdrawal to the pre-1967 borders.

Those who criticize the Jordanian option say that because such an alternative could not satisfy the Palestinians' national aspirations, most Palestinians would oppose such a solution by using force against Jordan. Moreover, the critics claim, a solution that involves this option might topple the Hashemite rule, a chance King Hussein is not likely to take.[19] Others express concern that the Jordanian option might Palestinize Jordan. In that case it would be unlikely that Israel would peacefully coexist with a Palestinian state on its border.[20]

Indeed, one of the reasons for Hussein's 1988 dissociation from the West Bank was the fear that the *intifada* would spread to the East Bank and that the incorporation of the West Bank and the Gaza Strip into a Jordanian-Palestinian federation would add to the weight of the Palestinian population in Jordan.[21] Little wonder, then, that even though Jordan rushed to sign an agreement with Israel on the agenda of their future bilateral talks, King Hussein embraced the Gaza-Jericho agreement with noticeable caution.

Nonterritorial Compromise

Whereas the option of a territorial compromise is based on the premise that some Israeli withdrawal from the occupied territories is necessary, the nonterritorial option is based on the refusal to negotiate any agreement that carries with it the prospect of withdrawal from the West Bank or Gaza. A nonterritorial, or functional compromise thus seeks to avoid any new partition of the area between the Mediterranean and the Jordan River, bypassing completely the question of territorial partition. Instead, it provides for some kind of functional division of authority between Jews and Arabs.[22]

Those who advocate such a compromise believe that a territorial compromise—typically designed to meet security needs only—is unfeasible because in such a compromise one or both sides must cede land. Since land is usually associated with territorial and national aspirations and since a territorial compromise by definition involves an element of finality, a territorial compromise may often be too difficult to realize. But in a functional compromise neither side has to give up land or national aspirations, making it easier to achieve a compromise within an existing territorial structure.[23]

Mark Heller has grouped the nonterritorial compromise into four main themes: (1) autonomy, which permits the Palestinians in the West

Bank and Gaza to regulate personal, educational, religious, welfare, judicial, and some economic matters but permits no separate status for these territories as political entities; (2) federal themes, which would create a political entity (or entities) in these territories separate from Israel but leave the control of the most critical functional areas in the hands of an Israeli authority; (3) confederal themes, which would provide a still greater degree of autonomy for the established political entity(ies) but limit their division of power; and (4) condominial themes, which would formalize the de facto division of authority in these areas, while granting their residents a greater degree of autonomy in local and regional matters than is currently practiced. Since a functional compromise could free the Israelis of the burden of occupation and defuse the Palestinian issue without ending Israel's control of the West Bank and Gaza, such a compromise is not without appeal.[24]

The most prevalent nonterritorial option Israel proposed is the autonomy plan, envisioned by the first Likud government. The plan is based on the twenty-six-point proposal Prime Minister Begin introduced to the Knesset in December 27, 1977. It rested on two premises: the land west of the Jordan River is an integral part of Israel and is nonnegotiable; the Palestinian Arabs do not constitute a separate entity and are therefore not entitled to self-determination. Under these restrictions the best the Palestinians can achieve is autonomy.

Begin's autonomy plan was limited, permitting the inhabitants of the West Bank and Gaza to run their own internal affairs, but only within the sovereign borders of Eretz Yisrael. To secure Israel's sovereignty over the West Bank and Gaza, Begin made sure that the issues of final borders and Palestinian sovereignty would be left open while Israel remained responsible for the area's security.[25]

Under the plan the Palestinians would run their own affairs through an eleven-member administrative council elected by Palestinians from the West Bank and Gaza for a five-year period. The council would replace the military government in Judea, Samaria, and Gaza and would be responsible for education, religious affairs, finance, transportation, housing and construction, industry, commerce, agriculture, health, labor, social welfare, refugee rehabilitation, justice, and local police.[26]

The plan also permitted Arab inhabitants of the West Bank and Gaza to be offered either Israeli or Jordanian citizenship. Those becoming Israeli citizens would be entitled to vote for and be elected to the Knesset; Jordanian citizens would enjoy the same rights within Jordan. A joint committee of Israelis, Jordanians, and the administrative council would decide which legislation would remain in force and which would be abolished. Israeli residents would be able to acquire land and settle in the West Bank and Gaza, and Arabs in these territories who became Israeli citizens would have rights in Israel. Immigration, including that of Arab refugees, would be regulated in "reasonable numbers" by a committee representing Israel, Jordan, and the administrative council. Residents of the autonomous areas and Israel would have freedom of movement as well as economic freedom within these areas. Free access to holy shrines would be guaranteed to Christians, Muslims and Jews.[27] (The plan excluded East Jerusalem and the Golan Heights, which were formally incorporated into Israel.)

The hawks in Israel feared that the modified version of the autonomy plan incorporated into the Camp David agreements might endanger Israel's future control over the West Bank and Gaza. Indeed, concerned that the provision for Palestinian autonomy laid the foundation for a Palestinian state, Begin's hard-line critics sought to force his government into a course of action that guaranteed permanent Israeli control over the territories. Thus, soon after the Camp David agreements had been signed, Begin moved quickly to ensure that the autonomy plan would not wipe out Israel's right to annex the West Bank and Gaza: In May 1979 he adopted the position of the hawkish group in his cabinet, led by Ariel Sharon, Haim Landau, and Zevulun Hammer. This position safeguarded Israel's claim of sovereignty over the entire territory after the transitional period.[28]

Opinions about Begin's own understanding of his autonomy plan vary. Some believe that Begin changed his mind about the autonomy plan and intentionally undermined the autonomy negotiations once he realized that the autonomy clause in the Camp David agreements he could jeopardize the future of the whole of Eretz Yisrael—a realization that eventually caused his resignation.[29] Others believe that Begin in fact viewed Palestinian autonomy, as defined in the Camp David accords, as a final settlement rather than an interim arrangement.[30]

Although Begin's successor, Shamir, was strongly opposed to the Camp David agreements and the autonomy plan—he boycotted the Knesset session in which the agreements were endorsed—as prime minister he had little choice but to recognize the agreements. He thus advocated autonomy for the Arab inhabitants of Judea, Samaria, and Gaza for a five-year interim period, as set forth in the Camp David accords. But he called for the deferment of the final determination of the status of these areas until the end of the transitional period. Shamir's view on any form of Palestinian self-determination was made clear in an article he wrote in 1982, in which stated that "the state known today as the Kingdom of Jordan is an integral part of what once was known as Palestine; its inhabitants therefore are Palestinian—not different in their language, culture, or religious and demographic composition from other Palestinians. ... It is merely an accident of history that this state is called the Kingdom of Jordan and not the Kingdom of Palestine."[31]

In its party platform for the 1984 elections, the Likud reaffirmed its claim of sovereignty over Judea, Samaria, and Gaza, and it pledged to realize this claim at the proper time. Moreover, it rejected any plan to surrender parts of "western Israel" to a "foreign rule." Such a plan, according to Likud, undermined Israel's right to the Land of Israel, fostered the unavoidable creation of a Palestinian state, threatened Israel's civilian population, and endangered the existence of Israel.[32]

As for the autonomy arrangements, these were reaffirmed to guarantee that no territorial partition would ever again occur in western Israel and that under no circumstances would a Palestinian state be established there. It stated that "the autonomy plan under the agreements was not a state, not a sovereignty, nor was it self-determination. Self-determination was provided to the Arab nation through the existence of twenty-one independent Arab states."[33]

These same principles were reiterated in the party's platform for the 1988 election. That platform also reaffirmed Likud's refusal to conduct peace talks under the auspices of an international conference. Instead, the platform revalidated the government's commitment to direct negotiations with the Arabs.[34]

The 1992 Likud platform reaffirmed Israel's right and claim to sovereignty over Judea, Samaria, and Gaza and reconfirmed the Camp David agreements as the bases for negotiations (with representatives of Palestinian inhabitants of Judea, Samaria, and Gaza) on an interim agreement.

Although the autonomy plan is widely accepted in Israel, its proponents are divided on a number of controversial subjects: ownership of the water and land, control of the entrance passages, the source of authority, and the nature of the constitutional and administrative institutions.[35] These issues have been discussed under the Madrid formula and will of course be further negotiated under the Gaza-Jericho agreement.

Some analysts are not terribly optimistic about the workability of the autonomy concept. For example, a 1989 study done by the Jaffee Center for Strategic Studies at Tel Aviv University concluded that the majority of the Palestinians view the Camp David autonomy proposal as a means for the legitimization of permanent Israeli control over the West Bank and Gaza rather than an interim arrangement geared at an imminent Israeli withdrawal from these areas. The only autonomy scheme the Palestinians might accept—especially after the PLO's 1988 declaration of independence—is one closer to sovereignty, and only as an interim stage toward a guaranteed independence, a scheme not accepted by most Israelis.[36]

Others argue that Palestinian autonomy would rapidly turn into a semisovereign state quickly recognized by the international community. The burden of preventing such a development, a task that much more difficult than confronting the *intifada* would fall on Israel.[37]

In theory Israel could unilaterally enforce the Camp David autonomy on the Palestinians. But such a move could invite unrest, including increased Palestinian terrorist activity, the radicalization of the Israeli Arabs, retaliation by the Arab states, and the worsening of U.S.-Israeli relations.[38]

Of course these views were expressed before the 1992 elections in Israel, the 1993 Israeli-PLO agreement on Palestinian self-rule in Gaza and Jericho, and the 1994 peace agreement between Israel and Jordan. Still, the effective implementation of the autonomy plan depends largely on the ability of the international community to improve the daily life of the Palestinian inhabitants and on the ability of the PLO to curb terrorist activities against Israelis.

Annexation and Transfer

In addition to the territorial compromise and autonomy, two other options exist: annexation and transfer. Because of their impracticality, these schemes are not as widely espoused. Nonetheless, they have become more attractive, at least to the extreme Right since the beginning of the *intifada*.

Those who favor de jure annexation of the West Bank and Gaza—Ariel Sharon from Likud, some in the National Religious Party, Tehiya, and Tzomet—do not necessarily propose the expulsion of Arabs from the West Bank and Gaza. Instead, they recommend the unilateral implementation of Israeli law in all of the occupied territories, the same way Israeli law was implemented in East Jerusalem in 1967 and in the Golan Heights in 1981.

The purpose of annexation is to formalize and finalize the Israeli presence in the territories and thus to fulfill the aspiration for the existence of Greater Israel. Although annexation is technically feasible—Israel can impose such a "solution" unilaterally—its wisdom is seriously challenged by highly respected Israeli strategists. Annexation would invite reproach not only from the Arab states, including Egypt, but also from the rest of the international community, including the United States. It would create a society that would be religiously and nationally divided—a society that, from a demographic point of view, would not be able to sustain the democratic institutions on which Israel was founded. The cost of annexation would therefore surpass its benefits.[39]

Equally disturbing are the possible reactions of the Palestinians in the West Bank and Gaza. In response to annexation the Palestinians might launch a rebellion more violent than the *intifada* or accept the move only in return for equal political and civil rights, including the right to vote for equal political and civil rights, including the right to vote for the Knesset. The purpose of such demands would be to transform Israel into a binational state as a step toward the Palestinian control over the country.[40]

Transfer, or expulsion, is supported by the extreme Right: Moledet, some members of Likud, the NRP, Tehiya, Tzomet, and what is left of the Kach movement after the assassination of Rabbi Meir Kahane. The essence of the transfer idea is to relocate some or all of the Arabs in the occupied territories to neighboring Arab states. By expelling the Arabs, Israel would rid itself of the demographic problem of controlling the West Bank and Gaza. Those who advocate transfer justify their idea on two grounds: First, Israel has already absorbed 600,000 or so Jews from Arab countries without a reciprocal population exchange by the Arabs; second, the return of the Arabs of Eretz Yisrael to the lands of their ancestors does not constitute an expulsion. In fact, those who call for transfer believe that it is the best option to guarantee peaceful coexistence between the two societies. They refer to other population exchanges that had occurred in recent history, such as those between Turkey and Greece (after the emergence of a separate Turkish Cypriot state in 1975).[41]

Key Israeli strategists believe that no Arab country would agree to accept Arabs expelled from Israel (Kach advocated the expulsion of all the Arabs of Eretz Yisrael, including Israeli citizens) or from the Israeli occupied territories. Furthermore, any attempt to transfer the Arabs would be met with harsh criticism from the international community, not to mention the severe reaction Israel could expect from the Arabs. Such a move would undoubtedly radicalize the Arab world, including the more moderate factions of the PLO, resulting in increased terrorist activities against Israel, if not an all-out Arab war against Israel.[42]

Factional Division and Election Campaigns

In the four election campaigns from 1977 to 1988, all major parties used the territorial debate to rally popular support for a particular position. Likud—which exploited the territory/security issue as the justification for its settlement policy and expanded territorial control—along with other territorial parties focused on the Greater Israel symbol to show that permanent Israeli control over the occupied territories is a matter of national survival. For example, Likud election posters in 1977, reiterated the claim to Judea, Samaria, and Gaza and restated the need for "secure and defensible" borders; a map depicted the strategic value of keeping the West Bank. In its 1981 posters the party reassured voters that the territorial changes in the West Bank and Gaza, which had been implemented by the first Begin government, in the form of 144 new settlements, were there to stay. The Labor Alignment, in contrast, used the same symbol to demonstrate that such control is a matter of demographic and national peril. Labor posters showed a map without clear border lines.

The ultraright party Tehiya, which for the first time in 1981, outdid Likud when it blamed that party for withdrawing from the Sinai and destroying Jewish settlements there. Kach depicted on its posters a Torah-shaped boundary that included all the areas of the Promised Land mentioned in the Bible.

The same pattern was repeated in 1984 and again in 1988. Likud, which in 1988 opposed Labor's support for the Shultz peace initiative, cited the Arabs' threat to throw the Jews into the sea, warning that territorial compromise could allow the Arabs to make good that threat. Labor in turn used a map with the Jordan River as Israel's eastern boundary, conveying that only a territorial compromise was capable of safeguarding the Zionist vision.

The NRP, too, concentrated on the notion of a Greater Israel, calling it a tenet of faith rather than principle. In its campaign posters Moledet represented a clear alternative: either the "transfer" of the Israeli Jews to the sea or the expulsion of the Arabs to the East Bank. Tehiya promised to be the only party capable of securing Greater Israel against the *intifada*.[43]

In 1992 polls indicated that a considerable number of voters were concerned primarily with economic and social problems, such as unemployment, immigration absorption, and housing shortages. Thus Labor's campaign focused on domestic performance and leadership rather than on divisive ideological issues. By contrast, the Likud turned to position issues, trying to corner Labor on problems related to the future of the occupied territories.[44] It tried to draw the public's attention to Labor's platform of land for peace and the unilateral implementation of Palestinian autonomy within six to nine months after the elections. Likud was also opposed to Rabin's promise to halt the creation of "political settlements" in the territories, accusing Labor of "putting the Land of Israel on an end-of-season sale."[45] But after polls indicated that such tactics were counterproductive, Likud redirected its strategy toward generating doubts about the character and performance of the Labor leaders.[46] Other parties on the right and the left shifted their campaign tactics as well, concentrating on the need to change the country's national priorities.[47]

Likud's stable position from 1977 to 1992 (with the exception of the setback it suffered in the 1984 elections as a result of the Lebanon debacle) suggested that of the existing alternatives regarding the occupied territories, the nonterritorial option gained the most credibility in those years. Yet Labor's victory in 1992 was the result of changing priorities among the voters more than a widespread endorsement of the territorial compromise option. In fact 1992 election results indicated that the Israeli public remained nearly evenly divided on the issue. However, a successful implementation of the Gaza-Jericho plan and a confident Labor government may transform the territorial compromise option into a preferred choice.

In 1977 the Likud won forty-three Knesset seats (35.8 percent of the total vote) against Labor's thirty-two seats (26.6 percent of the total). For the Likud, this was an increase of four Knesset seats, a 3.5 percent increase over the number it won in 1973. Labor lost nineteen seats, or 15.8 percent of the total vote in comparison to the 1973 elections.

In 1981 a record number of thirty-two lists ran for election. Of these only ten won representation in the Knesset. The Likud won forty-eight Knesset seats (37.1 percent of the total) against forty-seven seats (36.6 percent of the total) won by the Labor Alignment. As Daniel Elazar noted, although Labor's total was close Likud's, Labor and its coalition partner, the Citizen's Right Movement (CRM) only reached the 1977 combined total of Labor and the Democratic Movement for Change (DMC), in itself a far lower figure than the Labor Alignment had won in its heyday.[48] Likud, in contrast, gained over and above what it and Ariel Sharon's Shlomtzion Party won in 1977. It did so despite the secession of the Likud's right-wing members to form Tehiya and part of its La'am faction to form another new list, Telem. At least four of the five seats won by those two parties must be added to the Likud total to get an authentic picture of the results. Moreover, most of the thirteen seats of the religious camp represented people committed to a coalition with Likud. In effect, the Jewish vote went three to two against Labor.[49] Together, the Likud, the NRP, Tehiya, and the Kach—all in favor of the Israeli annexation of the West Bank and Gaza—won fifty-nine seats, an impressive 45.9 percent of the total vote.

In 1984 twenty-seven lists ran for election, fifteen of them winning Knesset representation. This time both the Likud and Labor—still the two strongest parties—declined in strength. The Labor Alignment won forty-four seats (35.4 percent of the total), while Likud won forty-one seats (32 percent of the total). But together the nationalist front—composed of Likud, the NRP, Tehiya/Tzomet, Morasha/Matzad (a new religious nationalist front, composed of two groups that had left existing religious parties), and Kach—won fifty-two seats, or 43.3 percent of the vote.

On September 14 Prime Minister Peres presented to the Israeli president the new National Unity government, formed by the two largest parties. It was a rotation government, appointing Shimon Peres as prime minister and Yitzhak Shamir as vice premier and foreign minister for its first two years switching these roles for the second half of the government's term.

Despite predictions that the National Unity government would fall soon after its creation, it lasted for a full four-year term, but not without

TABLE 8.3 Parties Elected in Israel in 1981–1992, with Number of Seats in the Knesset

Party/List Left	1981	1984	1988	1992
Hadash	4	4	4	3
New Democratic Party	–	–	1	2
Progressive List for Peace	–	2	1	–
Citizens Rights	1	3	5	–
Shinui	2	3	2	–
Yahad	–	3	–	–
Agudat Yisrael	4	2	5	–
Meretz	–	–	–	12
Labor	47	44	39	44
Likud	48	41	40	32
National Religious	6	4	5	6
Ometz	–	1	–	–
Torah Flag	–	–	2	–
United Torah Jewry	–	–	–	4
Shas	–	4	6	7
Tami	3	1	–	–
Morasha	–	2	–	–
Telem	2	2	–	–
Tzomet	–	–	2	7
Tzomet/Tehiya	–	5	–	–
Tehiya	3	–	3	–
Moledet	–	–	2	3
Kach	–	1	–	–
Right				
Total Seats	120	120	120	120

Sources: Asher Arian, *Politics in Israel* (Chatham: Chatham House, 1989); *The Elections in Israel 1992* (Albany: SUNY Press, 1995).

its share of crises: As shown previously, Peres's call for an international peace conference and his peace plans as foreign minister nearly toppled the government, Likud and its supporters fearing that these initiatives could end in territorial compromises they were not prepared to make.

Except for a significant gain for the religious front and increased polarization, hardly any change occurred in the 1988 elections. Indeed, the Israeli public was as divided about the peace process as it had been in 1984.[50] This time, however, the two-year-old *intifada* was an added issue that polarized the Israeli voters between those who demanded more forceful measures against the uprising and those who advocated a political solution. Likud tried to maintain its edge by delegitimizing Labor; it accused Labor of secret plans to negotiate with the PLO and charged Labor with bias toward the parties who advocated a two-state solution.[51] For its part, Labor blamed the *intifada* on Likud's rigidity and pledged to prevent the establishment of additional Jewish settlements in areas heavily populated by Palestinians.[52]

As in 1984, fifteen of the twenty-seven lists that competed in the 1988 elections won Knesset seats. Likud emerged as the largest party, winning forty seats (or 31 percent of the total), while Labor was the second largest, winning thirty-nine seats (30 percent of the total). Labor lost five seats to its partner for twenty years, Mapam, which quit the alignment and ran on its own.

The ultranationalist front lost the Kach, which was disqualified from running by the Central Election Commission and the Israeli Supreme Court because of its racist stand. But it gained the newly formed list of Moledet, which won two seats. Together, the nationalist front—Likud, NRP, Tehiya, Tzomet, and Moledet—won fifty-two seats, or 42 percent of the total vote.

Although the votes for the Likud and the Labor Alignment were almost evenly divided, voters perceived Likud as the party better fit to handle the Arab-Israeli conflict.[53]

Soon after coalition negotiations had begun, it appeared as if the Likud would form a government with the religious bloc. But after prolonged and complex negotiations, Shamir was in a position to set up either a narrow-based government jointly with the right-wing and religious parties or a broad coalition together with the Labor Alignment. Eventually, both Shamir and Peres favored the creation of another National Unity government. The new agreement nominated Shamir as the sole prime minister for the full term of the government and Peres as vice premier and finance minister. In June 1990, after the fall of the National Unity government, Shamir succeeded in forming an ultranationalist coalition, which sent the Labor Alignment back into the opposition. On the ultranationalist front the coalition was formed by Likud, Tehiya,

Tzomet, and the Movement to Advance the Zionist Idea (an offshoot of Modai); on the religious front were the NRP, Shas, Degel Hatorah, and two independent Knesset members formerly of Shas and NRP. When most Israelis were preoccupied with the Gulf war, Shamir quietly added the superhawkish Moledet to the cabinet.[54]

The new government upheld the Camp David agreements and the initiative of May 14, 1989, as the framework for the continuation of the peace process. It rejected the establishment of an additional Palestinian state in Gaza and in the area between Israel and Jordan, and it renounced direct or indirect negotiations with the PLO.[55]

The Knesset approved the new government on June 11, 1990. But in June 1992 Israelis voted the right-wing government of Yitzhak Shamir out of office. Of the two major competing parties, Labor won forty-four Knesset seats (37 percent of the total vote) while Likud won thirty-two seats (27 percent of the total vote). The result of this change was the 1993 agreement between Israel and the PLO.

Notes

1. Yaakov Bar-Siman-Tov, "Peace as a Significant Change in Foreign Policy: The Need for Legitimacy," *Jerusalem Journal of International Relations* 12, 3 (September 1990): 20–21.

2. On March 18, 1992, the Knesset passed a law allowing the direct election of the prime minister by 1996. But after Haim Ramon, an independent candidate who had seceded from Labor, won the Histadrut elections in spring 1994, some leading figures in Israel called for the repeal of the new election law. Ramon's victory raised the question whether a directly elected prime minister would adhere to his or her party platform.

3. Asher Arian and Michal Shamir, eds., *The Elections in Israel–1988* (Boulder, Colo.: Westview, 1990), p. 1.

4. Gad Barzilai and Bruce Russett, "The Political Economy of Israeli Military Action," in ibid., p. 29.

5. Asher Arian, Ilan Talmud, and Tamar Hermann, *National Security and Public Opinion in Israel* (Boulder, Colo.: Westview, 1988), pp. 38–39.

6. Asher Arian, "A People Apart: Coping with National Security Problems in Israel," *Journal of Conflict Resolution* 44, 4 (December 1989): 605–631.

7. K. J. Holsti, *International Politics* (Englewood Cliffs, New Jersey: Prentice Hall, 1988), p. 45.

8. Milton J. Esman and Itamar Rabinovich, "The Study of Ethnic Politics in the Middle East," in Milton J. Esman and Itamar Rabinovich, eds., *Ethnicity, Pluralism, and the State in the Middle East* (Ithaca: Cornell University Press, 1988), pp. 3–24.

9. Norman Hill, *Claims of Territory in International Law and Relations* (New York: Oxford University Press, 1945), pp. 35–52.

10. Ibid., pp. 81–115.

11. Shimon Peres, *Tomorrow Is Now* (Jerusalem: Keter, 1978), p. 256, and his speech to the twenty-ninth annual policy conference of AIPAC of May 16, 1988, C-SPAN Broadcasting; Rabin, The Leon Charney Report, CCN LTD/JMS Productions, September 26, 1993.

12. *Facts on File* 28, 1459 (October 10–16, 1968): 425–426.

13. *Middle East Record*, 4 (Jerusalem: Israeli Universities Press, 1968).

14. Quoted from Labor's platform for the tenth Knesset.

15. David Newman, *Population, Settlement and Conflict: Israel and the West Bank* (Cambridge: Cambridge University Press, 1991), p. 23.

16. Don Peretz, "Israeli Peace Proposals," in Willard A. Belling, ed., *Middle East Peace Plans* (New York: St. Martin's Press, 1986), pp. 30–31.

17. Labor's platform for the twelfth Knesset.

18. Labor's platform for the thirteenth Knesset.

19. *Israel, the West Bank, and Gaza: Israel's Option for Peace* (Hebrew) (Tel Aviv: Jaffee Center for Strategic Studies, Tel Aviv University, 1989), pp. 129–130.

20. Yehezkel Dror, *A Grand Strategy for Israel* (Hebrew) (Jerusalem: Academon, 1989), pp. 280–281.

21. *Israel, the West Bank, and Gaza*, pp. 129–130.

22. Mark Heller, *A Palestinian State* (Cambridge: Harvard University Press, 1983), p. 40.

23. This summary is based in part on information obtained in a private conversation with Aharon Levran, Editor, *The Middle East Military Balance*, 1988, Jaffee Center for Strategic Studies, Tel Aviv, January 16, 1990.

24. Heller, *A Palestinian State*, pp. 40–41.

25. Peretz, "Israeli Peace Proposals," pp. 17–18.

26. Ibid.

27. Ibid., p. 19.

28. Shimon Shamir, "Israeli View of Egypt and the Peace Process: The Duality of Vision," in William Quandt, ed., *The Middle East Ten Years After Camp David* (Washington D.C.: Brookings Institution, 1988), pp. 187–216.

29. Private conversation with then MK Ezer Weizman, Caesaria, July 4, 1991.

30. Harold H. Saunders, *The Other Wall* (Washington, D.C.: American Enterprise Institute, 1985), p. 44.

31. Yitzhak Shamir, "Israel's Role in a Changing Middle East," *Foreign Affairs* 60, 4 (spring 1982): 789–801.

32. Likud platform for the eleventh Knesset.

33. Ibid.

34. Likud platform for the twelfth Knesset.

35. Private conversation with then MK Shimon Peres, Tel Aviv, July 3, 1991.

36. *Israel, the West Bank, and Gaza*, pp. 49–61.

37. Dror, *A Grand Strategy*, pp. 282–283.

38. Ibid.

39. Ibid., p. 278.

40. *Israel, the West Bank, and Gaza*, p. 66.

41. *In Eretz Israel* (a Likud publication), 180 (September–October 1987): 29.

42. *Israel, the West Bank, and Gaza*, p. 67.

43. Hanna Herzog, "Was It on the Agenda? The Hidden Agenda of the 1988 Campaign," in Asher Arian and Michal Shamir, eds., *The Elections in Israel–1988* (Westview Press, Boulder, Colo.: 1990), pp. 37–62.

44. Jonathan Mendilow, "The 1992 Campaign: Valance and Position Dimensions," in Asher Arian and Michal Shamir, eds., *The Elections in Israel 1992* (Albany: SUNY Press), 1995.

45. Sammy Smooha and Don Peretz, "Israel's 1992 Knesset Elections: Are They Critical?" *Middle East Journal* 47, 3 (summer 1993): 444–463.

46. Mendilow, "The 1992 Israeli Electoral Campaign."

47. Ibid.

48. Daniel J. Elazar, "The 1981 Elections: Into the Second Generation of Statehood," in Howard R. Penniman and Daniel J. Elazar, eds., *Israel at the Polls, 1981* (Washington, D.C.: American Enterprise Institute, 1986), p. 8.

49. Ibid.

50. The religious parties won eighteen seats (15 percent of the total vote). Of these, thirteen seats went to non-Zionist religious parties. For details on the religious votes, see Arian and Shamir, eds., introduction to *The Elections in Israel–1988*; Robert O. Freedman, "Religion, Politics, and the Israeli Elections of 1988," *Middle East Journal* 43, 3 (summer 1989): 406–422; and Don Peretz and Sammy Smooha, "Israel's Twelfth Knesset Elections: An All-Loser Game," *Middle East Journal* 43, 3 (summer 1989): 389–405.

51. Peretz and Smooha, "Israel's Twelfth Knesset Elections."

52. Labor's platform for the twelfth Knesset.

53. Michal Shamir and Asher Arian, "The Intifada and Israeli Voters: Policy Preference and Performance Evaluation," in Arian and Shamir, *Elections in Israel–1988*, p. 84.

54. Coalition Agreement, Israel's Twenty-Fourth Government, June 8, 1990.

55. *Basic Policy Guidelines for Israel's Twenty-Fourth Government* (Jerusalem: Israel Ministry of Foreign Affairs, June 11, 1990).

9

The Growth of the Israeli Right: The Emergence of Gush Emunim and the Rise of Likud

The astonishing Israeli victory in the Six-Day War provoked a religious awakening among Orthodox and secular Jews alike. That resulted in the rise of messianic nationalism, reinforcing and legitimizing the belief held by the nationalist camp that the Land of Israel should never be repartitioned. But it also resulted in the creation of an influential extraparliamentary movement that helped put Likud in power in 1977 and succeeded in delegitimizing the territorial compromise option, thereby effectively undermining the peace process until the 1992 defeat of Likud.

The Effect of the Six-Day War: The Revitalization of Revisionist Zionism

When Prime Minister Begin explained to the Israeli citizens why he had rejected the 1982 Reagan peace plan, he did so with a messianic message:

> I feel that our forefathers stand beside me in this battle: Bar Kochba and the Maccabee warriors, and all our ancestors who shed their blood for Eretz Yisrael. Yes, I am waging the war for Eretz Yisrael. At my side stand Herzl, Jabotinsky and Nordau, Berl Katznelson and Tabenkin, all participants in the war for Eretz Yisrael. ... I feel contentment, exaltation and faith, a sense of mission (and) I am just the prime minister in this historic battle.[1]

Begin's melodramatic tone reflected on the painful Jewish experience in Palestine, an experience that has shaped the attitude of many Israelis toward the peace process. Although they were not the only inhabitants of the Land of Canaan, it was there that the Israelites developed spiritually and culturally, it was there that they established their first monarchy, and it was there that they yearned to reestablish their independence after centuries of exile and dispersion.

The Jews were exiled after the destruction of their first monarchy by the Babylonians, in the sixth century B.C. When the Persian dynasty conquered Babylon in 539 B.C., exiled Jews were permitted to return to their land to rebuild their national and cultural identity. But in the second century B.C., Eretz Yisrael fell to the Syrian Seleucids. After a successful revolt by the Maccabees, the Jews regained their independence until 63 B.C., when Judea became part of the Roman Empire. Between A.D. 66 and 73, those Jews who refused to accept foreign domination—the Zealots—staged the Great Revolt but were defeated. Rather than being captured alive by the Romans, those who had fled and fortified themselves on Massada chose to commit mass suicide. So ingrained is the Massada legacy in Israeli political culture that youth groups in Israel still sing a folksong vowing never to let Massada fall again, and army recruits take their oath of allegiance on top of Massada. Between A.D. 132 and 135, under the leadership of Bar Kochba, the Jews rebelled again, with catastrophic results. Although defeated and dispersed, the Jews still considered Eretz Yisrael their homeland and Jerusalem its spiritual center. It was thus natural that Zionism—the Jewish national movement—envisioned the return of the Jews to Zion and the establishment of a Jewish national home there.

Two millennia after the destruction of Judea, Jewish independence was reestablished in Palestine when in 1948 the State of Israel was founded, with Jerusalem its capital. That the state was established soon after the Holocaust gave it special meaning: The existence of an independent Jewish state would safeguard all Jews everywhere.

But since independence, the most intense fear for Jews in Israel has been the Arab commitment to "liberate" Palestine. Indeed, from 1948 to 1982 the Israelis fought six wars with the Arabs—the 1948 war of independence, the 1956 Sinai campaign; the 1967 Six-Day War, the 1970 war of attrition, the 1973 Yom Kippur War, and the 1982 Lebanon war—not to mention fedayeen wars (fighting Arab commando groups operating against Israel) and wars against terrorism. Since 1967, Palestinian nationalism in particular has provoked the Israelis, primarily because it brings up the Palestinians' claim to the right of return to the land the Israelis consider their own.

Begin's emotional response to the Reagan plan reflected his own convictions that the Jewish people had always existed and will forever exist in a hostile, anti-Semitic world; that in such a world the Jews can rely only on themselves; that a powerful Israel must always exist to protect the Jews; and that any means are legitimate for the protection of Israel and all Jews. But it also reflected a new kind of sociopolitical thinking that began to emerge in Israel after the Six-Day War. According to this attitude, the cession of any part of the territories gained in the Six-Day War would be unacceptable not only to the religious and the right-wing Israeli population that has grown dramatically as a result of the Six-Day War but also to segments of the secular Zionist population. This thinking produced a new Revisionist Zionist ideology that conformed both to the Revisionist Zionism founded by Ze'ev Jabotinsky (1880–1940) and to religious Zionism, advocated by the NRP and other religious nationalistic parties.

The revitalization of Revisionist Zionism was less surprising than the process of spiritualization that overtook a society as secular as the Israeli society was meant to be.[2] In this process the collectivity reacquaints itself with its religious past to the point where its identification with its spiritual background becomes as important as other ideals or even overshadows them.

Religious Awakening and the Rise of Messianic Nationalism

To be sure, religion has always influenced national identity. Prior to the rise of nationalism, almost every ancient religion was a state religion, and long after the establishment of the great world religions, denominationalism helped to determine interstate relations. Moreover, religion often served as a powerful vehicle for both the nationalization and denationalization of societies.[3]

What is unique in the case of Israel, however, is the rapidity and depth of the process of spiritualization and the influence it has had on the Israeli polity. In Israel until 1967 a secular-socialist brand of nationalism dominated culture and politics. This was replaced almost overnight by messianic nationalism that permitted, or better yet, encouraged the rise of a radical Right and Jewish fundamentalism.

Religious identification has always been inherent in the Israeli polity: Judaism, which is widely recognized as a religion and a nationality, is central to Zionism and its fulfillment—the State of Israel. But as Charles Liebman and Eliezer Don-Yehiya have argued, this identification agitated the secularist Labor Zionists, who rejected any association between tradition and national self-redemption. Nonetheless, as early as the Yishuv period (the pre-state period, meaning "settlement"), the secular Zionist leadership still had to draw national symbols from traditional Jewish culture in order to reinforce the historic and contemporary links among Judaism, the Jewish people, and the Israeli polity.[4]

Indeed, because of the strong link between the Jewish experience and tradition, the Labor Zionists had to develop a civil religion that relied on the Jewish experience. Paradoxically, however, it repudiated tradition altogether. A civil religion is a system of symbols a government develops in order to legitimate its view and mobilize the population for its accomplishments. Although a civil religion can be constructed out of new symbols, traditional symbols offer a sense of continuity with the past, which may serve to legitimate the people's right to the land itself and to a distinct identity. The Labor Zionist civil religion deliberately inverted these symbols.[5]

But after the establishment of the State of Israel, the civil religion was modified to integrate the entire Jewish population, religious and secular alike. Although it shifted from the confrontational approach of the Yishuv, it still did not focus on the centrality of Judaism in the Israeli polity but on the centrality of the state (statism, or *mamlakhtiut*).[6]

That changed in the aftermath of the 1967 Arab-Israeli war, when a more conservative trend in public opinion emerged. Its influence reached a peak with the Likud's victory in 1977. In fact, Daniel Elazar saw the Likud under Begin's leadership as the party that expressed and represented Israel's new civil religion, and Begin himself as the leader who advanced the Jewish character of the state to an unprecedented extent. In this respect Begin personified the official expression of Israel's civil religion and its transformation into one that drew heavily upon Jewish religious expression in its traditional form.[7] The goal of the new civil religion was to unite Israeli society around the Jewish tradition, rejecting Labor's attempts to unify society around the symbolism of statehood alone.[8]

How did the transformation from a secular Labor nationalist ideology to a religious nationalist ideology—or what has become known as New Zionism—come about after the Six-Day War? Why was that war—as Amnon Rubinstein pointed out—such an important turning point in the history of both Israel and Zionism?[9]

To grasp the effect the Six-Day War has had on the Israeli polity one must first look at the period that immediately antecedes the war. That period brought the Israelis in touch with the fear of total annihilation, a fear the Jewish people have experienced throughout history. As Amos Elon described it, "for two or three weeks prior to the Six-Day War, Israelis had shared a sense of anguish and dread as deep as only a nation of refugees can feel, down to the marrow of their bones."[10] In the Israeli psyche there is a connection between the Holocaust and the Six-Day War, many Israelis having been seized by the immense fear that Egypt was preparing another holocaust.[11] In this context Jay Gonen, a psychohisto-rian, labeled that war "the holocaust that did not happen."[12] The link between the two events was also expressed by young soldiers immedi-ately after the war.[13]

In the trying days immediately preceding the war, the Israelis felt iso-lated and abandoned. Abba Eban, who in 1967 was the Israeli representa-tive in the United Nations, described this feeling: "In Greek tragedy the chorus would at least express consternation about events which it was powerless to affect. Here we could not even hope for a mild expression of concern. Israel was being told in the plainest possible terms not to expect any assistance or even moral support from the United Nations."[14] Eban's account may well explain the motto that surfaced in Israel after the 1967 victory: "a people that dwells alone." Certainly, as the international com-munity condemned Israel for occupying the areas it had conquered in the Six-Day War, the Israelis' distrust of outsiders took stronger hold, many dismissing the criticism of a world that had stood idly by when the Nazis slaughtered 6 million Jews.[15] Thus defiance rather than compliance with international pressure became the norm for the Israeli polity, as reflected in the government's reaction to international peace initiatives. As Asher Arian has shown, what he called the "people apart syndrome," was a potent source of political inflexibility.[16]

Another effect the war had on the Israeli polity was the result of the Israelis' encounter with Jewish holy places liberated from Jordan. In the religious camp this gave the war a messianic meaning or a sign that redemption was on its way. It inspired a movement to settle Judea and Samaria and signaled the transformation of the nature and politics of the religious sector in Israel.[17]

But the movement to settle these territories was not confined to the religious camp: the Whole Land of Israel Movement that arose after the Six-Day War included not only religious fundamentalists but also mili-tary hard-liners and former Labor members who shared the same polit-ico-ideological traits, advocating holding on to the occupied territories.[18] Secular Israelis did not remain unmoved by the rediscovery of their ancestry. The famous snapshot of young Israeli soldiers weeping at the Wailing Wall became a national symbol, as many in Israel began to regard that scene as a religious awakening among the secular Israeli-born youth. The spiritual uplift within the secular camp in turn stimulated a wide-scale national debate regarding the future purpose of Zionism. Of course the religious sector directly influenced this debate.[19]

Indeed, within a short time after the Six-Day War, the religious camp in Israel succeeded in recruiting enthusiastic followers from the old Labor Zionists, gaining unprecedented political and ideological influence. That influence became even stronger as a result of the 1973 Yom Kippur War.

The shock the country suffered and the hard-won victory in that war elevated the position of the religious camp, as many in Israel believed that triumph after a near defeat was the result of divine intervention. The outcome was the rise of a Jewish fundamentalist group named Gush Emunim and the rise of Likud to a position of dominance.

The Rise and Influence of Gush Emunim

Gush Emunim (Bloc of the Faithful) was established in spring 1974 by a group of religious fundamentalist Jews in order to prevent a new partition of Eretz Yisrael.[20] While its immediate inspiration was the post-Six-Day War movement to settle Judea and Samaria, the shock of the Yom Kippur War and the threat that war posed to the 1967 territorial gains gave the movement a special urgency, at least in the eyes of its founders.

Aided by its supporters, Gush Emunim has evolved into one of the most influential interest groups in Israel, capable of determining the fate of perhaps the most important issue shaping the future of Israel, namely, peace with the Arabs. The Gush, which has best been described as a religious Zionist revivalist or revitalization movement,[21] is composed mainly of the younger generation of the religious Zionist segment of Israeli society, particularly the Young Guards of the NRP.

Similar to the old revisionists who viewed the Zionist leaders of their time as insufficiently active and formed their own branch of Zionism, so Gush Emunim's founders were dissatisfied with the NRP's lack of activism, especially in terms of foreign and defense policies, and formed their own branch of religious Zionism. The NRP remained faithful to its position that every Jew has the right to settle anywhere in Eretz Yisrael and encouraged its affiliates to settle in the West Bank. But as a member of the Labor coalition, the party accepted the rule of the majority, which opposed the settlement of Jews in densely Arab populated areas in the West Bank and Gaza[22] The NRP and the Gush therefore benefited from one another: Through its support of Gush Emunim, the NRP could still sustain an activist settlement policy, while the Gush gained from the party's religious claim to the Promised Land.

They trace that claim to biblical times, when God promised Abraham the Land of Canaan (Genesis 12:1–7); the Israelites finally arrived there after enduring centuries of misery under alien rule.

The Gush's primary goal has been the Jewish resettlement of biblical Israel, the area between the Jordan River and the Mediterranean Sea, to which they believe the Jewish people are originally connected.[23] This goal is based on the idea that as part of the process of messianic redemption, it is the sacred duty of every Jew to inhabit and possess every part of the Holy Land.

The concept of redemption itself entails the notion of "fused time." In contrast to the secular Zionist notion of linear history, "fused time" is a cyclical concept that explains the Jewish link to the land in the remote past. This cyclical approach to history contributes religious legitimacy to the idea of resettling biblical Israel by Jews, since return to the land is also a return in time and is considered a moral commandment.[24] Historical events that have taken place between biblical times and the present are immaterial; the Arab political and moral claim to the Land of Palestine is reduced to historical irrelevancy, since that claim is based on a linear model of history.[25]

Settlement of the land, however, constitutes only one stage in the pursuit of a "complete spiritual and conceptual revolution," after which the entire Jewish population will ultimately form Gush Emunim. Indeed, the Gush is preparing itself for the control of Zionism and of the State of Israel.[26]

Viewing the Zionist enterprise as the initial stage in the process of redemption, the Gush and its followers firmly believe that there is no difference between the Jewish pioneers of the Labor movement who settled Palestine during the Yishuv period and the Jewish settlers of Judea and Samaria. Not to settle these areas is unbefitting the Zionist credo and therefore should be avoided at all costs.[27] The settlement issue is thus above the law of the state.[28]

It is perhaps ironic that the Gush's concept of the state is not very different from the Islamic notion of the state. According to Gush Emunim, the national entity is supreme over that of the individual, whose existential purpose is to carry out divine commands. It does not recognize the separation between the religious and the temporal, and it aspires to a state based on Jewish religious law.[29] Similarly, in Islam the religious role of the state stems from the concept of the *umma*—the community of Muslims, consisting of the collectivity of individuals bound to one another in their mission of the Prophet Muhammad. The head of the *umma* is Allah alone, and his commands embody the law and the constitution of the *umma*, which is the basis of all Islamic political doctrine. The idea of a separation between religion and state is thus meaningless.[30]

Can the Palestinian question and a prospective peace with the Arabs be reconciled with Gush Emunim's convictions? The idea that any group other than the Jews can have rights to the Land of Israel seems completely incompatible with the concept of Jewish chosenness embraced by Gush leaders.[31] The movement does not view the Arab-Israeli conflict as a normal interstate dispute over borders and political rights or a conflict that can be settled through compromise and negotiation. Instead, the Arab-Israeli conflict is seen as a metaphysical struggle, and any notion of resolving it through territorial compromise not only weakens and endangers Israel but contradicts God's commands upon the Jewish people to inherit the land. This in turn delays the eventual redemption not only of Israel but of the whole world.[32]

In practical terms this view translates into two approaches to a peaceful settlement. The first is a temporary peace based on the Arabs' fear of Israel's military strength (it is temporary because the Arabs still do not abandon their desire to destroy Israel); this is the kind of peace Prime Minister Begin envisioned during the Lebanon war. The second is "real peace," involving the realization of Israel's inheritance of the whole land, a prelude to the complete messianic redemption of the Jews.[33]

Sprinzak cited a view that is less fanatical, but fundamentalist nonetheless. According to Sprinzak, the Palestinians' demand for self-determination to be exercised within any part of Eretz Yisrael is meaningless to Gush Emunim: Since the Land of Israel belongs to the Jews by divine order, the universal principle of self-determination does not apply to Eretz Yisrael.[34] Instead, Palestinian nationalism must be considered, if at all, as part of Arab nationalism, and the Palestinian demand for self-determination must be assessed throughout the whole of the Middle East.[35]

Since the Gush views the Palestinian question not as a problem of a nation but of *gerim* (non-Jewish residents of Eretz Yisrael, who according to the Torah should be treated by the people of Israel with no more than tolerance and respect), it sees three alternatives for the Arabs of Eretz Yisrael: (1) to acknowledge publicly the Gush's version of the legitimacy of the Zionist doctrine and to receive full civil and political rights that do not include the right to self-determination; (2) to obey the laws of the state without formal recognition of Zionism and in return be granted full rights of resident aliens, which do not include political rights; (3) to be offered economic incentives to immigrate to Arab countries.[36]

Whichever view individual followers might adhere to, Gush Emunim in general rejects any outside attempt to persuade Israel to negotiate with King Hussein and the Palestinians.[37] Indeed, the Gush views successful attempts to move the peace process forward as an imminent danger.[38] Because of their desire to eliminate the State of Israel, the Palestinians represent for Jews the most destructive and dangerous current of Arab hostility and thus are condemned to defeat, which in their case will be through self-destruction.[39]

The 1977 Elections and the Likud's Rise to Power

In 1977 Likud rose to power after three decades as the most vocal member in the Israeli opposition. The party was formally established in summer 1973 as an affiliation of a number of existing nationalistic and right-of-center parties. These included Herut, Likud's predecessor and the largest faction of the Likud; the Liberal Party, which was Herut's partner in the Gahal bloc, formed in 1965; La'am, created in 1969 by former members of Rafi—a faction led by David Ben-Gurion, which split from Mapai in 1963; the Free Center—a faction that split from Herut in 1969; and the Greater Israel Movement. Shlomtzion, a faction led by Ariel Sharon, joined Herut after the 1977 elections. The bond holding this alignment together was the desire to incorporate into Israel all of the occupied territories.[40]

Three main factors helped Likud to win the 1977 elections. From the early 1970s a process of delegitimation had gradually deprived the Labor Alignment of the political domination it had enjoyed since the Yishuv period.[41] That process involved a growing public perception that the Labor Alignment no longer exercised power rightfully. Second, a slow process that began in the 1960s, when Herut had adopted an effective legitimation strategy, finally awarded Likud legitimacy.[42] Large segments of the Israeli population came to see Likud as the alternative party capable of fulfilling the function of the political order. Finally, the composition of the Israeli electorate underwent two significant transformations. One was a demographic change: Part of Likud's strength was based on the vote of the Sephardic Jews who were expelled from Arab countries after the 1956 Arab-Israeli war.[43] The other was the rise of the Israeli Right,[44] which enabled Begin and the Likud to safeguard the political status quo.

How did the rise of an influential Israeli Right contribute to the Likud's rise to power, and why did Likud keep reinforcing this shift to the right? One answer lies in the relationship between the political atmosphere that engulfed Israel after the Six-Day War and the teachings of the Likud Party. The Likud is a territorial party, that is, it is interested primarily in territorial matters. The party is known for its extreme position on Jewish control of the West Bank of the Jordan River. This position goes back to 1949, when Begin refused to accept the demarcation lines of the armistice agreement.[45] After the Six-Day War the issue of Jewish control over the area resurfaced. Because Begin was a member of the National Unity government that was formed during the trying days that preceded the war, Begin's stance became increasingly legitimate. In fact, it has been pointed out that the decisive Israeli victory of 1967 helped Begin to bring about the Herutization of the right-of-center political bloc.[46]

But it was Begin's departure from the National Unity government in August 1970 that helped popularize his extreme position. He resigned after the government decided to accept a U.S. proposal to resume the Jarring talks, which had began in November 1967 and terminated in April 1969.[47] Soon after his resignation, Begin and his Herut Party became the backbone of Israel's annexationist movement, attracting many other

members, some of whom were not early supporters of Begin. By 1973
these forces were united under Begin's leadership in the newly formed
Likud Party. They were strengthened after the trauma of the 1973 Arab-
Israeli war.

Although the Likud did not win the 1973 elections, it formed the first
ultranationalistic opposition in Israel's history, and Begin became the recognized leader of a large bloc of political parties united under the banner
of "Greater Israel."[48] Coupled with the declining image of Labor (because
of the 1973 war, a number of scandals, and a transformation in Israel's
demographic makeup), the steady rise of Likud was quite natural in the
prevailing atmosphere. Once in power, with the support of the religious
and right-wing camps, Begin could transform Likud's ideology into state
policy.[49]

Begin's successor, Shamir, was also motivated by territorial considerations. Like Begin, he was not ready for territorial compromises. Peres
epitomized Shamir's preoccupation with territory:

> I had an argument with Shamir even on Taba. I asked him, why is this
> small piece of territory so important? There is doubt that it was ours; it has
> no strategic value, it was not promised to us in the Bible; it is nothing more
> than a strip of land where people go to sunbathe. But he insisted that the
> area is ours. This notion is built on obsession not on conception. It is
> hopeless. Our mistake was that we thought that Shamir could be edu-
> cated.[50]

Others in the Knesset also believed that Shamir did not want to return
any land and that he was not interested in the peace process. Instead, he
was building the West Bank and Gaza according to his own outlook,
which until the 1992 elections was more successful in the Knesset than the
outlook of Peres or Rabin.[51]

How did the Likud manage to implement its hawkish policies in a
democracy that is almost evenly divided on the issues of peace, security,
and territorial rights? The answer rests in Likud's ability to manipulate
the implementation of its policies through a strong collaboration with
Gush Emunim and its supporters. For it was Gush Emunim that ambi-
tiously aspired to the leadership of a massive drive for the colonization of
the whole of the West Bank.[52]

Collaboration Between Likud and Gush Emunim
and the Strengthening of the Right

The close relationship between Gush Emunim and the Likud, coupled
with the enormous encouragement Gush received from religious parties
and the parties of the extreme right (such as the NRP, Morasha, Tehiya,

Tzomet, Kach, Moledet, and even a Jewish underground), in effect created an ultranationalist alliance in the Israeli polity capable of undermining any peace initiative. With the exception of the NRP, all of these parties emerged on the Israeli political scene after the Likud had risen to power in 1977.

Although Gush Emunim was just one small protest group that sprang up between the 1973 war and Likud's ascendancy, it remained the only group that the newly elected Menachem Begin revered and encouraged. Indeed, once in power Begin's government reinforced its political dominance through adherence to ultranationalistic policies, mainly by using the Gush as a surrogate to promote its own ideology and by legitimizing Gush Emunim and bolstering its position in the Israeli polity.[53]

The major area of collaboration between Likud and Gush Emunim was settlement activity in the occupied territories. This is hardly surprising, since for the Likud the settlement drive was not just a means of establishing an Israeli presence in strategically vital areas but a means to realize the party's ideological obligations. From that standpoint Likud viewed the establishment of settlements in the West Bank and Gaza as a way to reaffirm the claim to Jewish sovereignty over all of Eretz Yisrael.[54]

In practical terms the settlement drive guaranteed the incremental de facto annexation of the West Bank and Gaza. Combined with the tactic of economic interdependence—the creation of Arab dependency on the Israeli-established infrastructure in the region—settlement safeguarded Israel's control over the territories.[55]

It also served the Likud as a means to attract coalition partners and to maintain political stability: By making settlement activity part of its coalition obligations, the Likud assured itself the continuous support of the religious and right-wing bloc, without which no Likud government—with the exception of a National Unity government—could survive.

Prior to Likud's rise to power, Gush Emunim was forbidden by the Labor government to establish new settlements in areas that were heavily populated by Palestinians.[56] Not accidently, Gush Emunim was actively involved in the 1977 campaign. It insisted that "the devotees of Eretz Yisrael vote only for lists whose plank on the integrity of the Land is lucid."[57] At the heart of the Gush's demand was the end of the ban to settle in Samaria. That demand was answered with the establishment of the new Likud government.

To be sure, the Likud government did not start the settlement of the West Bank and Gaza. Rather, the Labor-led government had begun to establish Jewish settlements in the occupied territories soon after the Six-Day War as part of its national defense strategy. But it was the Likud-led government that envisioned a massive settlement drive in these areas in order to reinforce the right of all Jews to settle in any part of biblical Eretz

Yisrael. In fact, the Likud government was engaged in the most far-reaching settlement expansion in Israel's history. During the first ten years of the Israeli occupation, from 1967 to 1977, the Labor government established twenty-four settlements in the West Bank. By contrast, during the first ten years of Likud's rule, from 1977 to 1987, the government established 150 settlements there.[58] During this latter period the number of Jewish settlers grew from roughly 3,000 to about 70,000.[59]

How exactly did the Gush help Likud implement its de facto annexation of territory? Soon after assuming power, the Likud government announced a plan to settle more than a million Jews in the West Bank within a twenty-year period. But the task of realizing this goal—at least during the first term of the Likud government—fell to Gush Emunim. Indeed, during that period over half of the new settlements established were affiliated with the movement.[60]

David Schnall has argued that Prime Minister Begin utilized the existence of Gush Emunin to encourage settlement and land claims that his government could not easily undertake on its own. By condoning the Gush's activities, he could achieve territorial goals without direct involvement; and by claiming that its influence on the movement was limited, the Likud government had a ready excuse for not doing what it was reluctant to do anyway.[61] Asher Arian has pointed out that despite its ambitious settlement policy, the Likud had neither the personnel nor the organization to settle the West Bank and Gaza in a manner similar to that of the kibbutz movement during the first half of the twentieth century. The Likud government was therefore satisfied to identify itself with the Gush's pioneers.[62]

Similarly, Ian Lustick has suggested that the ultranationalism and active messianism of Gush Emunim was able to fill the ideological vacuum created by the Likud's inability to implement its annexationist objectives. Coupled with the practical expertise and pioneering zeal of the settlers, this provided the first Likud government with a valuable resource.[63]

Still, no agreement among scholars exists regarding the impact of Gush Emunim on the Israeli political system. The Gush's apologists believe that the movement's influence has already eroded.[64] Others regard Gush Emunim as an aggressive extraparliamentary body that succeeded more than any other movement of its kind in achieving its political goals, a movement whose impact was felt not only in the political and policy-related spheres but also in the ideological, social, religious, and economic sectors.[65] I shared this latter view.

Within a relatively short period, Gush Emunim not only succeeded in terms of its specific settlement aspirations, but also became a powerful actor on the political stage in Israel. Moreover, because of the legitimacy the Likud government bestowed on it from 1977 to 1992, the Gush was both accepted in government circles and absorbed into the institutional framework.[66]

Despite its refusal to identify with any single political party, the Gush enjoyed parliamentary representation through parties such as the NRP, Tehiya, and Morasha and through the support of MKs of other parties.[67] Most significant, the Gush won the solid support of Sharon and Levy, the two hawkish Herut members who challenged Shamir's leadership. Sharon, the minister of agriculture and chairman of the Ministerial Committee of Settlements at the time, was the driving force behind the settlement campaign. Although he has always defended the right of the Jews to settle in all of Eretz Yisrael, Sharon has been concerned mostly with Israel's security. For him, this meant Israeli control over the occupied territories in order to guarantee that a Palestinian state is never created there. And it is his belief that only through the establishment of Jewish settlements can control over these territories be realized. "Those settlements," Sharon argued, "are stronger than any political definition and any written agreement."[68]

Be that as it may, in 1993 the number of Jewish settlers in the territories was estimated at about 130,000. In 1980 they established the Council of Jewish Settlements in Judea, Samaria, and Gaza known as Yesha. Yesha is a semiofficial governing body whose main feature is a legal association called Amana (Covenant).[69] It provides the government with significant administrative and economic resources and is also directly involved in the implementation of government policies in the West Bank and Gaza.[70] Although its members belong to a number of political parties, its hard core belongs to the nationalist parties, especially Tehiya and the NRP.[71]

Sprinzak noted that while the settlers may conduct most of their activities under the name of Yesha, most are members of Gush Emunim.[72] Similarly, Giora Goldberg and Efraim Ben-Zadok asserted that Gush Emunim does represent the majority of the settlers; that the local leadership in Judea and Samaria—as reflected in Yesha—is composed largely of Gush Emunim activists; that no prominent ideological trends other than that of Gush Emunim exists in Judea and Samaria; and that even in settlements not affiliated with Amana, the identification with Gush Emunim is virtually total.[73] It is well to note, however, that the majority of the 130,000 settlers moved to the West Bank not out of ideology but because of government economic incentives.

Aside from that, there is much empirical evidence to show the Gush's leverage in the Likud governments, especially on the settlement issue. First, in 1977 the government adopted the Gush's settlement plans for the West Bank.[74] After the 1981 elections, in which the movement actively campaigned, a superhawkish alliance led by Begin, Sharon, and Shamir, dominated the new government. This new government undertook a still more ambitious drive to settle Judea and Samaria.[75]

The Camp David agreements were anathema to the settlers. Thus, from that time until the creation of the 1984 National Unity government, Israel founded new settlements, expanded existing ones, or promised to do both during all new peace initiatives; it legislated guarantees to protect existing and future settlements; it cooperated with the Jewish settlers on the questions of the establishment of unauthorized settlements and illegal purchase of Arab land; and it collaborated with the settlers on the release of underground Jewish terrorists and on increased activity against the Arab inhabitants of the West Bank and Gaza.

But a growing number of Israelis objected to the Likud government's expenditure on settlements rather than more pressing needs. They also became farther removed from the Gush's ideology and were opposed to the national sacrifice of protecting the Jewish settlers in an increasingly hostile environment (see Chapter 12). Thus, since its defeat in the 1992 elections, the Right, including Gush Emunim, has been attempting to regroup and strengthen itself. But it is unable to offer the Israelis a better option than the Gaza-Jericho agreement. Indeed, aside from threatening to abrogate the agreement once back in power or alerting the public to the dangers it imposes on Israel's very survival, the Likud leader, Binyamin Netanyahu, has not offered any viable alternative to the plan. Rather, sharing the views of his predecessors (Shamir and Begin), Netanyahu opposes any territorial compromise in the West Bank and objects to peace negotiations with Arafat and to the elections of a Palestinian self-governing council in the territories. He prefers a limited West Bank autonomy through the transferring of municipal, economic, and social powers to the Palestinians, not as an interim stage but as a permanent solution. Still, if terrorist attacks on Jewish settlers and other Israelis will continue, the Right may be able to prevent the implementation of the Gaza-Jericho plan even if it cannot offer a better plan.

■ ■ ■

The victory in the 1967 Six-Day War provoked a religious awakening in Israel, strengthening the idea that Eretz Yisrael should never be partitioned again. That resulted in the creation of Gush Emunim, an influential extraparliamentary movement that helped put Likud in power in 1977. Together, and with the help of other right-wing political parties, Likud and Gush Emunim succeeded in undermining the peace process until the 1992 return of Labor to power. The ability of the Right to revitalize itself and to effectively undermine the Jaza-Jericho plan depends on a growing sense of vulnerability among Israelis. But for the time being the Right is unable to construct a more acceptable plan.

Notes

1. Jerusalem Domestic Service (Hebrew), appeared in English in *Foreign Broadcast Information Service/Daily Report: Middle East and Africa* (Washington, D.C.: United States Department of Commerce/Technical Information Service), September 10, 1982, p. 27.

2. Yoram Peri, "From Political Nationalism to Ethno-Nationalism: The Case of Israel," in Yehuda Lukacs and Abdalla M. Battah, eds., *The Arab-Israeli Conflict* (Boulder, Colo.: Westview, 1988).

3. Salo Wittmayer Baron, *Modern Nationalism and Religion* (New York: Harper Brothers, 1947), pp. 15–17; Hans Kohn, *The Idea of Nationalism* (New York: Macmillan, 1944), p. 15.

4. Charles S. Liebman and Eliezer Don-Yehiya, "The Dilemma of Reconciling Traditional Cultural and Political Needs," *Comparative Politics* (October 1983): 53–66.

5. Ibid.

6. Ibid.

7. Daniel Elazar, "Religious Parties and Politics in the Begin Era", in Steven Heydemann, ed., *The Begin Era: Issues in Contemporary Israel* (Boulder, Colo.: Westview 1984).

8. Ibid.

9. Amnon Rubinstein, *From Herzl to Gush Emunim and Back* (Hebrew) (Jerusalem: Shoken, 1980), p. 89.

10. Amos Elon, *The Israelis* (New York: Penguin Books, 1981), p. 5.

11. Ibid., p. 216.

12. Jay Gonen, *A Psychohistory of Zionism* (New York: Mason, Charter, 1975), p. 166.

13. Ibid., p. 167; Elon, *The Israelis*, p. 216.

14. Abba Eban, *An Autobiography* (New York: Random House, 1977), p. 379.

15. Rubinstein, *From Herzl to Gush Emunim*, pp. 93–95.

16. Asher Arian, "A People Apart: Coping with National Security Problems in Israel," *Journal of Conflict Resolution* 44, 4 (December 1989): 605–631.

17. Rubinstein, *From Herzl to Gush Emunim*, p. 90.

18. Ehud Sprinzak, "The Emergence of the Israeli Radical Right," *Comparative Politics* 21 (January 1989): 173.

19. Rubinstein, *From Herzl to Gush Emunim*, pp. 91–111.

20. Ehud Sprinzak, "Gush Emunim: The Tip of the Iceberg," *Jerusalem Quarterly* 21 (Fall 1981): 28–47.

21. Myron J. Aronoff, *Israeli Visions and Divisions* (New Brunswick, N.J.: Transaction Books, 1989), p. 76; Ehud Sprinzak, "The Iceberg Model of Political Extremism," in David Newman, ed., *The Impact of Gush Emunim* (New York: St. Martin's Press, 1985), p. 30.

22. Yitzhak Rabin, *Pinkas Sheirut* (Hebrew) (Tel Aviv: Maariv Library, 1979), p. 549.

23. For the different interpretations by religious leaders of Gush Emunim regarding the delineation of the Promised Land, see Ian S. Lustick, *For the Land and the Lord: Jewish Fundamentalism in Israel* (New York: Council on Foreign Relations, 1988), pp. 104–110.

24. Stewart Reiser, *The Politics of Leverage* (Cambridge: Center for Middle Eastern Studies, Harvard University, 1984), p. 35.

25. Ibid.

26. Giora Goldberg and Efraim Ben-Zadok, "Gush Emunim in the West Bank," *Middle East Studies* 22, 1 (January 1986): 52–73.

27. Aronoff, *Israeli Visions and Divisions*, pp. 72–73.

28. Goldberg and Ben-Zadok, "Gush Emunim in the West Bank," p. 60.

29. Ibid.

30. James A. Bill and Carl Leiden, *The Middle East: Politics and Power* (Boston: Allyn and Bacon, 1974), p. 3.

31. Lustick, *For the Land and the Lord*, pp. 76–79.

32. Ibid., p. 81.

33. Ibid., pp. 81–82.

34. Sprinzak, "Gush Emunim: Tip of the Iceberg," p. 38.

35. Sprinzak, "The Iceberg Model," p. 32.

36. Ibid.

37. Lustick, *For the Land and the Lord*, pp. 129–131.

38. Ibid., p. 150.

39. Ibid., pp. 76–79.

40. Gershon R. Kieval, *Party Politics in Israel and the Occupied Territories* (Westport, Conn.: Greenwood Press, 1983), p. 138.

41. Yonathan Shapiro, "The End of a Dominant Party System," in Asher Arian, ed., *The Elections in Israel–1977* (Jerusalem: Jerusalem Academic Press, 1980), pp. 23–38.

42. Ariel Levite and Sidney Tarrow, "The Legitimation of Excluded Parties in Dominant Party Systems: A Comparison of Israel and Italy," *Comparative Politics* 15, 3 (April 1983): 295–327.

43. For the demographic factor in the 1977 elections, see Asher Arian, "The Israeli Electorate, 1977," in Arian, *The Elections in Israel–1977*.

44. Ibid., pp. 253–276.

45. Ilan Peleg, "The Impact of the Six Day War on the Israeli Right: A Second Republic in the Making?" in Lukacs and Battah, *The Arab-Israeli Conflict*, p. 55.

46. Ibid., p. 58.

47. For a discussion of the Jarring mission, see Saadia Touval, *The Peace Brokers* (Princeton, N.J.: Princeton University Press, 1982), pp. 153–164.

48. Peleg, "Impact of the Six-Day War," pp. 58–59.

49. Ibid., p. 60.

50. Private conversation with then MK Shimon Peres, Tel Aviv, July 3, 1991.

51. This conclusion is based in part on a private conversation with then MK Ezer Weizman, Caesaria, July 5, 1991. After his defeat in the 1992 elections, Shamir

admitted his intention to complete the de facto annexation of the West Bank and Gaza. *Ma'ariv,* June 26, 1992.

52. Kieval, *Party Politics,* p. 156.

53. Ian Lustick, "Gush Emunim Ideology—From Religious Doctrine to Political Action," *Middle Eastern Studies* 18, 3 (July 1982): 265–275.

54. Kieval, *Party Politics,* pp. 142–143.

55. For the aggregate sum of land acquisition and settlement activity during the first Begin government, see Ian Lustick, "Israel and the West Bank After Elon Moreh: The Mechanics of De Facto Annexation," *Middle East Journal* 35, 4 (autumn 1981): 557–577; and Lustick, "The West Bank and Gaza in Israeli Politics," in Steven Heydemann, ed., *The Begin Era: Issues in Contemporary Israel* (Boulder, Colo.: Westview, 1984), p. 86.

56. Shmuel Sandler, "The Protracted Arab-Israeli Conflict: A Temporal-Spatial Analysis," *Jerusalem Journal of International Relations* 10, 4 (December 1988): 54–78.

57. Yael Yishai, "Drafting the Platform: The Territorial Clause," in Asher Arian and Michal Shamir, eds., *The Elections in Israel–1984* (New Brunswick, N.J.: Transaction Books, 1986), p. 245.

58. Aronoff, *Israeli Visions and Divisions,* p. 76.

59. Arian, "Israel's National Unity Government and Domestic Politics," in Asher Arian and Michal Shamir, eds., *The Elections in Israel–1988* (Boulder, Colo.: Westview, 1990), p. 217. Although part of this activity took place under the National Unity government, in that period the settlement program was carried out at a much slower pace than during Likud's rule.

60. Gershon Shafir, "Institutional and Spontaneous Settlement Drive," in Newman, *The Impact of Gush Emunim,* p. 161.

61. David Schnall, "An Impact Assessment," in Newman, *The Impact of Gush Emunim,* p. 22.

62. Arian, *Politics in Israel,* pp. 87–88.

63. Lustick, *For the Land and the Lord,* p. 9.

64. Eliezer Don-Yehiya, "Jewish Messianism, Religious Zionism and Israeli Politics: The Impact and Origin of Gush Emunim," *Middle Eastern Studies* 23, 2 (April 1987): 215–234.

65. Sprinzak, "Gush Emunim: Tip of the Iceberg"; Lustick, *For the Land and the Lord,* p. 8.; Schnall, "An Impact Assessment," p. 22. For an excellent discussion on what Sprinzak calls the movement's "invisible realm," see Ehud Sprinzak, *The Ascendance of Israel's Right* (New York: Oxford University Press, 1991), pp. 130–132.

66. Newman, *The Impact of Gush Emunim,* p. 1. For a discussion on the process by which the Gush managed to intermix its policies with the policies of the government, see Sprinzak, "Gush Emunim: Tip of the Iceberg," pp. 40–46. In addition, see Myron J. Aronoff, "The Institutionalization and Cooptation of a Charismatic, Messianic, Religious-Political Revitalization Movement," in Newman, *The Impact of Gush Emunim.* Aronoff shows how the movement institutionalized itself since 1977.

67. Aronoff, *Israeli Vision and Division,* p. 87.

68. Kieval, *Party Politics in Israel,* p. 154.

69. For a discussion on Yesha and Amana, see Sprinzak, *The Ascendance of Israel's Right,* ch. 5.

70. Lustick, *For the Land and the Lord,* p. 10.

71. Sprinzak, *The Ascendance of Israel's Right,* ch. 6, and Yishai, "The Territorial Clause," p. 245.

72. Sprinzak, "Gush Emunim: Tip of the Iceberg," p. 34.

73. Goldberg and Ben-Zadok, "Gush Emunim in the West Bank," p. 57.

74. Shafir, "Institutional and Spontaneous Settlement Drive," pp. 161–165.

75. Sprinzak, "The Iceberg Model," p. 34.

10

The First Fallout: The Near Collapse of the National Unity Government

Secretary of State Shultz's idea to convene an international Middle East peace conference produced two conflicting foreign policies in Israel, still governed by a National Unity government at the time. Likud strongly rejected the conference idea, whereas Labor enthusiastically supported it. As a result, the first National Unity government nearly collapsed; it survived only because the Labor Party did not have the votes it needed to form a new government. Prime Minister Shamir's rejection of the conference thus prevailed, even though the idea had been endorsed by all the major players in the Arab-Israeli conflict.

The Political Crisis over the International Conference Plan

The internal tension that erupted in Israel over the idea of an international conference turned into a political crisis after rotation occurred in October 1986, when Peres assumed the vice premiership and the foreign ministry and Shamir became prime minister. Shamir came under tremendous pressure from those who believed that the concept of Palestinian autonomy went too far. This camp was conspicuously represented by Likud ministers Sharon and Levy as well as the Tehiya Party. The result was a conflicted foreign policy carried out at the same time by both Shamir and Peres. Although this posed tremendous difficulties for the Reagan administration, the administration refrained from meddling in Israel's internal politics, leaving Israelis to work out their differences themselves.[1]

The rift over the conference idea broadened in April 1987, when Shamir faulted Peres for accepting the idea of the international conference, describing the conference notion as "suicide, insane and monstrous." He also accused Peres of dictating the idea through "shrewd and clandestine tactics."[2]

In response some Labor ministers called for the dismantling of the government, but Peres hoped to prevent a crisis. Instead, Labor agreed to a compromise according to which the party ministers would sustain a relationship with Likud, however stormy, until a carefully prepared and concrete proposal for the specifics of the international conference could be submitted to the cabinet for a vote. On his side Shamir tried to avoid a crisis by rejecting Tehiya's initiative for early elections. Both Likud and Labor preferred to stay in the government rather than face the uncertainties of new elections.

But the debate intensified when Likud leaked details of a plan for an international conference, which Likud attributed to Peres, though it was submitted to the Israeli government as a U.S. proposal for the next phase of the peace process. Likud's accusation came after the United States presented to Israel a draft proposal for the conference idea and after Hussein and Peres had secretly agreed on the conference procedures. Shamir also blames Peres for surrendering Israeli security assets, including the Golan Heights and East Jerusalem.

In a countercampaign Peres presented his full plan to the inner cabinet on May 11. At the same time he introduced a letter from Secretary Shultz that indicated immediate U.S. support for Peres's plan. He also assured the Israelis that the conference would lead to direct negotiations between Israel and its neighbors without coercion or pressure. He reiterated the U.S. commitment regarding conditions for a recognizing the PLO and including the Soviet Union in the political process.

Aside from his belief that his agreement with King Hussein provided an opportunity Israel should not miss, Peres's justification for holding an international conference rested on the 1973 decision of the Meir government and the 1977 decision of the Begin government to support the same idea. But Peres added certain stipulations: (1) Negotiations would be direct, face to face, without any preconditions; (2) after the opening of the conference, negotiations would be conducted within the framework of bilateral committees, with the Palestinian issue negotiated between the Israeli delegation and the Jordanian-Palestinian delegation, which would exclude PLO members. The negotiations themselves were to be based on UN Resolutions 242 and 338 and on the participants' renunciation of violence and terrorism.

For Peres, the conference had three purposes. The first was to invite the warring parties to settle the Jewish-Arab conflict in a peaceful way. This included the settlement of the Palestinian problem "on all its aspects," in line with the Camp David formula.

The second was to invite the parties to agree to establish bilateral committees in order to negotiate peace. The third was the actual formation of these committees—which were to include a Jordanian-Palestinian committee, a Syrian-Israeli committee, a Lebanese-Israeli committee, and, if possible, a committee to discuss regional issues such as irrigation and development. The creation of each of these bilateral groups was not to depend on the establishment of any of the others. In that way the participation of the Jordanian-Palestinian committee in negotiations would not be tied to the participation of the Syrian-Israeli or Lebanese-Israeli committees.

Peres also insisted that the conference could not force a solution on the parties, nor could it revoke any decisions the parties agreed on. In case of a breach in regulations, the United States, together with Israel, was to withdraw from the conference. Further, the participation of the Soviet Union and China was conditioned on establishment of diplomatic relations between these countries and Israel. Finally, Peres pledged that Labor would refuse to return to the 1967 borders, would reject the repartition of Jerusalem, would refuse to uproot Jewish settlements, and would prevent the participation of the PLO in the conference.[3]

But because the cabinet was evenly divided on the international conference, Labor decided not to bring the issue to a vote. Shamir interpreted this decision as the cabinet's renunciation of the Peres proposal, thereby stripping the foreign minister of any mandate to pursue the idea further. But Peres continued to direct the Israeli foreign ministry without change. On May 13, 1987, Labor officially demanded the resignation of Shamir, accusing him of obstructing the peace process. The move was merely symbolic, as Labor did not expect to win the number of votes needed for early elections. But at the same time Labor held overt negotiations with other parties regarding the possibility of calling for early elections. Peres himself left for a two-week visit to the United States, where he reportedly agreed with Shultz on a number of private moves to stimulate the peace process.

Still, the crisis was not over: Shinui—a small left-of-center party—pulled out of the government in the hope that its departure would precipitate Labor's withdrawal from the government and thus force new elections. But on May 19 the National Unity government defeated three motions of no confidence advanced by a number of small left-wing parties.

Concluding that there was no chance to bring the government down, the Labor Alignment decided to remain in the coalition for the time being.[4] Labor's decision was based on the assessment of a special team that examined the possibility of holding new elections and on the explicit commitment Shamir had from the religious parties, who promised to support a narrow-based coalition headed by Likud should Labor withdraw from the government. On top of this, polls indicated that both Labor and Likud were losing voters to the smaller and more ideological parties of both left and right.

To justify his party's remaining, Peres declared that Labor would not leave the government to a right-wing Likud that had come to represent the ideology of Gush Emunim, Tehiya, and religious extremism. He also called for a national referendum on the peace process—a call that Shamir rejected on the basis that the idea did not conform to the Israeli political system. His assertion was confirmed by a team of jurists who ruled that the idea was illegal.

In October Peres—in the United States for the forty-second General Assembly—continued to pursue the issue of the international conference, meeting with Secretary of State Shultz and the Soviet foreign minister, Eduard Shevardnadze. But as Shultz's February visit to the region neared, Shamir agreed to a tactical change in his position and declared his readiness to support the convening of an international conference, but only as a formality for the conclusion of negotiations on permanent agreements.

Shamir also formulated his own three-part proposal. The first part included a plan for solving the problem of Palestinian refugees through the construction of 41,000 housing units for the 280,000 refugees in Judea, Samaria, and Gaza who still resided in camps. This was to be carried out with the help of a special international fund and completed within eight to ten years. The second part contained a plan for peace with Jordan. According to Shamir's proposal, negotiations with Jordan would span a three-year period, at which time autonomy would be established in Judea, Samaria, and Gaza. By the third year joint agreements for de facto peace relations with Jordan would be secured in contracts. At the end of three years, Israel would negotiate with Jordan toward permanent settlement for Judea, Samaria, and Gaza. The third part included a detailed autonomy plan based on the Camp David accords. It proposed to resume the autonomy talks at the point where negotiations with Egypt on the matter were stopped.

Shamir had no reason to believe that King Hussein or the Palestinians would accept any of the three parts of his plan. Because Palestinians form the majority of the Jordanian population and because Jordan is militarily weak, King Hussein was unable to negotiate with Israel on his own. Furthermore, the plan did not offer him any territorial gains during the first three years of negotiations. And the PLO has always maintained that the Palestinian problem was not a problem of refugees. The proposal, then, could be nothing more than a way to relieve some of Washington's pressure on Israel to participate in the peace process.

Nevertheless, on the eve of Shultz's arrival in Israel, the inner cabinet devoted its session to Shamir's plan. But sharp division between the Labor Alignment and Likud prevented an agreement. Labor accused Shamir of using the autonomy clause as an excuse to avoid negotiations, yet Peres pledged to remain in the government in order to promote the U.S. initiative.

As the controversy sharpened, Shamir was prepared to accept an "international event" sponsored by the two superpowers. This "event" would be a symbolic opening ceremony leading to direct negotiations. Although Shamir claimed his modified position was a concession to King Hussein, in reality Shamir accepted the idea only because he trusted Shultz, believing that the U.S. secretary of state was truly interested in Israel's well-being.[5]

But Peres and other Labor ministers demanded that the prime minister bring the original Shultz initiative to a vote before the inner cabinet prior to Shamir's departure for the United States, a demand Shamir flatly rejected. The hard-liners in Likud prevailed over the more moderate elements in the party.

The Influence of the Israeli Right
on the Domestic Debate

The crisis over the international conference idea dates back to the abrogation of the Amman accords in February 1986, which prompted an internal debate in Israel as to what direction the peace process should take. The agreement reached by King Hussein and Chairman Arafat set forth a framework for joint Jordanian-Palestinian participation in peace negotiations.

Peres, who was prime minister in 1986, thought that Israel should proceed with the peace process unilaterally and hand over to the inhabitants of the occupied territories autonomy over their internal affairs until formal arrangements could be reached. Alarmed, the Israeli Right quickly moved to secure the Israeli hold over Judea, Samaria, and Gaza. Soon after Hussein announced the abrogation of his agreement with Arafat, Geula Cohen from the ultraright Tehiya Party submitted to the Knesset a proposal to annex the territories.[6] That followed a challenge to Shamir's leadership within his own party, when two hawkish ministers from Herut—Sharon, minister of trade and industry, and Levy, deputy prime minister and minister of construction and housing—expressed doubts that Shamir would be capable of dealing with such vital issues when he assumed the position of prime minister under the rotation agreement.

In April 1986 Peres recognized the Palestinians as a nation, a move that prompted Tehiya to submit to the Knesset a no-confidence motion.

When rumors circulated that Egypt, Israel, and the United States were preparing autonomy for the Gaza Strip, Tehiya endorsed the expulsion of the Arab inhabitants of the West Bank and Gaza to Arab countries. For their part, the Jewish settlers in the occupied territories called for Israeli sovereignty over Gaza.

Less than a month after Peres revealed that secret diplomacy was under way between Israel and Jordan—a disclosure that Shamir validated—Sharon called for the annexation of the territories. Sharon always chose symbolic locations as settings for his announcements regarding the territories; this time he spoke from the Hebron Hills, the site chosen for a new industrial zone.

At the end of September, as rotation neared, Shamir came under pressure from Tehiya, Gush Emunim, and members of his own party to launch a massive settlement drive. Thus, before becoming prime minister, Shamir declared that the settlement drive would continue along with the search for peace. He also promised to consolidate the Jewish presence in all parts of the Land of Israel. On his first day in office as prime minister, despite a U.S. appeal against the expansion of settlements in the territories, Shamir visited Kokhav Ya'ir, where he promised to settle the entire Land of Israel so the country would be able to absorb its new immigrants.

Similarly, in mid-November Shamir declared that the Green Line could not be a line of peace and promised that land would not be partitioned again. In December, after Peres had promised Senator Ted Kennedy that Israel would not build new settlements in the territories, Shamir defiantly declared that expansion would indeed take place. By February 1987 Shamir's and Peres's opposing policies prompted discussions within both parties over the fall of the government. When on February 25 Peres left for a second visit to Cairo, Tehiya warned that if Peres continued to promote the idea of a peace conference, there would be no choice but to hold early elections. In reply Shamir vowed to thwart Peres's attempts to force the idea on the cabinet. On March 1, after a stormy cabinet session, Likud decided to launch a wide-scale information campaign in Israel and the United States against the international conference.

When Peres reassured the Israelis that Israel would not have to negotiate under pressure, Sharon dismissed it as fraud, arguing that Peres's plan would bring Israel back to the 1967 borders and to the climate of terror that existed in the country after independence. In reply Labor ministers reaffirmed their commitment to use the conference only as a preliminary phase for direct negotiations.

Meanwhile, Tehiya threatened to join the drive for early elections unless the government stopped Peres's efforts to convene an international conference and agreed to establish twenty-seven new settlements—a number that far exceeded the six settlements the government had approved. The latter demand was also voiced by the Council of Jewish Settlements and several MKs from Likud. Together, they requested that 30,000 more Jews be settled in Judea, Samaria, and Gaza during the remaining eighteen months left for the government. Gush Emunim insisted that the government be disbanded immediately unless the settlement movement was resumed.

On that same issue Tehiya on July 15 threatened to dissolve the Knesset and force new elections. It backed down after securing a pledge from Likud for a substantial expansion of settlements in the West Bank. This corresponded with increased support for Tehiya among the Israeli Right and the public's shift further to the right. But when Tehiya learned that Shamir had responded positively to Shultz's offer of a limited superpower role in the peace process, the party renewed its threats. The prime minister's office denied the report.

Still, in the initial cabinet debate over the Shultz initiative in January 1988, Shamir deviated from his unyielding position, asking the U.S. secretary of state to communicate to King Hussein that the territories were negotiable. Moreover, he informed the United States that he was prepared to grant the inhabitants of the territories full autonomy, except in foreign affairs and security matters.

But Sharon and Levy immediately revolted against Shamir, warning the country against the "Arab version" of autonomy that Shamir was ready to embrace. So did Yosef Shapira from Morasha, who feared the prime minister had been worn down by the *intifada*. Together, these ministers made it clear to Shamir that the Israeli Right would not permit him to do with the West Bank and Gaza what Prime Minister Begin had done with the Sinai. Sharon and Levy in particular demanded that the prime minster adhere to the autonomy plan as defined in the Camp David agreements and called for more aggressive settlement activity in the territories.

As usual Shamir acceded to the demand of his hard-line ministers and agreed that negotiations with Shultz would be restricted to the Camp David accords. Still, unwilling to reject the Shultz initiative outright (the initiative did not yet constitute a formal U.S. peace plan and was not voted on by the cabinet), he demanded that several clauses in the plan be changed, including: (1) the elimination of the international conference, (2) the postponement of Shultz's timetable for the implementation of autonomy, and (3) the elimination of a binding date for the beginning of negotiations on a permanent solution for the territories. When Shamir and Shultz finally met in Jerusalem, activists from Herut, Tehiya, and Gush Emunim demonstrated outside the prime minister's office, protesting against territorial concessions under the motto "Israel is not for sale."

Shamir repudiated the notion that a peace treaty might end Jewish settlement anywhere in Eretz Yisrael.

Meanwhile the discrepancy between the Labor Alignment and Likud over Shultz's plan brought about renewed debate over early elections. That possibility gave the hawkish members of Herut the opportunity to try to commit Shamir to a tougher position: Herut's platform committee decided to add to the movement's principles a commitment to act on the immediate implementation of Israeli law in all the territories. It rejected the autonomy concept as defined in the Camp David agreement or any other form of self-determination for the Palestinians. It also rebuffed any peace formula adopted from "outside." Other Herut ministers, however, were quick to deny that the modified platform reflected the party's official position. When Shultz's proposal became an official administration document on March 4, Herut activists began to campaign against the plan. In addition a number of Likud MKs ventured to dissolve the Knesset and to hold early elections. If successful, their motion would have been tantamount to the rejection of the Shultz plan. As ever, the most vocal opponents of the plan in Likud were Sharon and Levy, who accused the United States of breaking its commitments to the Camp David agreements. They were soon joined by Yitzhak Modai from Likud.

On the eve of his departure for Washington in mid-February, Shamir insinuated a reverse from his traditional opposition to the principle of territory for peace. Such suggestions, even if made in order to alleviate U.S. pressure, stimulated Sharon's revolt. A few days after Shamir left for the United States, Sharon announced his own plan: It defined the Jordan River as Israel's eastern security border and deployed the IDF along the River. It further determined that no foreign military forces, including UN forces, would be present west of the Jordan River; that Israel would bear sole responsibility for security in Greater Israel; that there would be no foreign sovereignty over any part of Judea, Samaria, and the Gaza Strip; that no second Palestinian state would be established west of the Jordan; that the refugee problem would be solved as part of a political settlement in the area; that the Golan Heights were an integral part of Israel; and that the Arab population in Judea, Samaria, and Gaza would be granted autonomy to conduct its internal affairs, and the citizens of these areas would retain their present nationality. Sharon also saw himself as a future candidate for the prime ministry.

Other Likud leaders had decided to negotiate with the small Knesset factions in order to create a narrow-based government without the Labor Alignment. They had the support of sixty MKs, including Meir Kahane of Kach. The result was familiar: Once more Shamir succumbed to pressure. Upon his return, in an emotional speech before a special Knesset plenary session, he called for national unity in order to deter those who were con-spiring to harm Israel and force the country to make concessions at the expense of national security.

But that was not enough for Sharon, who insisted that the government explicitly demand the establishment of the Jordan River as Israel's secu-rity border; continued Israeli control of the Golan Heights; expansion of Jewish settlements in Jerusalem, including the Muslim Quarter; and Israeli control of all parts of the city. As always, Sharon carefully chose the location from where to deliver his message: this time Jerusalem's Jewish Quarter, where the Herut central committee organized a seminar.

While not acceding to Sharon's demands, Shamir upheld his opposi-tion to the Shultz plan on the grounds that both the international confer-ence idea and the proposition that negotiations on the permanent arrangements for Judea, Samaria, and Gaza begin before the implementa-tion of the interim arrangements deviated from the Camp David agree-ments. In May new political strife erupted in Israel after President Reagan praised Foreign Minister Peres for his support of the Shultz initiative. But in the meantime the campaigning for the upcoming Israeli elections began. This time it was Hussein's dissociation from the West Bank together with the impact of the *intifada* that provided for a preelection political contest. Not unexpectedly Sharon—joined by the Tehiya Party—seized on Hussein's move as an opportunity to call for the annexation of the territories as a way to fill the vacuum the king had left. In the end the Likud platform endorsed the autonomy plan of the Camp David accords. The results of the 1988 elections revealed that the Israeli public was unde-cided about the direction the peace process should take. Soon after, a new political debate erupted over the Reagan administration's decision to open a dialogue with the PLO. Although the cabinet criticized that deci-sion, other voices in the political echelon welcomed it as an opportunity to end the deadlock in the peace process. Naturally, the NRP, Tzomet, Tehiya, and Moledet strongly opposed the U.S. move. But Peace Now joined by the parties of the Left, such as Shinui, Mapam, the CRM, and Hadash, called upon the government to join the United States and begin talks with the PLO.

■ ■ ■

Even though the National Unity government survived the conference controversy and even though conference did not materialize, interna-tional conditions would soon prompt the United States to initiate a new peace plan. More important, these conditions planted the seeds for the eventual Israeli recognition of the PLO five years later.

Notes

1. These conclusions are based in part on information obtained in private conversations with former assistant secretary of state for Near Eastern and African affairs Richard Murphy, New York, April 9, 1991, and Ambassador Samuel Lewis, Washington, D.C., April 26, 1991.

2. Unless otherwise documented, the data in this and the next chapter is compiled from the *New York Times*, *Ha'aretz*, *FBIS/DR*, and *JPS*, October 22, November 13, December 11–12, 1986; February 25, March 2, May 5–22, June 9, 12, 30, July 1, 10, 15–16, 20, October 19, November 4, December 31, 1987; February 1–2, 10, 16, 22, 25, March 3–5, 14–18, 28, May 21, April 6, 1988; January 3–26, February 1, 28, March 27, May 17–19, June 16, 22, 28–30, July 6, 10–24, August 9–10, September 19, October 5, 11–12, 20, December 1–13, 1989; February 12, March 5–16, 1990.

3. Labor Party, *The Struggle for the Continuation of the Peace Initiative* (Hebrew) (Tel Aviv: Labor Party, 1987).

4. Peres's inability to publicize his secret agreement with King Hussein limited his maneuverability in 1988. But in 1989 he was considering his party's resignation from the government over lack of progress in the peace process. A year later he did resign. Private conversation, Tel Aviv, July 3, 1991.

5. Private conversation with then health minister Ehud Olmert, Jerusalem, June 28, 1991.

6. On March 5, 1986, the Knesset rejected the proposal, which was supported by a number of cabinet members.

11

The Second Fallout: The Collapse of the National Unity Government

In March 1990 the coalition government fell after Prime Minister Shamir and his Likud Party refused to make a compromise according to which Israel could accept a peace initiative proposed by Secretary of State Baker. While a number of moderate Likud ministers supported a compromise, the hard-liners of the party—the so-called constraints ministers—were powerful enough to uphold Likud's rigid position.

Reaction to the Shamir-Rabin Plan

The Shamir-Rabin plan, which developed into the Israeli government initiative of May 14, 1989, was initially launched at a time when Israel had little choice but to react to regional and global changes. The most important of these changes were the PLO's acceptance of UN Resolutions 242 and 338 and its renunciation of terrorism, a changed American attitude toward the PLO, and the steady improvement of U.S.-Soviet relations.

Based on the Camp David agreements, the plan called for elections in the West Bank and Gaza, where a delegation representing the Palestinians in negotiations with Israel would be chosen. Negotiations would aim at establishing a transitional self-rule period, to be followed by talks on the permanent status of the territories. During the transitional period Israel would continue to be responsible for security, foreign affairs, and matters concerning Israeli citizens in the territories.

The plan was notable in that it extended beyond Likud's ideas of limited autonomy. But because it did not permit PLO representation, Shamir could be certain the Arabs would reject it, and he did not feel threatened by its possible adoption. Still, the need to react to a changed atmosphere had placed him in a serious predicament: The more evident it had become that Israel could not remain oblivious to a different environment, the more the Israeli Right was in danger of losing power. This jeopardized not only the existence of the government but Shamir's own position as Likud's leader.

To diffuse pressure from the United States and Labor, Shamir made a number of tactical moves to appear willing to adapt his narrow interpretation of the Camp David agreements. First, in January 1989 he declared that it was not necessary "to cling" to each and every word of the Camp David accords, as long as their framework was maintained. In February he made a similar statement.

Second, with Shamir's approval, Rabin was trying to arrange an indirect dialogue with the PLO leadership in Tunis (through the good offices of Palestinian figures from the territories) in order to weaken Arafat's opposition to negotiations between Israel and a non-PLO Palestinian representation. In fact, after the PLO had accepted UN Resolutions 242 and 338 in November 1988, the Israeli Left encouraged contacts with the PLO for the purpose of advancing the peace process. It was about that time that the Young Guards of the Labor Alignment demanded that the party drop from its platform any opposition to contacts with the PLO. On January 10, 1989, a delegation of left-wing MKs from Labor, Mapam, and the CRM left for Paris to participate in an international symposium that PLO representatives also attended. Later a group of Labor members recommended that Ezer Weizman, Labor's minister of science and development, lead a delegation of 100 Israeli figures from various political parties to meet with Arafat in Cairo to discuss the promotion of a peace agreement based on a tripartite confederation option. In mid-February a number of MKs from the Labor Alignment, Mapam, and Shinui met with Faisal al-Husseini, regarded by Israeli authorities as one of the most prominent PLO leaders in the West Bank and a chief coordinator of the *intifada*. On February 26 Weizman urged the inner cabinet to open a dialogue with the PLO. At the same time the Israeli defense establishment concluded that without a dialogue with the PLO, it would be impossible to advance the peace process toward a solution to the Palestinian problem or to end the *intifada*.

Finally, in April, on the eve of his Washington trip, Shamir pledged an innovative diplomacy regarding the interim arrangements. Government officials described that to mean full autonomy. But Shamir's ability to adapt to a changed environment was curtailed by strong opposition from the political far Right. As soon as he showed readiness to accept minimal formal UN participation in the peace process, Ariel Sharon, by now Shamir's chief Likud rival, warned that such a concession might jeopardize Israel's security. Tehiya submitted a no-confidence motion to the Knesset over Shamir's willingness to "negotiate the fate of Eretz Yisrael" under the auspices of an international conference. The Kach movement went as far as announcing its intention to form the State of Judea in the area comprising Judea, Samaria, and Gaza. In a gathering named the First Zionist Conference of the State of Judea, Kahane declared his movement's plan to be the "last resort" if Israel would not annex the territories. The meeting, patterned after the first Zionist Congress that gathered in Basel in 1897, even introduced the new Judean national anthem and Judean flags.

Such opposition spread despite the steps Shamir had taken in order to convince the far Right, especially Gush Emunim and its followers, of his commitment to hold on to the territories. These steps included renewed pledges to settle all parts of Eretz Yisrael and to redeem the country and a promise to establish eleven new settlements. Shamir also appointed his own special adviser on settlement affairs whose tasks were fostering settlement activities and consolidating settlement-related operations of various government ministries.

The final draft of his peace plan caused a serious rift within Likud between Shamir's camp and Likud members led by Sharon, Levy, and Modai, who joined forces with the extreme Right, including Tehiya, Kach, and Moledet. Their opposition was based on fear that the possible inclusion of East Jerusalem residents in the election plan would lead to the repartition of the city and to territorial compromise. Besides, the plan did not condition elections on the end of the *intifada*.

Taking the lead, Sharon pledged to block the election plan, which, he warned, could result in the emergence of a Palestinian state. He viewed the inclusion of East Jerusalem in the elections as a do-or-die issue, assisting terrorist leaders to operate out of Jerusalem.[1]

But the government endorsed the plan despite Sharon's warnings and immediately proceeded to lay down the guidelines for the elections. The territories were to be divided into ten districts, each of which would have one elected representative to negotiate the interim agreement with Israel. Additional representatives would be considered to join the delegation during the talks over the permanent solution, which would begin three years after the establishment of autonomy.

As the Knesset continued to debate the plan, thirteen Likud MKs demanded an urgent party session to formulate a unanimous position. It was then that Shamir began to capitulate to the Right, promising not to give an inch of land to the Arabs, not to negotiate with those involved in PLO activities, not to negotiate the implementation of the Israeli peace initiative as long as the *intifada* continued, and to ban Arab residents of East Jerusalem from participating in the election process in the territories.

Despite these assurances, Modai called on both Shamir and Peres to resign, and Sharon convened some thirty Likud activists (using his East Jerusalem residence as the symbolic setting) to demand Herut's central committee vote on the plan.[2]

When presenting the plan to the Knesset, Shamir reiterated his opposition to "another" Palestinian state (Likud considered Jordan to be Palestine); to negotiations with the PLO; and to any changes in the status of Judea, Samaria, and Gaza. But Levy claimed that the plan contradicted Likud's party platform, and Sharon demanded a written promise from Shamir that the *intifada* would be suppressed before the election process began and that residents from East Jerusalem would not be allowed to participate in the elections. Later he added a third demand: a clear statement that under no circumstances would the status of Jerusalem be negotiable.

As Likud's central committee convention neared, Shamir tried to manipulate between yielding to the pressure from Sharon's camp and adhering to the Israeli initiative. Thus, on June 16 he promised Herut's members of Likud's central committee to wipe out the Arab violence, but he also called for the initiation of Camp David in revised form. But on June 22 Sharon, Levy, and Modai demanded four changes in the government's plan: (1) violence must stop not only for the duration of elections but for as long as negotiations take place; (2) Arabs of East Jerusalem cannot participate in the voting; (3) no Palestinian state will ever be created between the Jordan and the Mediterranean; (4) Israel will not stop settlements.

In reply Shamir insisted that his peace initiative was a comprehensive proposal that was not open to changes. But Sharon countercharged that the initiative would lead to bloodshed and war rather than peace. The struggle was soon over: Seeking to avoid strife within the party, in his address before the central committee, Shamir reduced his entire initiative to "food for thought." Thus, "it was too premature to determine whether it will indeed become reality" and "too early and unjustified to turn the issue into a bitter, internal feud."[3] He then succumbed to the demands of his opponents, agreeing that (1) no negotiations could take place while violence continued and that the election process could be held only in complete calm; (2) Jerusalem was not part of the initiative, that is, the Arabs of East Jerusalem would not participate in the elections; (3) settlement activity would continue; and (4) in the negotiations of the permanent solution, Israeli representatives would insist in Israel's sovereignty over areas subject to negotiations. From then on Shamir adhered to this formula—in fact it had become the Likud's unified position—in spite of a commitment he later made to the Labor Alignment to comply with the government's initiative of May 14.

With the exception of Sharon, the Likud overwhelmingly endorsed the amended plan. It was also supported by Shas, Tehiya, NRP, Gush Emunim, and Moledet. But Labor, Mapam, Shinui, the CRM, and Hadash opposed the new plan. Some in the Labor Alignment called for the resignation of the party from the government; Mapam, Shinui, and the CRM submitted to the Knesset a vote of nonconfidence in the government (the motion was defeated on July 7).[4]

According to Labor, the participation of East Jerusalem Arabs in the vote would not necessarily jeopardize Jerusalem's unity and Israel's sovereignty over the city, and they therefore should be permitted to vote. Beyond the five or eight settlements to which the Labor Alignment conceded, the party strongly objected to the establishment of new settlements. Third, while it condemned violence, the party was against making the end of the *intifada* a condition for the continuation of the peace process. Fourth, it favored a territorial compromise in line with UN Resolution 242.

Initially, Peres and Rabin, along with other Labor Alignment ministers, decided to quit the government. But after two religious parties, Shas and NRP, called upon Labor and Likud to preserve the National Unity government, Labor issued an ultimatum: Unless Shamir renounced the resolution adopted by Likud's central committee, Labor would leave the government. The crisis ended on July 23, when Labor and Likud ministers ratified the government's original plan.

But the Labor Alignment took additional steps to rebut Likud's resolutions. On August 9 Labor's central committee adopted twelve principles. The party rejected the renunciation of the land-for-peace formula; reaffirmed Resolutions 242 and 338 as the basis for negotiations; allowed the participation of East Jerusalem Arabs in the proposed elections in the territories, provided that voting not be held in East Jerusalem itself; insisted that negotiations be held with the Palestinians without delay and without conditions (not necessarily before the end of the *intifada*); asked that observers from selected countries who maintain diplomatic relations with Israel be allowed to participate in the supervision of the election and that the elections be conducted in an atmosphere of nonviolence; called for Jerusalem to remain united under Israeli sovereignty; and demanded that no Palestinian state be established.[5] But before the government had the chance to discuss either Likud's or Labor's formulae, President Mubarak made public his ten-point plan.

Reaction to Mubarak's and Baker's Proposals

Prime Minister Shamir's initial reaction to the content of Mubarak's plan was to reaffirm the Israeli government plan as the only initiative to which Israel was bound. By contrast, Peres thought that with some exceptions the Egyptian initiative could serve as a basis for negotiations on the election plan.

To recollect, Mubarak's ten-point plan centered on elections in the occupied territories of a delegation to represent the Palestinians in negotiations with Israel. Among other things, his plan demanded that Palestinians from East Jerusalem be able to vote and to stand as candidates, that Israel accept international supervision of the election process, and that Israel commit itself to the negotiation of a permanent settlement based on Resolutions 242 and 338 and on the principle of land-for-peace.

When the "forum of four" (Ministers Shamir, Peres, Arens, and Rabin) began to discuss the content of Mubarak's initiative on September 13, the Egyptian suggestion that deported Palestinians be allowed to negotiate alongside other Arab residents from the territories became the focal point of controversy between the Labor Alignment and the Likud. Whereas Labor believed that deported Palestinians could be considered legitimate negotiating partners—since technically they were residents of the territories—the Likud thought that negotiating with deported Palestinians would imply recognition of the PLO. Furthermore, MKs from the Greater Israel movement, who feared that the ten-point plan would lead to the creation of a Palestinian state, demanded that Shamir initiate a cabinet decision based on the formula endorsed by Likud's central committee, even if that would lead to the fall of the government. Thus when Egypt officially presented its proposal to Israel, the Likud ministers decided to oppose it. Still, to avert an immediate crisis, the forum of four agreed to delay the decision on the plan until the inner cabinet could meet, following Arens's and Peres's return from Washington.

But on September 19 Shamir publicly rejected the ten-point plan on the grounds that Israel could not agree to the inclusion of foreign residents in negotiations or to the participation of East Jerusalem residents in the election plan. To avoid a crisis, on October 5 the Labor Alignment submitted to the inner cabinet a four-point proposal, according to which (1) the government of Israel was committed to the peace initiative it endorsed on May 14; (2) the government was ready to endorse Mubarak's proposal for a meeting between an Israeli and a Palestinian delegation in order to help realize its peace initiative; (3) the Israeli delegation would participate on the basis of the original government resolution; (4) the two countries would begin contacts to determine the composition of the Palestinian delegation at once.

But Likud ministers defeated the proposal, saying that since Egypt was coordinating the composition of the Palestinian delegation with the PLO, accepting the proposal would mean recognizing the organization.[6]

While other right-wing parties supported the position taken by the Likud ministers, Tzomet called for new elections, as half of the inner cabinet did promote Mubarak's initiative. Moledet took the opportunity to call for the repeal of the government initiative, arguing that it would lead to the establishment of a Palestinian state. But on the left, Mapam was initiating an emergency session of the Knesset plenum in order to oblige the government to exhaust the ongoing political process. The CRM called upon the Labor Alignment to set up an alternative government capable of furthering the peace process. For his part, following the rejection Peres tried unsuccessfully to persuade Agudat Israel (a non-Zionist religious party) to join Labor in a narrow-based coalition.

Meanwhile, Baker's proposal reached Israel. To recall, the plan called for a meeting in Washington of the foreign ministers of the United States, Egypt, and Israel. Thereafter Israel and a Palestinian delegation would meet in Cairo to discuss elections in the territories, in accordance with the Israeli government initiative. The constraints ministers, supported by the Eretz Yisrael Front (made up of about thirty right-wing MKs, including twenty from Likud) immediately opposed the plan. Without discussing the proposal in the cabinet, Shamir rebuffed it on the grounds that the PLO might become indirectly involved in the political process and that Baker's formula fell short of a public statement he made in a press conference on October 2. According to that statement, Israel, Egypt, and the United States would determine the makeup of the Palestinian delegation. Another of Shamir's concerns was the possibility that the dialogue would deviate to topics other than elections in the territories.

The Bush administration offered to conclude a binding bilateral understanding with Israel (similar to the 1975 memorandum of understanding) that would include U.S. guarantees concerning Shamir's two main objections to the proposal. Shamir rejected the offer, demanding instead that the guarantees be included in the five-point plan itself rather than as an addendum to the document.

Meanwhile, the Israeli press reported that in order to iron out differences with President Bush and to ensure the survival of the coalition government, some senior figures in the prime minister's office and in the Likud were leaning toward consent to the inclusion of two deportees in the Palestinian delegation to the Cairo talks, and others assented to the inclusion of East Jerusalem Arabs in the delegation. Indeed, sources close to the prime minister predicted that the Cairo meeting would take place during the first half of 1990.

On December 6 the United States notified Israel that Egypt had replied positively on the five-point plan. But as was evident from a series of interviews he gave to the Israeli press, Shamir refused explicitly to welcome the Egyptian reply as a step forward. He and other Likud ministers downplayed Cairo's response, distrusting that the Egyptians had indeed accepted Israel's refusal to talk to the PLO or to deal with the implementation of Shamir's plan only. The constraints ministers argued that in effect, through Egypt, Israel would be negotiating with the PLO.

In the meantime another coalition crisis erupted in Israel. On December 31 Shamir dismissed from the cabinet the Labor Alignment's science and technology minister, Ezer Weizman because of his contacts with PLO leaders. Weizman had reportedly advised the PLO to refrain from rejecting the election plan. His suggestion frustrated Shamir, who was hoping that the PLO would oppose Baker's plan, terminating the U.S.-PLO dialogue. To save the National Unity government, Shamir agreed to remove Weizman form the inner cabinet only. In reaction to this compromise, Tehiya and Moledet submitted to the Knesset a no-confidence vote, a motion that was defeated.

On January 25, 1990, the inner cabinet agreed to include two Palestinian deportees in the Palestinian delegation. In order to make it easier for Shamir and other Likud ministers to agree to such a move, the cabinet resolved that a group of ten deportees be allowed to return to their homes. But Shamir conditioned his acceptance of the idea on the exclusion of residents of East Jerusalem from the Palestinian delegation.

In the meantime the struggle within Likud between the Shamir-Arens camp and the constraint ministers, Sharon in particular, intensified, as the three ministers demanded that the Likud central committee be convened again, this time in order to review Shamir's response to Baker's proposals. But at the opening of the convention—in itself a showdown between Shamir and Sharon—Sharon resigned from the cabinet. As an outsider, Sharon became free to oppose the government on any issue.

Much as he acquiesced to the constraints ministers during the Likud central committee convention in July 1989, Shamir this time pledged not to implement the election plan as long as acts of violence against Israelis continued; not to permit any loopholes through which the PLO would be able to participate in the political process; not to accept any move that would present any doubt regarding the status of Jerusalem; to reject any proposition regarding the right of return or to deal with the Arab diaspora; and to strengthen Jewish settlements throughout Judea, Samaria, Gaza, and the Golan Heights according to the Likud platform.[7]

Although Shamir's pledges alleviated some of the pressure that had built up in Likud, he now faced the likely breakup of the coalition, which he could prevent by revoking his commitments to the central committee. To avoid such a repeal, Levy and his supporters within the party called for the complete rejection of the Baker plan. In fact, Levy threatened to call for another meeting of the Likud's central committee if any of Baker's proposals were accepted.[8]

Some in the administration believed Shamir could have mollified the constraints camp by compensating Levy with the position of foreign minister. But Shamir did not play that card for a long time, perhaps to encourage the constraints ministers to hold him back.[9] Given Shamir's suspicious nature, however, he could not have left foreign policy matters in Levy's hands in a government that was not controlled by the Likud and whose defense minister was a member of the Labor Alignment. Later, in the Likud government, Shamir did designate Levy to that post.[10]

At any rate, unable to stall a reply to Baker's proposals for much longer, the Likud ministers on March 6 agreed to participate in the Cairo meeting on the condition that the Labor Alignment agree to secure Israel's sovereignty over united Jerusalem, including an understanding that East Jerusalem Arabs would not participate in the election process either by voting or by being elected; and to prevent the PLO from taking control of the political process.

Labor adopted its own resolutions, by which (1) Israel would continue the peace process according to its initiative of May 14, 1989; (2) the status of Jerusalem as the sovereign and indivisible capital of Israel was not an issue for discussion; (3) Israel would not negotiate with the PLO; (4) the prime minister would convene the inner cabinet on March 7, 1990, to deliver a positive response to Baker; (5) Labor would not permit Likud to condition the acceptance of this resolution on Labor's acceptance of any deviation from the government peace initiative of May 1989.

When the inner cabinet convened on March 7, it failed to draft a compromise formula that could appeal to both parties. The next day—after a meeting with other Likud members, including Sharon, Levy, and other MKs associated with the constraints ministers—Shamir declared that his answers to Baker would have to await the government's decision on the issues of Jerusalem and the PLO. Meanwhile, thousands of right-wing demonstrators, led by MKs from Tehiya, Moledet, and Tzomet and leaders of the settlement movement, demanded that Israel abide by its commitment not to talk to the PLO and that Shamir reject Baker's plan. In fact, Moledet submitted a motion of no confidence in the government because of what it viewed as the government's acquiescence to Baker's demands.

March 11 was the final date, according to the Labor Alignment's ultimatum, for the government to decide on its response to Baker. Attempting to arrive at a compromise during the inner cabinet debate, Rabin suggested that the government submit a positive answer to Baker and only afterward coordinate its position. He also suggested that if during the Cairo talks the issue of voting by East Jerusalem residents was raised—the only remaining matter on which the two parties disagreed—a Knesset plenum should decide the issue.

But Shamir refused to administer a vote on Rabin's proposal. Thus, in a bid to avert an unavoidable cabinet crisis, Zevulun Hammer, the religious affairs minister of the NRP, drafted a plan he thought both parties could easily accept. According to the plan, in the talks with the Palestinians (1) Jerusalem was not negotiable and was not part of autonomy; (2) Israel would not negotiate with the Arab delegation if it announced that it was a delegation on behalf of the PLO; (3) Jerusalem would not be part of the election process, but if any of its Arabs inhabitants wanted to vote in another city, the issue would be submitted to the Knesset for a decision before the Israeli delegation departed for Cairo; (4) in response to Baker's proposals, the inner cabinet would agree on the composition of the Palestinian delegation.

But Shamir did not accept Hammer's proposal. Aware that the government could be toppled in the March 15 Knesset discussions concerning seven no-confidence motions (submitted by five left-wing and two right-wing parties) in reaction to the government's indecision, Shamir fired Shimon Peres. By dismissing Peres, Shamir, who was unsure about Labor's intentions to remain in the government, made certain that the Labor Alignment could not be part of a caretaker government in case the no-confidence votes passed. As expected, the rest of the Labor ministers collectively resigned from the government. Justifying his step, Shamir argued that with Labor's positions on the Baker proposals, particularly its stand on Jerusalem, the Likud was the only buffer between Israel and a Palestinian state.

While Tehiya, Tzomet, the NRP, and the new Party for the Advancement of the Zionist Idea (created by Modai after the resignation of Sharon)[11] immediately announced their support for a Likud-led, narrow-based government, Degel Hatorah and Shas offered a compromise that allowed Labor to return to the cabinet, canceled the no-confidence motions, and gave Baker an affirmative answer. The Shas proposal also recommended that the entire issue of Jerusalem not be negotiated at all.

Within Likud, the more moderate ministers (Olmert and Dan Meridor along with Arens) supported the Shas proposal, against the opposition of Levy, Modai, and Sharon. On March 15 Shamir and Peres met with the spiritual leader of Shas, Rabbi Ovadia Yosseff, who in a last bid to save the government, suggested that all the ministers resume their duties and that a weeklong interim period be assigned, after which Baker be given a positive answer. Shamir refused to accept this proposal, and the Labor Alignment proceeded with the no-confidence motion, resulting in the government's fall. The roll call in the Knesset vote was sixty for and fifty-five against. The motion passed only because five of the six Shas members abstained. Yitzhak Peretz, the immigrant absorption minister and Shas political leader, was the only Shas member to vote in support of the government.

Notes

1. Sharon referred to Sari Nusaybah, Hanna Seniora, and Faisal al-Husseini, whom many Israelis and Palestinians considered authentic Palestinian leaders.

2. In reaction the prime minister's office threatened that if the Herut central committee approved a vote of no confidence in Shamir, Shamir would resign, enabling Peres to assume the premiership.

3. Shamir's speech was translated in *Foreign Broadcast Information Service/Daily Report: Near East and South Asia* (Washington, D.C.: United States Department of Commerce/Technical Information Service), July 6th, 1989, p. 13.

4. The United States was operating on the assumption that the May 14 proposal was the legally binding basis for the Israeli government to proceed. *Development in the Middle East: Hearing Before the Subcommittee on Europe and the Middle East of the Committee on Foreign Affairs, House of Representatives,* 101 Cong. 1st sess., July 12, 1989.

5. In Likud Shamir and Levy compared the resolution to Fatah's convention.

6. In this regard Mark Heller correctly argued that no pre- or post-election negotiations about a future settlement could occur without the PLO's consent—whether formal or implied. Besides, Israel and the PLO were already engaged in a dialogue, however indirectly, through their discussions with third parties. See Mark Heller, "The Middle East: Out of Step with History," *Foreign Affairs* 69, 1 (1989/1990): 157.

7. For the full text of Shamir's address before the Likud central committee, see *FBIS/DR*, February 12, 1990.

8. For Levi's complete interview with the IDF radio station on March 4, 1990, see *FBIS/DR*, March 5, 1990.

9. Private conversation with Ambassador Samuel Lewis, Washington, D.C., April 26, 1991.

10. Private conversation with then health minister Ehud Olmert, Jerusalem, June 28, 1991.

11. On March 15 the new faction headed by Modai was accorded the status of an independent faction, but the five MKs who formed the faction still voted with Likud.

12

The End of Likud's Domination

On June 23, 1992, the Likud Party suffered a serious setback as Labor scored a substantial victory in the national elections. One important reason for Likud's defeat was the changing mood of the Israeli public: As a leading Israeli journalist observed, Israel ceased to be an ideological society. Indeed, with the exception of a small minority, the Israeli people now want to live a prosperous, normal, and tranquil life. They want to increase their income, have better housing, buy newer cars, enjoy leisure time, and improve the state's education and medical services. To a public with such a mind-set, the doctrine of Greater Israel has lost its charm.[1] But by the time Likud became attuned to the shifting mood, most voters had already made up their minds against the party.

Twenty-five lists competed in the 1992 election in Israel. Of the two major parties, Labor won forty-four Knesset seats (37 percent of the total vote) while Likud won thirty-two seats (27 percent of the total vote). Of the parties on the left, Meretz won twelve seats (10 percent of the total) Hadash won three seats (2 percent of the total); and the Arab Democratic Party (ADP) won two seats (2 percent of the total). On the right, Tzomet won eight seats (7 percent of the total vote); and Moledet three seats (2 percent of the total). Of the religious camp, Shas and NRP won six seats each (5 percent each of the total vote), and United Torah Jewry won four seats (3 percent of the total). Along with Meretz and Shas, Rabin's new government controlled sixty-one Knesset seats, but he also enjoyed the support of the left-wing Arab parties, the Arab Democratic Party and Hadash. Although they were excluded from Rabin's cabinet, these two parties pledged to refrain from trying to topple the government with calls for no-confidence votes.[2] Their support was certainly decisive when the Knesset approved the Gaza-Jericho agreement on September 23, 1993. Although the political change the 1992 elections signaled may not be as dramatic as the change that brought Likud to power in 1977, as Asher

Arian and Michal Shamir have pointed out, its potential political impact is no less significant. Rabin's working majority in the Knesset can secure Labor's national priorities as well as its new policies on a number of sensitive issues.[3] The recognition of the PLO by Rabin's government and the Gaza-Jericho agreement are cases in point.

As in previous elections, the two important but related issues in the 1992 electoral shift were security and economic prosperity. But this time the high unemployment among the recent immigrants from the former Soviet Union played into the hands of the Labor Party, which blamed the Likud government for spending huge amounts on building of political settlements in the occupied territories—settlements of ideological value only—rather than allocating funds toward improving the conditions of the new immigrants and the poor.

Some 260,000 of the 400,000 or so Soviet immigrants who arrived in Israel since 1988 were eligible to vote.[4] The immigrants of 1989–1992 were different from earlier Soviet immigrants in a number of ways, most significantly in their level of education: 61 percent of the more recent Soviet immigrants had thirteen or more years of education—two and a half times the Israeli average.[5] But the level of unemployment among these new immigrants reached 25 percent, or twice the national average. More than 42 percent had scientific and academic professional education—four times the Israeli average.[6] And while few of these professionals were successfully integrated into the scientific and academic communities, many others who were fortunate enough to be employed obtained low-paying, menial jobs that were typically filled by Palestinians from the West Bank and Gaza.

But high unemployment was not the only problem for the new immigrants: Faced with severe housing shortages, many were put up in police and army barracks; hotels; youth hostels; boarding, recreation, and prefabricated homes; and trailers. In July 1990 Housing Minister Sharon introduced to the Knesset a controversial five-year $13.5 billion housing plan for the new immigrants. But the proposal was torpedoed by Finance Minister Modai, who subsequently allocated $6.5 billion for that purpose. The government's decision to finance the plan in part by a 5 percent raise in personal income tax and a 2 percent increase in national sales tax (from 16 to 18 percent) enabled the Labor-led Histadrut—Israel's national trade union—to all but immobilize the country with a general strike. In the meantime the Likud government moved hundreds of new immigrants into the West Bank and Gaza in addition to preparing hundreds of housing units in the Golan Heights, violating a promise it had previously made to the United States.

By spring 1991 the government had publicly acknowledged that some of the newcomers were emigrating to other countries (Canada, Australia,

Germany), while tens of thousands of prospective Soviet immigrants were postponing or canceling their moves to Israel because of the lack of housing and employment. For these reasons, early on in the election campaign, Labor was able to focus on Likud's failing absorption policies.

Still, initial polling of these new voters indicated that on election day they would vote for Likud and other right-wing parties, primarily because of their abhorrence of socialism. But by March 1992 polls showed that their positions were shifting. On election day exit polls revealed that these immigrants' votes contributed significantly to the ability of Labor and Meretz to gain five critical mandates without which their victory would have been impossible.[7]

The new immigrants, however, were not the only voters disillusioned by Likud's national priorities, especially the huge settlement drive undertaken by Shamir and Sharon amid growing unemployment and a declining economy. In April 1990—as soon as he became the caretaker prime minister after the fall of the National Unity government—Shamir had set in motion a plan swiftly to begin construction of five new settlements in the West Bank and Gaza. Despite opposition from Labor MKs and the Unites States, on May 21, 1990, the Knesset granted his request and approved more than $17 million for that purpose.

According to a report issued in February 1991 by MKs Dedi Zuker and Haim Oron—a report that helped trigger the dispute with Washington over loan guarantees to Israel—from 1990–1993, the Housing and Construction Ministry planned to build close to 12,000 housing units in the territories. These units were to be built mostly in existing settlements in order to evade U.S. objection.[8] During fiscal year 1990–91, the construction of 2,149 housing units in the territories began, in addition to construction that had started in recent years but was not yet completed and the placement of 1,000 mobile homes in existing settlements. New settlements were also being planned in the West Bank. All told, the plan would enlarge the Jewish population in the territories by about 50,000.[9]

In March 1991 a Peace Now report on government spending on settlements indicated that the Housing Ministry's actual budget for the territories during FY 1990–91, was over $466 million ($200 million a year was the highest figure previously reported for government spending in the territories). The combined budget of other governmental agencies, including the ministries of agriculture, religious affairs, absorption, tourism, energy, education, and interior affairs and the Jewish Agency, were close to $46 million for that year.[10] In May the movement reported that at least 13,000 new housing units in the territories were planned for FY 1991–92. The report also stated that since the fall of the National Unity government (March 1990), four new settlements had been established in the West Bank and Gaza, and existing ones were undergoing the most widespread population growth and building expansion Israel had known. Payment terms and other financial benefits for housing in the territories were significantly more favorable than those within the Green Line.[11]

A January 1992 Peace Now report concluded that at least 13,000 housing units were under construction in 1991—a 60 percent increase over the previous total in twenty-two years of settlement. The government expenditure on settlements in 1991 (for housing, infrastructure, education, and other expenses) exceeded $1 billion. Furthermore, in its debate over the 1992 budget, the Knesset approved the building of 5,000 new housing units in the territories, out of a total of 7,500 units planned for that year. Taking into account the number of units that were transferred from the 1991 budget, the report concluded that at least one-fourth of the 1992 construction would take place in the settlements. The Knesset also allocated about $15 million for road building in settlement areas as a first stage in the construction of 130 kilometers of roads at a projected sum of $170 million. An amount of $30 million was approved for housing in new settlements and for expanding existing ones.[12]

A follow-up report covering settlement activity from January to March 1992 concluded that the government had made settlements its top priority. Construction had begun on approximately 1,330 housing units in the settlements; preparation for additional construction was under way at a number of sites. A total of more than 5,700 new units were planned for existing settlements, and two new settlements were established in March. As in the past, settlers enjoyed generous government loans and subsidies.[13] Finally, in its July 1992 report, Peace Now observed that 10,443 units were in various stages of construction and that preparation of land for additional construction and that construction of many bypass roads were continuing as well. Peace Now and the Israeli public in general welcomed the Labor government's shift in national priorities and its commitment to rechannel national funds from the settlements to more pressing needs.[14]

Views on the settlement question demonstrated an overall electoral shift: When asked the appropriate amount of spending on settlements, the gap between those who favored more spending and those who favored less spending was –29 percent of the total population, that is, 29 percent more respondents believed the government should spend less on settlements than those who answered that the government should spend more. In comparison, the gap between those who thought the government should spend more on jobs versus those who thought the government should spend less on jobs was +89 percent. Of the voters who selected Likud in 1988 but shifted to Labor in 1992, the parallel figure was –59 percent regarding settlements and +96 percent regarding new jobs.

On the issue of immigration absorption, +34 percent of all respondents thought the government should spend more rather than less. The same figure was true for those respondents who voted for Likud in 1988 but shifted to Labor in 1992.[15] The issue of immigration absorption influenced 69 percent of all voters and 68 percent of those who switched from Likud to Labor.[16]

Ultimately, the Likud government's obsession with settlements turned into not only an economic issue but also a foreign policy issue, as many voters began to view Likud's settlement policy as responsible for the Bush administration's refusal to sign the loan guarantees Israel badly needed in order to help house and retrain new immigrants. Labor could thus effectively argue that Rabin's willingness to work toward the realization of Palestinian autonomy and his offer to freeze settlements in the occupied territories—while retaining "in principle" the right to strengthen existing ones—would enable Israel to obtain the U.S. loan guarantees. This claim was realized in August, when Bush agreed to award the Rabin government the $10 billion in loan guarantees.

The issue of U.S.-Israeli relations influenced 62 percent of all voters and 63 percent of those who chose Likud in 1988 but switched to Labor in 1992.[17] It was thus no accident that the day after being elected, Rabin promised to move immediately to promote the peace process, repair Israeli relations with the United States, and shift funding from new settlements toward other needs, including the absorption of new immigrants.[18]

Finally, when discussing factors that influenced the 1992 elections, one cannot minimize Rabin's importance to the Labor Party. Rabin's leadership turned into a significant asset for Labor, since the party could stress that as a former army chief of staff who led Israel to its stunning victory in the 1967 Six Day War and as a hard-line former defense minister who took harsh measures to quell the *intifada*, the new Labor leader would not jeopardize Israel's security even when moving ahead with the peace process. Indeed, Rabin was perceived as more creative and innovative, more able to lead, and a better negotiator than Shamir. In general, 69 percent of all voters were influenced by Rabin's heading of Labor, whereas 80 percent of Likud's former supporters who voted Labor in 1992 were influenced by this factor. Of these voters 86 percent considered Rabin a better representative of their position concerning the territories.[19]

It is possible, however, that Rabin's leadership might not have advanced Labor's position if it were not for the increasing moderation in Israeli public opinion regarding the question of territorial compromise. According to Arian's documentation, since the turn of the decade, there has been a gradual growth in the percentage of Israelis willing to consider compromise, to return territories, and even to agree to an eventual Palestinian state.[20]

Although it is impossible to list the precise reasons behind this moderation, the *intifada* is certainly one. Even though the Israeli authorities managed to contain the uprising since the 1988 elections, the *intifada* nonetheless proved to be costly in both economic and political terms: The economic costs included those of military actions and disruption in production in the construction, textile, and tourism industries; foreign investment; and lengthy periods of military reserve service. On the political side Israel was widely condemned for its attempts to suppress the uprising, and its reputation as a democratic state was tarnished.[21]

Internally, the uprising polarized Israeli society— including the military—between those who favored tougher policies in the West Bank and Gaza and those who preferred milder tactics. Within the general public a considerable number of peace groups emerged after the *intifada* had begun. The number of soldiers who refused to serve in the territories because of their moral convictions grew as well. Not surprisingly, the uprising also influenced the Israeli Arabs, many of whom have come to identify more strongly with the Palestinians from the West Bank and Gaza. Others have become more nationalistic and more militant since the *intifada* began.[22]

Most important, the *intifada* resurrected the Green Line, as many Israelis—civilians and soldiers alike—realized that their personal safety depended on their separation from the West Bank and Gaza, altering their attitude toward the occupation. Lustick has determined that the uprising epitomized the deep divide between Israel and the territories despite twenty years of an occupation that many Israelis had perceived as irreversible. As a result, many in Israel have come to see that the only long-term solution to the Israeli-Palestinian problem is a political settlement.[23] This point was also articulated by a number of prominent Israeli pollsters, who concluded that the *intifada* had created growing insecurity in daily life, a situation that can partially explain the mounting desire for solutions and the rejection of the status quo.[24] What effect the *intifada* had on the voters is evident from Arian and Shamir's sampling: It influenced 86 percent of all voters, 44 percent of those who voted for Likud in 1988 but switched to Labor in 1992.[25]

■ ■ ■

Until the 1992 elections, the Israeli Right had managed to control the national agenda. The critical issue for the Right, and for a significant number of other Israelis, was territory. But as the June 1992 elections demonstrated, that issue was not as crucial to voters as were the continuous violence in the territories, pressing economic problems, and the difficulty of absorbing a huge number of new immigrants. Many voters were convinced that their national and personal safety would be protected by conceding on the territorial issue.

This suggests that under specific circumstances—when a considerable number of citizens perceive pursuit of certain issues as detrimental to the national interest—the importance of these issues declines, provided that the safety of the state is assured. This in turn suggests that a shift in national priorities may affect the country's attitudes on foreign policy issues. That means that the electoral shift in Israel altered the country's foreign policy behavior even though Labor's attitude on two major foreign policy issues is not exceedingly different from that of Likud. For example, like Likud, Labor is opposed to the future creation of a sovereign Palestinian state on Israel's eastern border. Like Likud, Labor will not alter the status of East Jerusalem. But unlike Likud, Labor showed its willingness to ease the entry into negotiations with the Arabs by moderating its position on the key issues of territory and settlements. Unlike Likud, Labor demonstrated its readiness to adapt its policies to a changed international environment in a purposeful way. And, most significant, unlike Likud, Labor recognized the PLO and negotiated a self-rule agreement with the organization.

In sum, as far as the peace process was concerned, the Israeli voters were faced with three alternatives: (1) keeping Likud in power, thereby adhering to the status quo politics; (2) returning to a National Unity government and the paralysis that such a government entailed; or (3) empowering a Labor-led government to move ahead with the peace process while still safeguarding Israel's security needs. As the elections results show, a plurality of Israelis chose the last alternative.

Notes

1. Yoel Marcus, "A Virus Has Penetrated," *Ha'aretz* (international ed.), September 29, 1993.

2. Sammy Smooha and Don Peretz, "Israel's 1992 Knesset Elections: Are They Critical?" *Middle East Journal* 47, 3 (summer 1993): 444–463.

3. Asher Arian and Michal Shamir, "Two Reversals: Why 1992 Was Not 1977," in Asher Arian and Michal Shamir, eds., *The Elections in Israel 1992* (Albany: SUNY Press, 1995), pp.17–53.

4. Arian and Shamir estimated that Labor won 100,000 votes from new immigrants and other first-time voters. Ibid.

5. Bernard Reich, Noah Dropkin, and Meyrav Wurmser, "Soviet Jewish Immigration and the 1992 Israeli Knesset Elections," *Middle East Journal* 47, 3 (summer 1993): 464–478.

6. Ibid.

7. Ibid.

8. On March 10, 1991, the Housing Ministry indicated that 10,000 new housing units were to be located in the territories, going against promises it had made to the Bush administration.

9. For the full report, see Document C3, *Journal of Palestine Studies* 20, 3 (spring 1991): 151–153.

10. For the full report, see Document C2, ibid. 20, 4 (summer 1991): 176–177.

11. Document C1, ibid. 21, 1 (autumn 1991): 172–177.

12. Document B2, ibid. 21, 3 (spring 1992): 150–158.

13. Document C1, ibid. 21, 4 (summer 1992): 161–163.

14. Document C8, ibid. 22, 1 (autumn 1992): 159–164.

15. Arian and Shamir, "Two Reversals."

16. Ibid.

17. Ibid.

18. *Keesing's Contemporary Archives* 38, 6 (1992): 38946.

19. Arian and Shamir, "Two Reversals."

20. *The Middle East in the 1990s, Hearing Before the Subcommittee on Europe and the Middle East, of the Committee on Foreign Affairs, House of Representatives,* 101 Cong., 2d sess., April 4, 1990.

21. Bernard Reich and Gershon Kieval, *Israel, Land of Tradition and Conflict* (Boulder, Colo.: Westview, 1993), p. 59.

22. Ibid., p. 29.

23. Lustick's testimony before the House Subcommittee on Europe and the Middle East, *The Middle East in the 1990s.* Asher Arian and Samuel Lewis, too, strongly believe that the *intifada* has had a long-term effect on Israeli public opinion with regard to the future of the West Bank and the Gaza Strip.

24. Giora Goldberg, Gad Barzilai, and Efraim Inbar, *The Impact of Intercommunal Conflict: The Intifada and Israeli Public Opinion, Policy Studies* 43 (Jerusalem: Leonard Davis Institute, 1991).

25. Arian and Shamir, "Two Reversals."

13

The Road to Peace

In this volume I have shown that although third parties can be instrumental in helping adversaries negotiate a compromise, they cannot choose the timing for such diplomacy. Instead, the warring parties themselves have to determine whether the time is ripe.

Two widely cited factors in this decision are the combatants' conclusion that the continuation of a status quo would only worsen their situation and their simultaneous desire to reach an agreement. But a third factor is equally important: *the domestic support for a negotiated solution.*

For example, after the 1973 war Egypt was too weak economically and politically to attempt another military solution without an assured military victory; for Israel it had become too difficult to keep holding on to the West Bank *and* Sinai. But most important, when both leaders decided to negotiate peace with one another, they enjoyed sufficient power in their own political systems to make the necessary concessions and yet sustain backing at home.[1]

In contrast, in the period that followed the Camp David agreement in Israel only the Labor Alignment and its supporters promoted the U.S. peace initiatives. However, not until the 1992 elections did Labor enjoy the domestic support it needed and was strong enough politically to push its position, even though the Israeli public had long been almost evenly divided on the peace process. Public opinion is formed by a common-sense perception of reality and how political leaders respond to such reality. Thus, declared shifts in superpower responsibilities and Scud attacks against Israeli population centers need no intermediaries to change attitudes in favor of peace.

Had the United States scrutinized the internal situation in Israel before making suggestions, it would have learned that there was no leadership in Israel capable of taking advantage of the U.S. initiatives. First, Begin, who was too preoccupied with his Lebanon adventure, was in no mood to confront the questions the Reagan initiative presented. Second, Shamir was too weak to disregard the concerns of the Israeli far Right, especially segments that challenged his leadership within his own party. Third, the National Unity government was paralyzed by the conflicting strategies the two main parties followed in the peace process. Finally, as it is presently well established, even though Shamir's ultraright government endorsed Israel's participation in the Madrid conference, Shamir intended to stretch the Madrid formula infinitely.

With the Oslo talks both Israel and the PLO recognized that negotiations were a positive-sum if nonsymmetrical game. Even though neither side could get *everything* it wanted, both agreed that an imperfect solution was better than no solution. Here, too, domestic support (or the expectation of such support) was vital to the agreement.

As for the U.S. peace initiatives, these were introduced under promising regional and international conditions, although sometimes these conditions were better than others. For example, the Reagan plan appeared when the PLO was badly weakened and did not have the power to jeopardize the peace process. It was further designed to enable Israel to end its unfortunate venture in Lebanon. The Shultz plan was initiated after the Arabs had begun to pay more attention to the Iran-Iraq war than to their conflict with Israel and after the outbreak of the *intifada*. Moreover, the United States submitted the plan only after having received the encouragement of local leaders (including leaders in Israel). It also had the enthusiastic support of the Europeans—enough to improve Israel's relations with the European Community instantly had Israel agreed to endorse the plan. Baker's election plan (which was based on the Israeli peace initiative of May 14, 1989) was introduced after the nineteenth PNC session, in which the PLO had demonstrated relative unity on the two-state solution, and after the beginning of a U.S.-PLO dialogue, following Arafat's recognition of Israel's right to exist and his denunciation of terrorism. Baker's plan also received the tacit endorsement of the PLO and help from the Egyptian government. Above all, each of these initiatives was based on the Camp David agreements, the only formal document signed by Israeli, Arab, and U.S. heads of state and ratified by the Israeli, Egyptian, and U.S. legislatures—and the only document ever to be signed by Israel and an Arab state in preparation for future peace processes.[2]

Why, then, did Israel reject every initiative until Madrid? Why did Israel not endorse the initiatives, even though they included workable elements that Israel could accept?

As I have argued in this volume, until the Likud government was driven into accepting the Madrid conference, the Israeli Right, led by Prime Ministers Begin and Shamir, gained the upper hand in the debate over the peace process. By the time Begin resigned in 1983, he had managed to delegitimize the concept of territorial compromise, particularly concerning the West Bank and Gaza. His successor—Yitzhak Shamir—was just as eager to continue the occupation of the disputed territories. But under pressure from both the United States and the Labor Alignment during the Likud-Labor partnership in the National Unity government, Shamir apparently agreed to negotiate some limited form of Palestinian autonomy. However, fearing that Palestinian self-rule would jeopardize Israel's grip over the territories, the Israeli Right effectively restrained Shamir and his Labor colleagues from accepting the U.S. peace initiatives. Despite extraordinary international and regional conditions that led him to accept the Madrid formula, Shamir had no serious intention of negotiating with the Arabs.

The ability of the Israeli Right to safeguard the status quo politics is traceable to the growth of right-wing ideology as a result of the Six-Day War, a shift that combined with other factors to facilitate the rise of Likud. Once in power the Likud government consciously and systematically strengthened and secured its right-wing policies. Its tactics included de jure but mostly de facto annexation of territory, the latter involving massive settlement activities in the West Bank and Gaza, and the cultivation of a special relationship with Gush Emunim, the vanguard of the settlement movement. The sound support that Gush Emunim secured from ultraright and right-wing parties, such as Tehiya, the NRP, and others, in turn created a forceful and influential right-wing axis capable of obstructing any meaningful progress in the peace process.

One result was that extremism became tolerable enough to permit the election of Meir Kahane of the Kach Party to the Knesset and allow "Kahanism" to become a considerable threat to democracy in Israel.[3] That threat later grew to the extent that the Knesset ousted Kahane and promulgated antiracist laws.

Meanwhile, within Likud, hawkish members such as Ariel Sharon and David Levy became powerful enough to challenge Shamir's leadership and to block any policies they deemed too moderate. In fact, after Begin's departure from politics in 1983, Shamir had to promulgate adamant policies to prove himself as the indisputable leader of his party, worthy to step into Begin's shoes. Indeed, Shamir was unable to moderate his positions on the international conference idea and the question of Palestinian autonomy because moderation was not acceptable to the Israeli far Right. In 1992 Shamir lost his working majority when two far right parties decided to leave the government because of their apprehension of the Madrid formula.

The first National Unity government nearly collapsed over the international conference idea. It survived only because Peres, who did not have the votes to form a new coalition chose to drop the idea and remain in the government. But the second National Unity government did not survive the debate over Palestinian elections in the territories, Peres and his colleagues deciding they could no longer be partners with Likud.

Surely, the collapse of the National Unity government was a relatively small price for Shamir to pay. A costlier risk was strong resistance by the Right, which had become a formidable force on the Israeli political scene. In fact, the Jewish settlers and their supporters could threaten civil war or resist militarily if the government agreed to withdraw from even parts of Judea and Samaria.[4] They had called for a civil rebellion against the Labor-led government in their attempt to undermine the Gaza-Jericho agreement, even though the agreement excluded Jewish settlements from the jurisdiction of the interim self-government and provided that they remain under Israeli authority.

One can of course argue that the Egyptian-Israeli peace treaty and the return of the Sinai to Egypt demonstrate that the ideological shift to the right did not restrain Israel from making territorial compromises. But such an argument is disputable on a number of grounds. First, it was to Begin's benefit to give up the Sinai—a territory of moderate economic significance for which Israel had been generously compensated by the United States—in order to secure the West Bank and Gaza through the autonomy clause of the Camp David agreements. Second, for most Israelis, the Sinai had never acquired the same religious and ideological value as did the West Bank and Gaza. Indeed, the Sinai was never considered part of Eretz Yisrael by most right-wingers. In addition, the Sinai contained very few Jewish settlements. Third (regardless of the second factor), the return of the Sinai to Egypt provoked strong opposition from religious and hawkish Knesset and cabinet members, who had vowed never again to allow the dismantling of Jewish settlements in Eretz Yisrael. Fourth, peace with Egypt never challenged the integrity of the Zionist state. Indeed, as a disciple of Ze'ev Jabotinsky (the father of the Revisionist movement), Begin, who for over thirty years was the leader of the Israeli opposition, was widely trusted as a guardian of hard-line Zionism. Fifth, by concluding peace with Egypt and returning the Sinai, Israel had neutralized its strongest enemy.

Fifteen years after signing the Camp David agreements, Israel controlled additional territory in the West Bank and Gaza, in spite of Begin's pledge at the time to withdraw forces and civilians alike from these areas. Indeed, until it lost the 1992 elections, Likud was relying on the time factor together with the settlement movement to complete the process of de facto annexation of the West Bank and Gaza.[5] It is therefore safe to speculate that had Labor lost in 1992, the permanent status of the West Bank and Gaza would have been determined not by negotiations but by established facts in the territories.

We have, then, the general conclusion that no matter how favorable the international constellation might be for successful third-party mediation, the domestic landscape must be just as favorable. But we can make a number of other, perhaps more specific conclusions concerning the effectiveness of third-party peace initiatives. First, because peace initiatives in regional conflicts are often the result of the self-interest of the third-party, they can generate a great deal of cynicism on the part of the protagonists, enough to undermine their validity. Therefore, although self-interest should not prevent the third-party from being an honest broker, when presenting a new peace initiative the third-party must not appear immersed in its own interests to the point of neglecting the deep concerns of the primary parties. For example, the Reagan plan reflected Reagan's own preoccupation with the Soviet influence in the Middle East without giving enough thought to Begin's concerns about Israel's security. Similarly, when introducing the Shultz plan, the Reagan administration initially failed to take into account Likud's fear that an international conference could become a stage for the Arabs to manipulate a unified anti-Israeli position. By the time the United States addressed these concerns—when the proposed conference had turned into nothing more than an opening ceremony for direct bilateral talks—the position of the Israeli Right had become too strong to permit the conference. Last, when Baker refused to give Shamir the guarantees Shamir wanted—because of the United States' desire to safeguard its broader diplomatic capacity with the Arabs—Shamir could not view the United States as an honest broker. That helped the Likud justify its refusal of Baker's initiatives.

Second, without the existence of a prenegotiation period, a third-party ought not initiate, let alone publicize, any new peace plans.[6] As David Kimche has noted, "there are no guarantees for successful negotiations, even with the most thorough pre-negotiations, but ... a comprehensive delineation of topics to be discussed and goals to be reached can go a long way toward preventing a breakdown of talks."[7]

Indeed, one mistake the Americans made repeatedly was to publicize their initiatives before they had reached an understanding with the protagonists about what kind of agreement would be acceptable. This was particularly true for the Reagan plan, which Begin instantly rejected as a violation of Camp David and a number of Arab states criticized as another version of Camp David. By contrast, this is where the Oslo negotiations were most successful. For they enabled the Israelis and Palestinians—as Herbert Kelman had suggested years before—to persuade one another that negotiations are safe, that they do not represent an uncertain path that might end up in disaster, and to recognize each other in order to move to the negotiating table.[8]

The importance of the prenegotiation stage was also evident in the

Camp David agreements: By 1977 the basic nature of the potential peace between Israel and Egypt had been secretly discussed for some years between Moshe Dayan (Israel's foreign minister at the time) and Hassan Tuhami (President Sadat's adviser). During these informal explorations Egypt learned that Israel was ready to give up the Sinai for peace, while Israel learned that if Sadat would get the Sinai back, he would make substantial concessions for peace. At that point negotiations centered on the depth of concession the leaders were prepared to make for peace.[9]

Still, the need to predetermine the agenda is not without problems. When introducing a new peace initiative, the third-party must avoid potentially explosive issues, allowing for preliminary discussions to keep the parties from rejecting the initiative outright. For example, a major mistake the United States made when it initiated the Reagan and the Baker plans was raising the topic of East Jerusalem—by far the most sensitive issue for almost all Israelis, as very few (if any) would agree to the repartition of Jerusalem. The gap between the need for prenegotiations on the one hand and vagueness on the other can be filled by skillful diplomacy. Such was the case in the Oslo negotiations, which allowed the parties to decide on an agenda for negotiations that left to a later date such sensitive issues as the status of East Jerusalem and the future of Jewish settlements.

Finally, the negotiating process itself is a long and laborious one. The third-party should be prepared to expect setbacks before any breakthrough can occur. Such a breakthrough can happen only when (1) the external environment is so extraordinarily encouraging as to compel the rivals to enter negotiations and (2) the domestic situations of the disputing parties are supportive of such a move.

Regarding the domestic landscape on the Arab side, from the announcement of the Reagan plan until 1988, King Hussein and the PLO chairman Yasir Arafat did try to formulate a joint approach to peace. But not until the Madrid conference could Arafat make good on his intention to give King Hussein a mandate to negotiate for the Palestinians. Arafat feared that any sign of diplomatic concessions on peace with Israel might bring about the disintegration of the PLO because of the stance of hardline factions within the organization. This position, however, changed because of the *intifada*, when the growing frustration of Palestinians from the West Bank and Gaza and the increased popularity of Hamas threatened the legitimacy of the PLO as the exclusive Palestinian leadership. But even though extremist Palestinian groups may attempt to sabotage the implementation of the Gaza-Jericho plan, there are signs that the process that has begun in Madrid (let alone Oslo) has raised the expectations of many Palestinians in the occupied territories for a political solution, which they believe will improve their economic and social circumstances.[10]

As for King Hussein, the role Washington assigned to him during most of the peace process was to negotiate not only on behalf of Jordan but also on behalf of the Palestinians. But because the Arab League had designated the PLO as the sole legitimate representative of the Palestinian people and because Jordan was militarily and politically weak, King Hussein had no mandate to negotiate for the Palestinians. Nor was the king strong enough to negotiate a separate agreement with Israel as did President Sadat. That changed, however, with the Israeli-PLO agreement, which set Hussein free to negotiate an agreement with Israel on his own. Indeed, one day after the Israeli-PLO agreement was signed, Jordan began to normalize relations with Israel.

Before the Madrid conference Syria had no reason to enter the peace process. First, Syria has been able to live without the Golan Heights—hardly an inhabitable region—while assuming the role of an all-Arab crusader. The Syrian regime could appeal to Syrian patriotism, Arab nationalism, and Islamic sentiments among both the civilian population and the military—all this in order to rally the Syrians around the regime. Moreover, the holy war against Israel in which Syria has been engaged has helped the Alawite Syrian regime to neutralize the growing opposition of the Sunni majority.[11] But the end of the Cold War, combined with the Syrian need for economic aid from the West and the victory of the U.S.-led coalition in the Gulf war, changed Assad's mind about entering the peace process. Neither the country's cooperation with the West in the Gulf war nor its participation in the Madrid conference created upheavals within the Syrian public. No longer a hostage to the Palestinian cause, Syria could now earnestly move forward with its own negotiations with Israel, in spite of Damascus' relentlessness. The Clinton administration and the EC are thus in a comfortable position to move ahead with the peace process. And if their basic interests in the region are unchanged, they should nonetheless redefine them by paying particular attention to Iran.

Having recovered from its war with Iraq and heartened by Iraq's devastation, Iran is resurging as the most influential power in the region (and one that either had or may soon acquire nuclear capability). With support from the Sudan, Iran is funding and otherwise supporting a number of Islamic fundamentalist movements that threaten the stability of moderate and nonmoderate Arab actors, including those involved in the peace process—namely, the PLO, Egypt, Jordan, and even Syria.

It is therefore critical that the United States and its European allies help Israel and the PLO to implement their agreement. The sooner the process is continued, the less time Iran and its allies have to foil it. Should the peace process collapse, another war in the Middle East may be imminent.

Notes

1. For explanations of Sadat's motivation to negotiate with Israel—and to do so under U.S. auspices—see Moshe Dayan, *Breakthrough* (New York: Alfred A. Knopf, 1981); Eitan Haber et al., *The Year of the Dove* (New York: Bantam, 1979); Mohamed Heikal, *Autumn of Fury* (New York: Random House, 1983); William Youssef Kosman, *Sadat's Realistic Peace Initiative* (New York: Vantage Press, 1981); Louis Kriesberg, *Social Conflict* (Englewood Cliffs, N.J.: Prentice-Hall, 1982); Yoel Marcus, *Camp David: The Key to Peace* (Hebrew) (Jerusalem: Shoken, 1979); William Quandt, *Camp David: Peace Making and Politics* (Washington, D.C.: Brookings Institution, 1986); Jihan Sadat, "Pathway to World Peace," lecture in Great Neck, New York, October 30, 1988; Shimon Shamir, "Israeli View of Egypt and the Peace Process: The Duality of Vision," in William Quandt, ed., *The Middle East Ten Years After Camp David* (Washington, D.C.:, Brookings Institution, 1988); Avraham Tamir, *A Soldier for Peace* (New York: Harper and Row, 1988); Natan Yanai, ed., *On the Peace Process and Israel's Future* (Hebrew) (Tel Aviv: Ministry of Defense, 1988); Saadia Touval, *The Peace Brokers* (Princeton: Princeton University Press, 1982); Ezer Weizman, *The Battle for Peace* (New York: Bantam, 1981).

2. This conclusion is based in part on a private conversation with then MK Ezer Weizman, Caesaria, July 5, 1991.

3. In 1984 Kach won 1.2 percent of the vote, or one Knesset seat. Kahanism views the Arab population as a malignancy that threatens Israel's survival. It calls for a total separation of Arabs and Jews through the expulsion of all Arabs from all of Eretz Yisrael. For the philosophy behind Kahanism, see Meir Kahane, *They Must Go* (Miami Beach: Copy Service, 1987).

4. Samuel Lewis, "Israeli Political Reality and the Search for Middle East Peace," *SAIS Review* 7, 1 (winter/spring 1987): 67–80; Ehud Sprinzak, *The Ascendance of Israel's Radical Right* (New York: Oxford University Press, 1991), p. 312. After the Israeli-PLO agreement became public, some members of the settlement movement did threaten a civil war.

5. This conclusion is partly based on a private conversation with then MK Ezer Weizman, Caesaria, July 5, 1991.

6. For definitions of the prenegotiation stages, see Brian Tomlin, "The Stages of Prenegotiation: The Decision to Negotiate North American Free Trade," in Janice Gross Stein, ed., *Getting to the Table* (Baltimore: Johns Hopkins University Press, 1989); Gross Stein in her introduction to *Getting to the Table*, p. x; William Zartman, "Prenegotiation: Phases and Functions," in ibid., p. 4.

7. David Kimche, "The Importance of Prenegotiation: Observations of a Former Diplomat," *Jerusalem Journal of International Relations* 13, 4 (December 1991): 65–70.

8. Herbert C. Kelman, "The Palestinianization of the Arab-Israeli Conflict," in Yehuda Lukacs and Abdalla M. Battah, eds., *The Arab-Israeli Conflict* (Boulder, Colo.: Westview Press, 1988), pp. 339–340.

9. Tamir, *Soldier for Peace*, ch. 2; private conversation with ambassador Samuel Lewis, Washington, D.C., April 26, 1991.

10. Yossi Torfstein, "First Rays of Light," *Ha'aretz* (international ed.), October 6, 1992.

11. Moshe Maoz, *Modern Syria* (Hebrew) (Tel Aviv: Reshafim, 1972), pp. 93–95.

Appendixes

Appendix A:
The Israeli Government
Peace Initiative, May 14, 1989[1]

The Government's Resolution:

It is decided to approve the attached peace initiative of the Government of Israel.

A Peace Initiative by the Government of Israel

Generals:

1. This document presents the principles of a political initiative of the Government of Israel which deals with the continuation of the peace process; the termination of the state of war with the Arab states; a solution for the Arabs of Judea, Samaria and the Gaza district; peace with Jordan; and a resolution of the problem of the residents of the refugee camps in Judea, Samaria, and the Gaza district.

2. The document includes:

A. The principles upon which the initiative is based.

B. Details of the processes for its implementation.

C. Reference to the subject of the elections under consideration. Further details relating to the elections as well as other subjects of the initiative will be dealt with separately.

Basic Premises:

3. The initiative is founded upon the assumption that there is a national consensus for it on the basis of the political guidelines of the Government of Israel, including the following points:

A. Israel yearns for peace and the continuation of the political process by means of direct negotiations based on the principles of the Camp David Accords.

B. Israel opposes the establishment of an additional Palestinian state in the Gaza district and the area between Israel and Jordan.

C. Israel will not conduct negotiations with the PLO.

D. There will be no change in the status of Judea, Samaria and Gaza other than in accordance with the basic guidelines of the Government.

Subjects to Be Dealt with in the Peace Process:

4. A. Israel views as important that the peace between Israel and Egypt, based on the Camp David Accords, will serve as a cornerstone for enlarging the circle of peace in the region, and calls for a common endeavor for the strengthening of the peace and its extension, through continued consultation.

B. Israel calls for the establishment of peaceful relations between it and those Arab states which still maintain a state of war with it for the purpose of promoting a comprehensive settlement for the Arab-Israeli conflict, including recognition, direct negotiations, ending the boycott, diplomatic relations, cessation of hostile activity in international institutions or forums and regional and bilateral cooperation.

C. Israel calls for an international endeavor to resolve the problem of the residents of the Arab refugee camps in Judea, Samaria and the Gaza district in order to improve their living conditions and to rehabilitate them. Israel is prepared to be a partner in this endeavor.

D. In order to advance the political negotiation process leading to peace, Israel proposes free and democratic elections among the Palestinian Arab inhabitants of Judea, Samaria and the Gaza district in an atmosphere devoid of violence, threats and terror. In these elections a representation will be chosen to conduct negotiations for a transitional period of self-rule. This period will constitute a test for co-existence and cooperation. At a later stage, negotiations will be conducted for a permanent solution, during which all the proposed options for a settlement will be examined, and peace between Israel and Jordan will be achieved.

E. All the above-mentioned steps should be dealt with simultaneously.

F. The details of what has been mentioned in (d) above will be given below.

The Principles Constituting the Initiative:

Stages:

5. The initiative is based on two stages:

   A. Stage A—A transitional period for an interim agreement.

B. Stage B—Permanent solution.

6. The interlock between the stages is a timetable on which the Plan is built: the peace process delineated by the initiative is based on Resolutions 242 and 338 upon which the Camp David Accords are founded.

Timetable:

7. The transitional period will continue for 5 years.

8. As soon as possible, but not later than the third year after the beginning of the transitional period, negotiations for achieving a permanent solution will begin.

Parties Participating in the Negotiations in Both Stages:

9. The parties participating in the negotiations for the First Stage (the interim agreement) shall include Israel and the elected representation of the Palestinian Arab inhabitants of Judea, Samaria and the Gaza district. Jordan and Egypt will be invited to participate in these negotiations if they so desire.

10. The parties participating in the negotiations for the Second Stage (Permanent Solution) shall include Israel and the elected representation of the Palestinian Arab inhabitants of Judea, Samaria and the Gaza district, as well as Jordan; furthermore, Egypt may participate in these negotiations. In negotiations between Israel and Jordan, in which the elected representation of the Palestinian Arab inhabitants of Judea, Samaria and the Gaza district will participate, the peace treaty between Israel and Jordan will be concluded.

Substances of Transitional Period:

11. During the transitional period the Palestinian Arab inhabitants of Judea, Samaria and the Gaza district will be accorded self-rule by means of which they will, themselves, conduct their affairs of daily life. Israel will continue to be responsible for security, foreign affairs and all matters concerning Israeli citizens in Judea, Samaria and the Gaza district. Topics involving the implementation of the plan for self-rule will be considered and decided within the framework of the negotiations for an interim agreement.

Substances of Permanent Solution:

12. In the negotiations for a permanent solution every party shall be entitled to present for discussion all the subjects it may wish to raise.

13. The aim of the negotiations should be:
   A. The achievement of a permanent solution acceptable to the nego-
      tiating parties.
   B. The arrangements for peace and borders between Israel and
      Jordan.

Details of the Process for the Implementation
of the Initiative

14. First and foremost dialogue and basic agreement by the Palestinian
Arab inhabitants of Judea, Samaria and the Gaza district, as well as Egypt
and Jordan if they wish to take part, as above-mentioned in the negotiations, on the principles constituting the initiative.

   15. A. Immediately afterwards will follow the stage of preparation and
      implementation of the election process in which a representa-
      tion of the Palestinian Arab inhabitants of Judea, Samaria and
      Gaza will be elected. This representation:
      I. Shall be a partner to the conduct of negotiations for the tran-
         sitional period (interim agreement).
      II. Shall constitute the self-governing authority in the course of
         the transitional period.
      III. Shall be the central Palestinian component, subject to agree-
         ment after three years, in the negotiations for the permanent
         solution.
   B. In the period of the preparation and implementation there shall
      be a calming of the violence in Judea, Samaria and the Gaza dis-
      trict.

16. As to the substance of the elections, it is recommended that a proposal of regional elections be adopted, the details of which shall be determined in further discussions.

17. Every Palestinian Arab residing in Judea, Samaria and the Gaza
district, who shall be elected by the inhabitants to represent them—after
having submitted his candidacy in accordance with the detailed document which shall determine the subject of the elections—may be a legitimate participant in the conduct of negotiations with Israel.

18. The elections shall be free, democratic and secret.

19. immediately after the election of the Palestinian representation,
negotiations shall be conducted with it on an interim agreement for a
transitional period which shall continue for 5 years, as mentioned above.
In these negotiations the parties shall determine all the subjects relating
to the substance to the self-rule and the arrangements necessary for its
implementation.

20. As soon as possible, but no later than the third year after the establishment of the self-rule, negotiations for a permanent solution shall begin. During the whole period of these negotiations until the signing of the agreement for a permanent solution, the self-rule shall continue in effect as determined in the negotiations for an interim agreement.

Notes

1. *Jerusalem Post*, May 15, 1989.

Appendix B:
Main Points of the U.S. Letters of Assurance on the Terms of the Madrid Peace Conference, October 1991[1]

US Letter of Assurance to Israel

1. The US sees the objective of the Middle East negotiation as the attainment of genuine peace and reconciliation between the peoples of the region, accompanied by peace treaties and full diplomatic relations.

2. The opening conference will have no power to make decisions, hold votes, or impose positions.

3. Negotiations will be direct only.

4. The US will not support linkage between the various bilateral negotiations.

5. No party need sit with another party against its wishes.

6. The US has no intention of bringing about a dialogue between Israel and the PLO or negotiations between them.

7. Palestinians taking part in negotiations must be residents of the West Bank or the Gaza Strip who accept phased direct negotiations in two tracks and are ready to live at peace with Israel.

8. The US will not support the creation of an independent Palestinian state.

9. Israel holds its own interpretation of Security Council Resolution 242, alongside other interpretations.

10. Israel is entitled to secure and defensible borders.

11. The US will take steps to enlarge the circle of peace in the Middle East.

12. The US will take steps to bring the Arab economic boycott to an end and to have UN Resolution 3379 equating Zionism and racism annulled.

13. The US will consult closely with Israel and show due consideration for Israel's positions in the peace process.

202

Appendix B

14. The US reconfirms ex-president Gerald Ford's written commitment to ex-premier Yitzhak Rabin of September 1975 regarding the importance of the Golan Heights to Israel's security.

15. The US would be ready to give its own guarantees to any border agreed upon between Israel and Syria.

16. Israel is entitled to a secure border with Lebanon and Security Council Resolution 425 on Lebanon must be implemented in a manner assuring the stability and security of the border.

17. The US is committed to Israel's security and to the maintenance of Israel's qualitative edge.

US Letter of Assurance to Syria

1. The peace conference and the talks that follow must be based on Security Council Resolutions 242 and 338.

2. The object of the conference is to prepare for direct bilateral Arab-Israeli talks within two days and also for multilateral talks within two weeks. The bilateral talks will run on two parallel tracks: direct talks between Israel and the neighboring states, and direct talks between Israel and "the Palestinians."

3. The US intends to work actively towards a comprehensive settlement of the Arab-Israel conflict and do everything it can to keep the two-track process going in that direction. The US is not an advocate of linkage between the "various forms of negotiations," but believes that speedy action in all negotiations to arrive at an agreement is needed and would serve the interest of a comprehensive settlement.

4. The conference will convene under US-Soviet auspices and can reconvene with the approval of all parties.

5. The role of the UN consists in the dispatch by the UN secretary-general of a representative to attend the conference as an observer.

The US and the USSR will keep the secretary-general informed of the progress of the negotiations. Any agreements reached by the parties will be registered at the UN secretariat and communicated to the security council, whose endorsement will be sought by the participating parties. The US, cognizant of all parties' interests in the success of this process, will not, as long as the process is actively under way, support any parallel or conflicting action by the Security Council.

6. The final settlement can be reached only on the basis of mutual concessions during the negotiations. The US will throughout these negotiations continue to be committed to the fact that Security Council Resolution 242 and the land-for-peace principle are applicable to all fronts, including the Golan Heights.

7. The US does not intend to recognize or accept any unilateral action on the part of Israel vis-a-vis the extension of its laws, sovereignty or administration on the territory of the Golan Heights.

8. The US will continue to oppose Israeli settlement activity in the territories occupied in 1967, which remains an obstacle to peace.

9. The US is prepared to serve as guarantor of the security of whatever borders Israel and Syria agree on.

10. The US will continue to act as a mediator that genuinely seeks a settlement of the Arab-Israeli conflict on the basis of recognition of all parties' "needs and requirements." The US and USSR will remain the "moving force" in this process to help the parties make progress towards a comprehensive peace settlement.

The US and USSR are ready to remain in constant touch with any of the parties at any time, and the US is also ready to participate in the negotiations in any of their stages with the approval of the parties involved.

US Letter of Assurance to Lebanon

• An assurance that Security Council Resolution 425, which calls for an Israeli withdrawal of Israeli troops from Lebanon, has nothing to do with resolution 242 and will be treated as a separate issue.

• As assurance that the withdrawal of Israeli troops and the withdrawal of Syrian troops from Lebanon are two separate issues, the former addressed by resolution 425 and the latter by the Taef agreement, which also calls for the withdrawal of all non-Lebanese forces from Lebanon.

US Letter of Assurance to the Palestinians

• Palestinians and Israel must respect each other's security, identity, and political rights.

• Bilateral talks will begin four days after the opening of the conference.

• Multilateral talks will open two weeks after the opening of the peace conference.

• We believe that Palestinians should gain control over political, economic, and other decisions that affect them and their fate.

• The US will seek to avoid prolongation and stalling by any party. All negotiations should proceed as quickly as possible toward agreement.

• The US doesn't seek to determine who speaks for Palestinians in this process. We are seeking to launch a political negotiating process that directly involves Palestinians and offers a pathway for achieving the legitimate political rights of the Palestinian people and for participation in the determination of their future. We believe that a joint Jordanian-Palestinian delegation offers the most promising pathway toward this end.

• Palestinians will be free to announce the component of the joint delegation and to make a statement during the opening of the conference. They may also raise any issue pertaining to the substance of the negotiations during the negotiations.

• The US understands how much importance Palestinians attach to the question of East Jerusalem. Thus we want to assure you that nothing Palestinians do in choosing their delegation members in this phase of the process will affect their claim to East Jerusalem or be prejudicial or precedential to the outcome of the negotiations.

• The US is opposed to the Israeli annexation of East Jerusalem and extension of Israeli law on it and the extension of Jerusalem's municipal boundaries. We encourage all sides to avoid unilateral acts that would exasperate local tensions or make negotiations more difficult or preempt their final outcome.

• The US believes that Palestinians of East Jerusalem should be able to participate by voting in elections of an interim governing authority. The US further believes that Palestinians from East Jerusalem and Palestinians outside the occupied territories who meet the three criteria should be able to participate in the negotiations on final status. The US supports the right of Palestinians to bring any issue including East Jerusalem to the table.

• The purpose of negotiations on transitional arrangements is to affect the peaceful and orderly transfer of authority from Israel to Palestinians. Palestinians need to achieve rapid control over political, economic, and other decisions that affect their lives and to adjust to a new situation in which Palestinians exercise authority in the West Bank and Gaza. For its part the US will strive from the outset and encourage all the parties to adopt steps that can create an environment of confidence and mutual trust, including respect for human rights.

• Negotiations between Israel and Palestinians will be conducted in phases beginning with talks on interim self-governing arrangements. The talks will be conducted with the objective of reaching agreements within one year. Once agreed the interim self-governing arrangements will last for a period of five years. Beginning the third year of the period of self-governing arrangements, negotiations will take place on permanent status. It is the aim of the US government that permanent status negotiations will be concluded by the end of the transitional period.

• Palestinians are free to argue whatever outcome they believe best meets their requirements. The US will accept any outcome agreed by the parties. In this regard and consistent with long-standing US policies, confederation is not excluded as a possible outcome of negotiations on final status.

• The US believes that no party should take unilateral actions that seek to predetermine issues that can only be reached through negotiations. In this regard the US has opposed and will continue to oppose settlement activity in territories occupied in 1967 which remain an obstacle to peace.

• Any party will have access to the sponsors at any time.

• We are prepared to work hard with you in the period ahead.

Notes

1. *Journal of Palestine Studies* 21, 2 (winter 1992), Documents IA-ID.

Appendix C:
Declaration of Principles
on Interim Self-Government
Arrangements

Final agreed draft of August 19, 1993[1]

The Government of the State of Israel and the Palestinian team (in the Jordanian-Palestinian delegation to the Middle East Peace Conference) (the 'Palestinian Delegation'), representing the Palestinian people, agree that it is time to put an end to decades of confrontation and conflict, recognize their mutual legitimate and political rights, and strive to live in peaceful coexistence and mutual dignity and security and achieve a just, lasting and comprehensive peace settlement and historic reconciliation through the agreed political process. Accordingly, the two sides agree to the following principles:

Article I
AIM OF THE NEGOTIATIONS

The aim of the Israeli-Palestinian negotiations within the current Middle East peace process is, among other things, to establish a Palestinian Interim Self-Government Authority, the elected Council (the 'Council') for the Palestinian people in the West Bank and the Gaza Strip, for a transitional period not exceeding five years, leading to a permanent settlement based on Security Council Resolutions 242 and 338.

It is understood that the interim arrangements are an integral part of the whole peace process and that the negotiations on the permanent status will lead to the implementation of Security Council Resolutions 242 and 338.

Article II
FRAMEWORK FOR THE INTERIM PERIOD

The agreed framework for the interim period is set forth in this Declaration of Principles.

Article III
ELECTIONS

1. In order that the Palestinian people in the West Bank and Gaza Strip may govern themselves according to democratic principles, direct, free and general political elections will be held for the Council under agreed supervision and international observation, while the Palestinian police will ensure public order.

2. An agreement will be concluded on the exact mode and conditions of the elections in accordance with the protocol attached as Annex I, with the goal of holding the elections not later than nine months after the entry into force of this Declaration of Principles.

3. These elections will constitute a significant interim preparatory step toward the realization of the legitimate rights of the Palestinian people and their just requirements.

Article IV
JURISDICTION

Jurisdiction of the Council will cover West Bank and Gaza Strip territory, except for issues that will be negotiated in the permanent status negotiations. The two sides view the West Bank and Gaza Strip as a single territorial unit, whose integrity will be preserved during the interim period.

Article V
TRANSITIONAL PERIOD
AND PERMANENT STATUS NEGOTIATIONS

1. The five-year transitional period will begin upon the withdrawal from the Gaza Strip and Jericho area.

2. Permanent status negotiations will commence as soon as possible, but no later than the beginning of the third year of the interim period, between the Government of Israel and the Palestinian people representatives.

3. It is understood that these negotiations shall cover remaining issues, including: Jerusalem, refugees, settlements, security arrangements, borders, relations and cooperation with neighbors, and other issues of common interest.

4. The two parties agree that the outcome of the permanent status negotiations should not be prejudiced or preempted by agreements reached for the interim period.

Article VI
PREPARATORY TRANSFER OF POWERS
AND RESPONSIBILITIES

1. Upon the entry into force of this Declaration of Principles and the withdrawal from the Gaza Strip and the Jericho area, a transfer of authority from the Israeli military government and its Civil Administration to the authorized Palestinians for this task, as detailed herein, will commence. This transfer of authority will be of preparatory nature until inauguration of the Council.

2. Immediately after the entry into force of this Declaration of Principles and the withdrawal from the Gaza Strip and Jericho area, with the view of promoting economic development in the West Bank and Gaza Strip, authority will be transferred to the Palestinians on the following spheres: education and culture, health, social welfare, direct taxation, and tourism. The Palestinian side will commence in building the Palestinian police force, as agreed upon. Pending the inauguration of the Council, the two parties may negotiate the transfer of additional powers and responsibilities, as agreed upon.

Article VII
INTERIM AGREEMENT

1. The Israeli and Palestinian delegations will negotiate an agreement on the interim period (the 'Interim Agreement').

2. The Interim Agreement shall specify, among other things, the structure of the Council, the number of its members, and the transfer of powers and responsibilities from the Israeli military government and its Civil Administration to the Council. The Interim Agreement shall also specify the Council's executive authority, legislative authority in accordance with Article IX below, and the independent Palestinian judicial organs.

3. The Interim Agreement shall include arrangements, to be implemented upon the inauguration of the Council, for the assumption by the Council of all of the powers and responsibilities transferred previously in accordance with Article VI above.

4. In order to enable the Council to promote economic growth, upon its inauguration, the Council will establish, among other things, a Palestinian Electricity Authority, a Gaza Sea Port Authority, a Palestinian Development Authority, a Palestinian Land Authority and a Palestinian Water Administration Authority, and any other Authorities agreed upon, in accordance with the Interim Agreement that will specify their powers and responsibilities.

5. After the inauguration of the Council, the Civil Administration will be dissolved, and the Israeli military government will be withdrawn.

Article VIII
PUBLIC ORDER AND SECURITY

In order to guarantee public order and internal security for the Palestinians of the West Bank and Gaza Strip, the Council will establish a strong police force, while Israel will continue to carry the responsibility for defending against external threats, as well as the responsibility for overall security of Israelis for the purpose of safeguarding their internal security and public order.

Article IX
LAWS AND MILITARY ORDERS

1. The Council will be empowered to legislate, in accordance with the Interim Agreement, within all authorities transferred to it.

2. Both parties will review jointly laws and military orders presently in force in remaining spheres.

Article X
JOINT ISRAELI-PALESTINIAN LIAISON COMMITTEE

In order to provide for a smooth implementation of this declaration of principles and any subsequent agreements pertaining to the interim period, upon the entry into force of this Declaration of Principles, a joint Israeli-Palestinian Liaison Committee will be established in order to deal with issues requiring coordination, other issues of common interest, and disputes.

Article XI
ISRAELI-PALESTINIAN COOPERATION
IN ECONOMIC FIELDS

Recognizing the mutual benefit of cooperation in promoting the development of the West Bank, the Gaza Strip and Israel, upon the entry into force of this Declaration of Principles, as Israeli-Palestinian Economic Committee will be established in order to develop and implement in a cooperative manner the programs identified in the protocols attached as Annex III and Annex IV.

Article XII
LIAISON AND COOPERATION
WITH JORDAN AND EGYPT

The two parties will invite the Governments of Jordan and Egypt to participate in establishing further liaison and cooperation arrangements between the Government of Israel and the Palestinian representatives, on one hand, and the governments of Jordan and Egypt, on the other hand, to promote cooperation between them. These arrangements will include the constitution of a Continuing Committee that will decide by agreement on the modalities of admission of persons displaced from the West Bank and Gaza Strip in 1967, together with necessary measures to prevent disruption and disorder. Other matters of common concern will be dealt with by this Committee.

Article XIII
REDEPLOYMENT OF ISRAELI FORCES

1. After the entry into force of this Declaration of Principles, and not later than the eve of elections for the Council, a redeployment of Israeli military forces in the West Bank and Gaza Strip will take place, in addition to withdrawal of Israeli forces carried out in accordance with Article XIV.

2. In redeploying its military forces, Israel will be guided by the principles that its military forces should be redeployed outside populated areas.

3. Further redeployments to specified locations will be gradually implemented commensurate with the assumption of responsibility for public order and internal security by the Palestinian police force pursuant to Article VIII above.

Article XIV
ISRAELI WITHDRAWAL FROM
THE GAZA STRIP AND JERICHO AREA

Israel will withdraw from the Gaza Strip and Jericho area, as detailed in the protocol attached as Annex II.

Article XV
RESOLUTION OF DISPUTES

1. Disputes arising out of the application or interpretation of this Declaration of Principles, or any subsequent agreement pertaining to the interim period, shall be resolved by negotiations through the joint Liaison Committee to be established pursuant to Article X above.

2. Disputes which cannot be settled by negotiations may be resolved by a mechanism of conciliation to be agreed upon by the parties.

3. The parties may agree to submit to arbitration disputes relating to the interim period, which cannot be settled through conciliation. To this end, upon the agreement of both parties, the parties will establish an Arbitration Committee.

Article XVI
MISCELLANEOUS PROVISIONS

1. This Declaration of Principles will enter into force one month after its signing.

2. All protocol annexed to this Declaration of Principles and Agreed Minutes pertaining thereto shall be regarded as an integral part thereof.

Done at Washington, D.C., this 13th day of September 1993.

For the Government of Israel   For the Palestinians

Witnessed by:

The United States of America   The Russian Federation

ANNEX I
PROTOCOL ON THE MODE
AND CONDITIONS OF ELECTIONS

1. Palestinians of Jerusalem who live there will have the right to participate in the elections process, according to an agreement between the
two sides.

2. In addition, the elections agreement should cover, among other things,
the following issues:

    a. the system of elections;

    b. the mode of the agreed supervision and international observation
    and their personal composition; and

    c. rules and regulations regarding election campaign, including agreed
    arrangements for the organizing of mass media, and the possibility
    of licensing a broadcasting and TV station.

3. The future status of displaced Palestinians who were registered on 4th
June 1967 will not be prejudiced because they are unable to participate
in the elections process due to practical reasons.

ANNEX II
PROTOCOL ON WITHDRAWAL OF ISRAELI
FORCES FROM THE GAZA STRIP AND JERICHO AREA

1. The two sides will conclude and sign within two months from the date
of entry into force of this Declaration of Principles, an agreement on

the withdrawal of Israeli military forces from the Gaza Strip and Jericho area. This agreement will include comprehensive arrangements to apply in the Gaza Strip and the Jericho area subsequent to the Israeli withdrawal.

2. Israel will implement an accelerated and scheduled withdrawal of Israeli military forces from the Gaza Strip and Jericho area, beginning immediately with the signing of the agreement on the Gaza Strip and Jericho area and to be completed within a period not exceeding four months after the signing of this agreement.

3. The above agreement will include, among other things:

   a. Arrangements for a smooth and peaceful transfer of authority from the Israeli military government and Civil Administration to the Palestinian representatives.

   b. Structure, powers, and responsibilities of the Palestinian authority in these areas, except: external security, settlements, Israelis, foreign relations, and other mutually agreed matters.

   c. Arrangements for the assumption of internal security and public order by the Palestinian police force consisting of police officers recruited locally and from abroad holding Jordanian passports and Palestinian documents issued by Egypt. Those who will participate in the Palestinian police force coming from abroad should be trained as police and police officers.

   d. A temporary international or foreign presence, as agreed upon.

   e. Establishment of a joint Palestinian-Israeli Coordination and Cooperation Committee for mutual purposes.

   f. An economic development and stabilization program, including the establishment of an Emergency Fund, to encourage foreign investment, and financial and economic support. Both sides will coordinate and cooperate jointly and unilaterally with regional and international parties to support these aims.

   g. Arrangements for a safe passage for persons and transportation between the Gaza Strip and Jericho area.

4. The above agreement will include arrangements for coordination between both parties regarding passage:

a. Gaza—Egypt; and

b. Jericho—Jordan.

5. The offices responsible for carrying out the powers and responsibilities of the Palestinian authority under this Annex II and Article VI of the Declaration of Principles will be located in the Gaza Strip and Jericho area pending the inauguration of the Council.

6. Other than these agreed arrangements, the status of the Gaza Strip and Jericho area will continue to be an integral part of the West Bank and Gaza Strip, and will not be changed in the interim period.

ANNEX III
PROTOCOL ON ISRAELI-PALESTINIAN COOPERATION
IN ECONOMIC AND DEVELOPMENT PROGRAMS

The two sides agree to establish an Israeli-Palestinian continuing Committee for Economic Cooperation, focusing among other things, on the following:

1. Cooperation in the field of water, including a Water Development program prepared by experts from both sides, which will also specify the mode of cooperation in the management of water resources in the West Bank and Gaza Strip, and will include proposals for studies and plans on water rights of each party, as well as on the equitable utilization of joint water resources for implementation in and beyond the interim period.

2. Cooperation in the field of electricity, including an Electricity Development Program, which will also specify the modes of cooperation for the production, maintenance, purchase and sale of electricity resources.

3. Cooperation in the field of energy, including an Energy Development Program, which will provide for the exploitation of oil and gas for industrial purposes, particularly in the Gaza Strip and in the Negev, and will encourage further joint exploration of other energy resources. This program may also provide for the construction of a Petrochemi-

cal industrial complex in the Gaza Strip and the construction of oil and gas pipelines.

4. Cooperation in the field of finance, including a Financial Development and Action Program for the encouragement of international investment in the West Bank and the Gaza Strip, and in Israel, as well as the establishment of a Palestinian Development Bank.

5. Cooperation in the field of transport and communications, including a Program, which will define guidelines for the establishment of a Gaza Sea Port Area, and will provide for the establishment of transport and communication lines to and from the West Bank and the Gaza Strip to Israel and to other countries. In addition, this Program will provide for carrying out the necessary construction of roads, railways, communication lines, etc.

6. Cooperation in the field of trade, including studies, and Trade Promotion Programs, which will encourage local, regional, and inter-regional trade, as well as a feasibility study of creating free trade zones in the Gaza Strip and in Israel, mutual access to these zones, and cooperation in other areas related to trade and commerce.

7. Cooperation in the field of industry, including Industrial Development Programs, which will provide for the establishment of joint Israeli-Palestinian Industrial Research and Development Centers, will promote Palestinian-Israeli joint ventures, and provide guidelines for cooperation in the textile, food, pharmaceutical, electronics, diamonds, computer and science-based industries.

8. A program for cooperation in, and regulation of, labor relations and cooperation in social welfare issues.

9. A Human Resource Development and Cooperation Plan, providing for joint Israeli-Palestinian workshops and seminars, and for the establishment of joint vocational training centers, research institutes and data banks.

10. An Environmental Protection Plan, providing for joint and/or coordinated measures in this sphere.

11. A program for developing coordination and cooperation in the field of communication and media.

12. Any other programs of mutual interests.

ANNEX IV
PROTOCOL ON ISRAELI-PALESTINIAN COOPERATION
CONCERNING REGIONALDEVELOPMENT PROGRAMS

1. The two sides will cooperate in the context of the multilateral peace efforts in promoting a Development Program for the region, including the West Bank and the Gaza Strip, to be initiated by the G-7. The parties will request the G-7 to seek the participation in this program of other interested states, such as members of the Organization of Economic Cooperation and Development, regional Arab states and institutions, as well as members of the private sector.

2. The Development Program will consist of two elements:

a) an Economic Development Program for the West Bank and the Gaza Strip

b) a regional Economic Development Program.

A. The Economic Development Program for the West Bank and Gaza Strip will consist of the following elements:

(1) A Social Rehabilitation Program, including a Housing and Construction Program.

(2) A Small and Medium Business Development Plan.

(3) An Infrastructure Development Program (water, electricity, transportation and communication, etc.)

(4) A Human Resources Plan.

(5) Other programs.

B. The Regional Economic Development Program may consist of the following elements:

(1) The establishment of a Middle East Development Fund, as a first step, and a Middle East Development Bank, as a second step.

(2) The development of a joint Israeli-Palestinian- Jordanian plan for coordinated exploitation of the Dead Sea Canal.

(3) The Mediterranean Sea (Gaza) - Dead Sea Canal.

(4) Regional Desalinization and other water development projects.

(5) A regional plan for agricultural development, including a coordinated regional effort for the prevention of desertification.

(6) Interconnection of electricity grids.

(7) Regional cooperation for the transfer, distribution, and industrial exploitation of gas, oil, and other energy resources.

(8) A Regional Tourism, Transportation and Telecommunication Development Plan.

(9) Regional cooperation in other spheres.

3. The two sides will encourage the multilateral working groups, and will coordinate towards its success. The two parties will encourage intercessional activities, as well as pre-feasibility and feasibility studies, within the various multilateral working groups.

AGREED MINUTES TO THE DECLARATION OF PRINCIPLES ON INTERIM SELF-GOVERNMENT ARRANGEMENTS

A. GENERAL UNDERSTANDINGS AND AGREEMENTS

Any powers and responsibilities transferred to the Palestinians pursuant to the Declaration of Principles prior to the inauguration of the Council will be subject to the same principles pertaining to Article IV, as set out in these Agreed Minutes below.

B. SPECIFIC UNDERSTANDINGS AND AGREEMENTS

Article IV

It is understood that:

1. Jurisdiction of the Council will cover West Bank and Gaza Strip territory, except for issues that will be negotiated in the permanent status negotiations: Jerusalem, settlements, military locations, and Israelis.

2. The Council's jurisdiction will apply with regard to the agreed powers, responsibilities, spheres and authorities transferred to it.

Article VI (2)

It is agreed that the transfer of authority will be as follows:

(1) The Palestinian side will inform the Israeli side of the names of the authorized Palestinians who will assume the powers, authorities and responsibilities that will be transferred to the Palestinians according to the Declaration of Principles in the following fields: education and culture, health, social welfare, direct taxation, tourism and any other authorities agreed upon.

(2) It is understood that the rights and obligations of these offices will not be affected.

(3) Each of the spheres described above will continue to enjoy existing budgetary allocations in accordance with arrangements to be mutually agreed upon. These arrangements also will provide for the necessary adjustments required in order to take into account the taxes collected by the direct taxation office.

(4) Upon the execution of the Declaration of Principles, the Israeli and Palestinian delegations will immediately commence negotiations on a detailed plan for the transfer of authority on the above offices in accordance with the above understandings.

Article VII (2)

The Interim Agreement will also include arrangements for coordination and cooperation.

Article VII (5)

The withdrawal of the military government will not prevent Israel from exercising the powers and responsibilities not transferred to the council.

Article VIII

It is understood that the Interim Agreement will include arrangements for cooperation and coordination between the two parties in this regard. It is also agreed that the transfer of powers and responsibilities to the Palestinian police will be accomplished in a phased manner, as agreed in the Interim Agreement.

Article X

It is agreed that, upon the entry into force of the Declaration of Principles, the Israeli and Palestinian delegations will exchange the names of the individuals designed by them as members of the Joint Israeli-Palestinian Liaison Committee.

It is further agreed that each side will have an equal number of members in the Joint Committee. The Joint Committee will reach decisions by agreements. The Joint Committee may add other technicians and experts, as necessary. The Joint Committee will decide on the frequency and place or places of its meetings.

ANNEX V

It is understood that, subsequent to the Israeli withdrawal, Israel will continue to be responsible for external security, and for internal security and public order of settlements and Israelis. Israeli military forces and civilians may continue to use roads freely within the Gaza Strip and Jericho area.

Notes

1. Israel Information Service, Information Division, Israel Foreign Ministry, Jerusalem.

Appendix D:
The Washington Declaration,
July 25, 1994, Washington, D.C.[1]

A. After generations of hostility, blood and tears and in the wake of years of pain and wars, His Majesty King Hussein and Prime Minister Yitzhak Rabin are determined to bring an end to bloodshed and sorrow. It is in this spirit that His Majesty King Hussein of the Hashemite Kingdom of Jordan and Prime Minister and Minister of Defense, Mr. Yitzhak Rabin of Israel, met in Washington today at the invitation of President William J. Clinton of the United States of America. This initiative of President William J. Clinton constitutes an historic landmark in the United States' untiring efforts in promoting peace and stability in the Middle East. The personal involvement of the President has made it possible to realise agreement on the content of this historic declaration. The signing of this declaration bears testimony to the President's vision and devotion to the cause of peace.

B. In their meeting, His Majesty King Hussein and Prime Minister Yitzhak Rabin have jointly reaffirmed the five underlying principles of their understanding on an Agreed Common Agenda designed to reach the goal of a just, lasting and comprehensive peace between the Arab States and the Palestinians, with Israel.

    1. Jordan and Israel aim at the achievement of just, lasting and comprehensive peace between Israel and its neighbours and at the conclusion of a Treaty of Peace between both countries.

    2. The two countries will vigorously continue their negotiations to arrive at a state of peace, based on Security Council Resolutions 242 and 338 in all their aspects, and founded on freedom, equality and justice.

    3. Israel respects the present special role of the Hashemite Kingdom of Jordan in Muslim Holy shrines in Jerusalem. When negotiations on the

permanent status will take place, Israel will give high priority to the Jordanian historic role in these shrines. In addition the two sides have agreed to act together to promote interfaith relations among the three monotheistic religions.

4. The two countries recognise their right and obligation to live in peace with each other as well as with all states within secure and recognised boundaries. The two states affirmed their respect for and acknowledgment of the sovereignty, territorial integrity and political independence of every state in the area.

5. The two countries desire to develop good neighbourly relations of cooperation between them to ensure lasting security and to avoid threats and the use of force between them.

C. The long conflict between the two states is now coming to an end. In this spirit the state of belligerency between Jordan and Israel has been terminated.

D. Following this declaration and in keeping with the Agreed Common Agenda, both countries will refrain from actions or activities by either side that may adversely affect the security of the other or may prejudice the final outcome of negotiations. Neither side will threaten the other by use of force, weapons, or any other means, against each other and both sides will thwart threats to security resulting from all kinds of terrorism.

E. His Majesty King Hussein and Prime Minister Yitzhak Rabin took note of the progress made in the bilateral negotiations within the Jordan-Israel track last week on the steps decided to implement the sub-agendas on borders, territorial matters, security, water, energy, environment and the Jordan Rift Valley.

In this framework, mindful of items of the Agreed Common Agenda (borders and territorial matters) they noted that the boundary sub-commission has reached agreement in July 1994 in fulfillment of part of the role entrusted to it in the sub-agenda. They also noted that the sub-commission for water, environment and energy agreed to mutually recognise, as the role of their negotiations, the rightful allocations of the two sides in Jordan River and Yarmouk River waters and to fully respect and comply with the negotiated rightful allocations, in accordance with agreed acceptable principles with mutually acceptable quality. Similarly, His Majesty King Hussein and Prime Minister Yitzhak Rabin expressed their deep satisfaction and pride in the work of the trilateral commission in its meeting held in Jordan on Wednesday, July 20th 1994, hosted by the Jordanian Prime Minister, Dr. Abdessalam al-Majali, and attended by Secretary of State Warren Christopher and Foreign Minister Shimon Peres. They voiced their pleasure at the association and commitment of the United States in this endeavour.

F. His Majesty King Hussein and Prime Minister Yitzhak Rabin believe that steps must be taken both to overcome psychological barriers and to break with the legacy of war. By working with optimism towards the dividends of peace for all the people in the region, Jordan and Israel are determined to shoulder their responsibilities towards the human dimension of peace making. They recognise imbalances and disparities are a root cause of extremism which thrives on poverty and unemployment and the degradation of human dignity. In this spirit His Majesty King Hussein and Prime Minister Yitzhak Rabin have today approved a series of steps to symbolise the new era which is now at hand:

1. Direct telephone links will be opened between Jordan and Israel.

2. The electricity grids of Jordan and Israel will be linked as part of a regional concept.

3. Two new border crossings will be opened between Jordan and Israel—one at the southern tip of Aqaba-Eilat and the other at a mutually agreed point in the north.

4. In principle free access will be given to third country tourists traveling between Jordan and Israel.

5. Negotiations will be accelerated on opening an international air corridor between both countries.

6. The police forces of Jordan and Israel will cooperate in combating crime with emphasis on smuggling and particularly drug smuggling. The United States will be invited to participate in this joint endeavour.

7. Negotiations on economic matters will continue in order to prepare for future bilateral cooperation including the abolition of all economic boycotts.

All these steps are being implemented within the framework of regional infrastructural development plans and in conjunction with the Jordan-Israel bilaterals on boundaries, security, water and related issues and without prejudice to the final outcome of the negotiations on the items included in the Agreed Common Agenda between Jordan and Israel.

G. His Majesty King Hussein and Prime Minister Yitzhak Rabin have agreed to meet periodically or whenever they feel necessary to review the progress of the negotiations and express their firm intention to shepherd and direct the process in its entirety.

H. In conclusion, His Majesty King Hussein and Prime Minister Yitzhak Rabin wish to express once again their profound thanks and appreciation to President William J. Clinton and his Administration for their untiring efforts in furthering the cause of peace, justice and prosperity for all the peoples of the region. They wish to thank the President personally for his warm welcome and hospitality. In recognition of their appreciation to the President, His Majesty King Hussein and Prime Minister Yitzhak Rabin have asked President William J. Clinton to sign this document as a witness and as a host to their meeting.

His Majesty King Hussein   Prime Minister Yitzhak Rabin

President William J. Clinton

Notes

1. Israel Information Service, Information Division, Israel Foreign Ministry, Jerusalem.

Appendix E:
Summary of the Main Points
of Peace Proposals

United Nations Resolution 242,
November 22, 1967

1. Focus: The establishment of a just and lasting peace in the Middle East.

2. The occupied territories: The resolution requested the withdrawal of Israeli armed forces from territories occupied in the Six Day War.

3. Mutual recognition: The resolution requested the recognition of the sovereignty, territorial integrity, and political independence of all states in the area and their right to live in peace within secure and recognized boundaries.

Prime Minister Begin's Autonomy Plan,
December 28, 1977

1. Focus: Palestinian autonomy in the West Bank and Gaza.

2. The occupied territories: The plan called for the abolition of the military government in Judea, Samaria, and the Gaza district but maintained Israel's claim of sovereignty to these areas.

3. Autonomy: The plan called for the establishment of an administrative autonomy by and for the residents of Judea, Samaria, and the Gaza district—subject to review after a five-year period. Autonomy would cover the following categories: education; religious affairs; finance; transportation; construction and housing; industry; com-

merce and tourism; agriculture; health, labor, and social welfare; rehabilitation and refugees; and the administration of justice and
supervision of local police forces.

4. Elections in the West Bank and Gaza: The residents of Judea,
Samaria, and Gaza would elect an administrative council composed of eleven members. The period of office of the council
would be four years from the day of its election.

The Camp David Accords,
September 17, 1978.

1. Focus: The establishment of a framework for peace in the Middle
East.

2. Basis for a peaceful settlement: United Nations Security Council
Resolution 242, in all its parts.

3. The occupied territories: The Israeli military government and its
civilian administration in the West Bank and Gaza would be
replaced by a self-governing authority.

4. Autonomy: A self-governing authority in the West Bank and Gaza
would be established to run the affairs of the Palestinian inhabitants in these areas for a five-year transitional period. No later than
the third year after the beginning of the transitional period, negotiations would take place to determine the final status of these areas.

5. Elections in the West Bank and Gaza: The self-governing authority
would be freely elected by the inhabitants of the West Bank and
Gaza to replace the existing Israeli military government there.

6. Palestinian participation in negotiations: The delegations of Egypt
and Jordan might include Palestinians from the West Bank and
Gaza or other Palestinians as mutually agreed.

The Reagan Peace Plan, September 1, 1982.

1. Focus: A just and lasting peace in the Middle East.

2. Basis for a peaceful settlement: United Nations Resolution 242 and the Camp David agreements.

3. The occupied territories: The Arab-Israeli conflict should be resolved through negotiations involving an exchange of territory for peace, applicable to all fronts, including the West Bank and Gaza.

4. Autonomy: Palestinian inhabitants of the West Bank and Gaza would have full autonomy over their own affairs during a five-year transitional period.

5. Elections in the West Bank and Gaza: The five-year period of transition would begin after free elections for a self-governing Palestinian authority.

6. Palestinian participation in negotiations: The United States supported a broad participation at the peace table as envisaged by the Camp David accords.

7. Israeli settlements: The United States called for the immediate adoption of a settlement freeze by Israel, denying that settlement activity was necessary for the security of Israel.

8. The establishment of a Palestinian state: The United States opposed the establishment of an independent Palestinian State in the West Bank and Gaza.

9. Annexation: The United States did not support annexation or permanent Israeli control of the West Bank and Gaza.

10. The status of Jerusalem: Jerusalem must remain undivided, but its final status should be decided through negotiations.

Peres-Hussein Agreement (the London Document), April 11, 1987

1. Focus: The convening of an international Middle East peace conference.

2. Basis for a peaceful settlement: UN Resolutions 242 and 338 and the renunciation of violence and terror. The international conference

would not impose a solution and would not veto any agreement reached by the sides; that the negotiations would be conducted in bilateral committees in a direct manner; and that the Palestinian issue would be discussed in a meeting of the Jordanian, Palestinian, and Israeli delegations.

3. Palestinian participation in negotiations: Palestinian representatives would be included in the Jordanian-Palestinian delegation.

The Shultz Initiative, March 4, 1988

1. Focus: The convening of an international Middle East peace conference.

2. Basis for a peaceful settlement: The acceptance of UN resolutions 242 and 338, and the rejection of violence and terrorism. Negotiations would be conducted by bilateral delegations; the conference could not impose solutions or veto agreements.

3. The occupied territories: The initiative supported the territories-for-peace formula.

4. Autonomy: The initiative called for a three-year transitional period.

5. Palestinian participation in negotiations: Palestinian representation would be part of a Jordanian-Palestinian delegation.

The Israeli Government Peace Initiative, May 14, 1989

1. Focus: The continuation of the peace process.

2. Basis for a peaceful settlement: UN Resolutions 242 and 338 and the Camp David agreements.

3. The occupied territories: There would be no change in the status of Judea, Samaria, and Gaza other than in accordance with the basic guidelines of the government.

4. Autonomy: A five-year transitional period would constitute a test for co-existence and cooperation. At a later stage (no later than three years), negotiations would be conducted for a permanent solution.

5. Elections in the West Bank and Gaza: Israel proposed free and democratic elections among the Palestinian Arab inhabitants in Judea, Samaria, and Gaza.

6. Palestinian participation in negotiations: In these elections a representative will be chosen to conduct negotiations for a transitional period of self-rule.

7. The establishment of a Palestinian state: Israel rejected the establishment of a Palestinian state in the Gaza district and the area between Israel and Jordan.

The Baker Proposals, October 10, 1989

1. Focus: A dialogue in Cairo between Israel, Egypt, and the United States to discuss elections in the West Bank and Gaza.

2. Basis for a peaceful settlement: The Israeli election plan of May 14, 1989.

3. Palestinian participation in negotiations: An elected Palestinian delegation from the West Bank and Gaza would participate in peace negotiations.

4. The status of Jerusalem: The plan itself did not mention Jerusalem, but the United States supported the participation of Palestinians from East Jerusalem in the elections.

The Madrid Conference, October 30, 1991

1. Focus: An opening to two-track bilateral peace negotiations between Israeli, Syrian, Lebanese, and joint Jordanian-Palestinian delegations; and multilateral talks between Arab, Israeli, and other negotiating teams on diverse regional issues.

2. Basis for a peaceful settlement: Security Council Resolution 242.

3. Palestinian participation in negotiations: Palestinians from the West Bank and Gaza participated as a segment of a joint Jordanian-Palestinian delegation.

4. Status of Jerusalem: The United States objected to the Israeli annexation of East Jerusalem and the extension of Israeli law there, and to the extension of Jerusalem's municipal boundaries.

Declaration of Principles on Interim Self-Government Arrangement.

Final draft agreed on August 19, 1993. Signed on September 13, 1993.

1. Focus: The implementation of Palestinian self-government authority in the Gaza Strip and Jericho area.

2. Basis of a peaceful settlement: UN Resolutions 242 and 338.

3. The occupied territories: Within two months from the time the Declaration of Principles takes effect, an agreement on the withdrawal of Israeli military forces from the Gaza Strip and Jericho area should be reached. Negotiations on the permanent status of the territories will begin as soon as possible, but not later than the beginning of the third year of the interim period, between the government of Israel and the Palestinians' representatives.

4. Mutual recognition: Prior to the signing of the agreement, Israel and the PLO officially recognized each other.

5. Elections: In order that the Palestinian people in the West Bank and Gaza Strip may govern themselves according to democratic principles, direct, free, and general elections are to be held for the Council under agreed supervision and international observation, while the Palestinian police will ensure public order.

6. Israeli settlements: The Council will have no jurisdiction over Jewish settlements. The issue will be negotiated in the permanent status negotiations.

7. Jerusalem: United Jerusalem will remain under Israeli jurisdiction. The issue is to be discussed in the permanent status negotiations, but Israel declared that Jerusalem will not be redivided.

The Washington Declaration, July 25, 1994

1. Focus: Israeli-Jordanian peace.

2. Basis for a peaceful settlement: UN Resolutions 242 and 338.

3. Jerusalem: Jordan upheld the role of protector of Muslim Holy Shrines in Jerusalem.

References

Abu-Amr, Ziad. "Hamas: A Historical and Political Background." *Journal of Palestine Studies* 22, 4 (summer 1993): 5–19.

Aly, Abdel Monem Said. "Egypt: A Decade After Camp David." In William Quandt, ed., *The Middle East Ten Years After Camp David.* Washington, D.C.: Brookings Institution, 1988.

Arian, Asher. *Politics in Israel.* Chatham: Chatham House, 1985.

——. "The Israeli Electorate, 1977." In Asher Arian, ed. *The Elections in Israel–1977.* Jerusalem: Jerusalem Academic Press, 1980.

——."Security and Political Attitude in Israel: 1986–1991." *Public Opinion Quarterly* (spring 1982): 116–128.

——. "A People Apart: Coping with National Security Problems in Israel." *Journal of Conflict Resolution* 44, 4 (December 1989): 605–631.

——. "Israel National Unity Government and Domestic Politics." In Asher Arian and Michal Shamir, eds. *The Elections in Israel–1988.* Boulder, Colo.: Westview Press, 1990.

Arian, Asher, and Michal Shamir. "Two Reversals: Why 1992 Was Not 1977." in Asher Arian and Michal Shamir, eds. *The Elections in Israel 1992* Albany: SUNY Press, 1995.

Arian, Asher, and Michal Shamir. *The Elections in Israel–1988.* Boulder, Colo.: Westview Press, 1990.

Arian, Asher, and Michal Shamir, eds. *The Elections in Israel–1984.* New Brunswick, N.J.: Transaction Books, 1986.

Arian, Asher, Ilan Talmud, and Tamar Hermann. *National Security and Public Opinion in Israel.* Boulder, Colo.: Westview Press, 1988.

Aronoff, Myron J. *Israeli Vision and Division.* New Brunswick, N.J.: Transaction Books, 1989.

——. "The Institutionalization and Cooptation of a Charismatic, Messianic, Religious-Political Revitalization Movement." In David Newman, ed. *The Impact of Gush Emunim.* New York: St. Martin's Press, 1985.

Atherton, Leroy Alfred Jr. "The Shifting Sands of Middle East Peace." *Foreign Policy* 86 (spring 1992): 114–133.

Baker, James. "Principles and Pragmatism: U.S. Policy Toward the Arab-Israeli Conflict." Address before the U.S.-Israel Public Affairs Committee (AIPAC), Washington, D.C., May 22, 1989.

Barnet, Richard J. *The Alliance.* New York: Simon and Schuster, 1983.

Baron, Salo Wittmayer. *Modern Nationalism and Religion.* New York: Harper Brothers, 1947.

234 *References*

Barron, Andrea. "Jewish and Arab Diaspora in the United States and Their Impact on U.S. Middle East Policy." In Yehuda Lukacs and Abdalla M. Battah, eds. *The Arab-Israeli Conflict.* Boulder, Colo.: Westview Press, 1988.

Basic Policy Guidelines for Israel's Twenty-Fourth Government. Jerusalem: Israel Ministry of Foreign Affairs, June 11, 1990.

Basic Policy Guidelines for the Rabin Government. Jerusalem: Israel Ministry of Foreign Affairs, July 13, 1992.

Bar-Siman-Tov, Yaacov. "Peace as a Significant Change in Foreign Policy: The Need for Legitimacy." *Jerusalem Journal of International Relations* 12, 3 (September 1990): 13–30.

Barzilai, Gad, and Efraim Inbar. "Do Wars Have an Impact? Israeli Public Opinion After the Gulf War." *Jerusalem Journal of International relations* 14, 1 (March 1992): 48–64.

Barzilai, Gad, and Bruce Russett. "The Political Economy of Israeli Military Action." In Asher Arian and Michal Shamir, eds. *The Israeli Elections–1988.* Boulder, Colo.: Westview Press, 1990.

Belling, Willard A., ed. *Middle East Peace Plans.* New York: St. Martin's Press, 1986.

Ben-Gurion, David. *Me'maamad le'am* [From class to nation]. TelAviv: Am Oved, 1974.

Ben-Zvi, Abraham. *Between Lausanne and Geneva: International Conferences and the Arab-Israeli Conflict.* Jerusalem: Jerusalem Post Press, 1989.

Bill, James A., and Carl Leiden. *The Middle East: Politics and Power.* Boston: Allyn and Bacon, 1974.

Brzezinski, Zbigniew. *Power and Principle.* New York: Farrar Straus and Giroux, 1983.

Burton, John W. "Resolution of Conflict." *International Studies Quarterly* 16 (March 1972): 5–30.

Bush, George. "The World After the Persian Gulf." Address before a joint session of Congress, Washington, D.C., March 6, 1991. United States Department of State, *Dispatch* 2, 1 (March 18, 1991).

Caplan, Neil. *Futile Diplomacy,* vol. 1, *Early Arab-Zionist Negotiation Attempts, 1913–1931.* London: Frank Cass, 1983. Vol. 2, *Arab-Zionist Negotiations and the End of the Mandate.* London: Frank Cass, 1986.

Carter, Jimmy. *Keeping Faith.* Toronto: Bantam, 1982.

———. *The Blood of Abraham.* Boston: Houghton Mifflin, 1985.

Clarke, Duncan L. "Entanglement: The Commitment to Israel." In Yehuda Lukacs and Abdalla M. Battah, eds. *The Arab-Israeli Conflict.* Boulder, Colo.: Westview Press, 1988.

Coalition Agreement, Israel's Twenty-Fourth Government, June 8, 1990.

Conant, Melvin A., and Fern Racine Gold. *The Geopolitics of Energy.* Boulder, Colo.: Westview Press, 1978.

Cooper, Richard N. "Oil, the Middle East, and the World Economy." In Joseph S. Nye Jr. and Roger K. Smith, eds. *After the Storm: Lessons from the Gulf War.* Lanham, MD.: Madison Books, 1992.

Danziger, Raphael, and Arthur Rubin, *The Clinton-Rabin Partnership in the Mideast Peace Process,* Washington, D.C.: AIPAC, 1993.

Dayan, Moshe. *Breakthrough.* New York: Alfred A. Knopf, 1981.

―――. *On the Peace Process and the Future of Israel.* (Hebrew) Natan Yanai, ed. Tel Aviv: Ministry of Defense, 1988.

Don-Yehiya, Eliezer. "Jewish Messianism, Religious Zionism and Israeli Politics: The Impact and Origin of Gush Emunim." *Middle Eastern Studies* 23, 2 (April 1987): 215–234.

Dror, Yehezkel. *A Grand Strategy for Israel.* (Hebrew) Jerusalem: Academon, 1989.

Eban, Abba. *Personal Witness.* New York: G. P. Putnam's Sons, 1992.

―――. *The New Diplomacy.* New York: Random House, 1983.

Eilts, Herman Fredrick. "The United States and Egypt." In William B. Quandt, ed. *The Middle East Ten Years After Camp David.* Washington, D.C.: Brookings Institution, 1988.

Elazar, Daniel J. "The 1981 Elections: Into the Second Generation of Statehood." In Howard R. Penniman and Daniel J. Elazar, eds. *Israel at the Polls, 1981.* Washington, D.C.: American Enterprise Institute, 1986.

―――. "Religious Parties and Politics in the Begin Era." In Steven Heydemann, ed. *The Begin Era: Issues in Contemporary Israel.* Boulder, Colo.: Westview Press, 1984.

Elon, Amos. *The Israelis.* New York: Penguin Books, 1981.

Esman, Milton J., and Itamar Rabinovich. "The Study of Ethnic Politics in the Middle East." In Milton J. Esman and Itamar Rabinovich, eds. *Ethnicity, Pluralism, and the State in the Middle East.* Ithaca: Cornell University Press, 1988.

Etzioni, Amitai. *Political Unification.* Huntington, N.Y.: Robert Krieger, 1974.

Fabian, Larry L. "The Middle East: War Danger and Receding Peace Prospects." *Foreign Affairs* 62, 3 (1983): 632–658

Fahmy, Ismail. *Negotiating for Peace in the Middle East.* Baltimore: John Hopkins University Press, 1983.

Feldman, Shai. *U.S. Middle East Policy: The Domestic Setting.* Boulder, Colo.: Westview Press, 1988.

Fisher, Ronald. "Third Party Consultation." *Journal of Conflict Resolution* 16, 1 (March 1972): 65–77.

―――. "Prenegotiation Problem-solving Discussions: Enhancing the Potential for Successful Negotiation." In Janice Gross Stein, ed. *Getting to the Table.* Baltimore: Johns Hopkins University Press, 1989.

Freedman, Robert O. "The Soviet Union and the Arab-Israeli Conflict." In Robert O. Freedman, ed. *World Politics and the Arab-Israeli Conflict* (New York: Pergamon Press, 1979).

―――. "Moscow and the Middle East in 1984." In Haim Shaked and Daniel Dishon, eds. *Middle East Contemporary Survey,* vol. 8: 1983–1984. Tel Aviv: Dayan Center for Middle Eastern and African Studies/Shiloah Institute, Tel Aviv University, 1986.

―――."The Middle East Peace Process." In Itamar Rabinovich and Haim Shaked, eds., *Middle East Contemporary Survey,* vol. 9: 1984–1985. Tel Aviv: Dayan Center for Middle Eastern and African Studies/Shiloah Institute, Tel Aviv University, 1987.

―――. "Religion, Politics, and the Israeli Elections of 1988." *Middle East Journal* 43, 3 (summer 1989): 406–422.

Freedman, Robert, ed., *Israel After Rabin.* Boulder, Colo.: Westview Press, 1995.

Garfinkle, Adam M. "West European Peace Diplomacy in the Levant. But Will They Come?" In Willard Belling, ed. *Middle East Peace Plans*. New York: St. Martin's Press, 1986.

Gazit, Mordechai. "The Middle East Peace Process." In Colin Legum, Haim Shaked, and Daniel Dishon, eds. *Middle East Contemporary Survey,* vol. 7: 1982–1983. New York: Holmes and Meier, 1985.

———. "The Middle East Peace Process." In Itamar Rabinovich Haim Shaked, eds. *Middle East Contemporary Survey,* vol. 9: 1984–1985. Tel Aviv: Dayan Center for Middle Eastern and African Studies/Shiloah Institute, Tel Aviv University, 1987.

Golan, Galia. *Yom Kippur and After.* Cambridge: Cambridge University Press, 1977.

Goldberg, Giora, and Efraim Ben-Zadok. "Gush Emunim in the West Bank." *Middle East Studies* 22, 1 (January 1986): 52–73.

Goldberg, Giora, Gad Barzilai, and Efraim Inbar. "The Impact of Intercommunal Conflict: The Intifada and Israeli Public Opinion". *Policy Studies* 43, Jerusalem: Leonard Davis Institute (February 1991).

Gonen, Jay. *A Psychohistory of Zionism.* New York: Mason, Charter, 1975.

Greilsammer, Ilan. "Campaign Strategies of the Israeli Religious Parties, 1981–1984." In Asher Arian and Michal Shamir, eds. *The Elections in Israel–1984.* New Brunswick, N.J.: Transaction Books, 1986.

Haber Eitan, Ze'ev Schiff, and Ehud Yaari. *The Year of the Dove.* New York: Bantam, 1979.

Hallaj, Muhammad. "Taking Sides: Palestinians and the Gulf Crisis." *Journal of Palestine Studies* 20, 3 (spring 1991): 41–47.

Heikal, Mohamad. *Autumn of Fury.* New York: Random House, 1983.

Heller, Mark. *A Palestinian State.* Cambridge: Harvard University Press, 1983.

———. "The Middle East: Out of Step with History." *Foreign Affairs* 69, 1 (1989/1990): 153–171.

Herzog, Hanna. "Was It On the Agenda? The Hidden Agenda of the 1988 Campaign." In Asher Arian and Michal Shamir, eds. *The Elections in Israel–1988.* Boulder, Colo.: Westview Press, 1990.

Hill, Norman. *Claims of Territory in International Law and Relations.* New York: Oxford University Press, 1945.

Hoffman, Stanley. *Primacy or World Order.* New York: McGraw-Hill, 1980.

Holst, Johan, *A Nuclear Freeze Zone in the Nordic Area.* Oslo: Norsk Utenrikspolitisk Institute, 1983.

———. *European Security and the Role of Arms Control.* Brussels: Center for European Policy Studies, 1984.

———. "Norwegian Defense Policy for the 1990s: A Conceptual Framework." *Scandinavian Review* 76, 2 (summer 1988): 30–42;

———. "Conventional Stability in Europe." *Scandinavian Review* 77, 2 (summer 1989): 7–18.

———. *Civilian-based Defense in a New Era.* Cambridge: Albert Einstein Institution, 1990.

———. *Exploring Europe.* Los Angeles, Calif: Rand/UCLA, 1990.

———. "Arms Control in the Nineties: A European Perspective." *Daedalus* 120, 1 (winter 1991): 83–110.

———. "Perusing a Durable Peace in the Aftermath of the Cold War." *NATO Review* 40, 4 (August 1992): 9–13.

———. "Middle East Peace Process: The Norwegian Channel." Address before the National Press Club, Washington, D.C., October 4, 1993.

Holsti, K. J, *International Politics*. Englewood Cliffs, New Jersey: Prentice Hall, 1988.

Holsti, Ole R., and James Rosenau. *American Leadership in World Affairs*. Boston: Allen & Unwin, 1984.

Ibrahim, Saad Eddin. "Domestic Developments in Egypt." In William B. Quandt, ed. *The Middle East Ten Years After Camp David*. Washington, D.C.: Brookings Institution, 1988.

Indyk, Martin. "The Postwar Balance of Power in the Middle East." In Joseph S. Nye Jr. and Roger K. Smith, eds. *After the Storm: Lessons from the Gulf War*. Lanham, MD.: Madison Books, 1992.

Israel, the West Bank and Gaza. JCSS Study Group. Tel Aviv: Jaffe Center for Strategic Studies, Tel Aviv University, 1989.

Israeli Delegation to the Peace Talks with the Palestinians, Draft of Agreed Statement of Principles, Washington, D.C., May 6, 1993, Document C4, *Journal of Palestine Studies*, 22, 4 (summer 1993).

Israel's Interim Self Government Proposal to the Palestinians Washington, D.C.: Embassy of Israel (September 17, 1992).

Kahane, Meir. *They Must Go*. Miami Beach: Copy Service, 1987.

Kelman, Herbert C. "Creating the Conditions for Israeli-Palestinian Negotiations." *Journal of Conflict Resolution* 26, 1 (March 1982): 39–79.

———. "The Palestinianization of the Arab-Israeli Conflict." In Yehuda Lukacs and Abdalla M. Battah, eds. *The Arab-Israeli Conflict*. Boulder, Colo.: Westview Press, 1988.

Kieval, Gershon R. *Party Politics in Israel and the Occupied Territories*. Westport: Greenwood Press, 1983.

Kimche, David. "The Importance of Prenegotiation: Observations of a Former Diplomat." *Jerusalem Journal of International Relations* 13, 4 (December 1991): 65–70.

Kissinger, Henry A. *American Foreign Policy*. New York: W. W. Norton, 1977.

———. *Years of Upheaval*. New York: Little, Brown, 1982.

Klienman, Aharon. *Statecraft in the Dark: Israel's Practice of Quiet Diplomacy*. Tel Aviv: Jaffe Center for Strategic Studies, Tel Aviv University, 1988.

Kosman, William Youssef. *Sadat's Realistic Peace Initiative*. New York: Vantage Press, 1981.

Kriesberg, Louis. *Social Conflict*. Englewood Cliffs, N.J.: Prentice-Hall, 1982.

———. "Strategies of Negotiating Agreements: Arab-Israeli and U.S.-Soviet Cases." *Negotiation Journal* 4, 1 (January 1988): 19–28.

Labor Party. *The Struggle for the Continuation of the Peace Initiative*. (Hebrew) Tel Aviv: Labor Party, 1987.

LaFeber, Walter. *America, Russia and the Cold War 1945–1990*. New York: McGraw Hill, 1991.

Lall, Arthur. *Modern International Negotiation*. New York: Columbia University Press, 1966.

Lenczowski, George. *The Middle East in World Affairs*. Ithaca: Cornell University Press, 1980.

Levite, Ariel, and Sidney Tarrow. "The Legitimation of Excluded Parties in Dominant Party Systems: A Comparison of Israel and Italy." *Comparative Politics* 15, 3 (April 1983): 295–327.

Lewis, Samuel W. "Israeli Political Reality and the Search for Middle East Peace." *SAIS Review* 7, 1 (winter/spring 1987): 67–80.

Liebman, Charles S., and Eliezer Don-Yehiya. "The Dilemma of Reconciling Traditional Cultural and Political Needs." *Comparative Politics* (October 1983): 53–66.

Long, David E. "Saudi Foreign Policy and the Arab-Israeli Peace Process: The Fahd (Arab) Peace Plan." In Willard A. Belling, ed., *Middle East Peace Plans*. New York: St. Martin's Press, 1986.

Lukacs, Yehuda, ed. *Documents on the Israeli-Palestinian Conflict 1967–1983*. Cambridge: Cambridge University Press, 1984.

Lukacs, Yehuda, and Abdalla M. Battah, eds. *The Arab-Israeli Conflict*. Boulder, Colo.: Westview Press, 1988.

Lustick, Ian. "Kill the Autonomy Talks." *Foreign Policy* 41 (winter 1980/1981): 21–43.

———. "Israel and the West Bank After Elon Moreh: The Mechanics of De Facto Annexation." *Middle East Journal* 35, 4 (autumn 1981): 557–577.

———. "Gush Emunim Ideology—From Religious Doctrine to Political Action." *Middle Eastern Studies* 18, 3 (July 1982): 265–275.

———. "The West Bank and Gaza in Israeli Politics." In Steven Heydemann, ed., *The Begin Era: Issues in Contemporary Israel*. Boulder, Colo.: Westview Press, 1984.

———. *For the Land and the Lord: Jewish Fundamentalism in Israel*. New York: Council on Foreign Relations, 1988.

Maoz, Moshe. *Modern Syria* (Hebrew). Tel Aviv: Reshafim, 1972.

Marcus, Yoel. *Camp David, the Key to Peace* (Hebrew). Jerusalem: Shoken, 1979.

———. "A Virus Has Penetrated." *Ha'aretz* (international ed.), September 29, 1993.

Mendilow, Jonathan, "The 1992 Israeli Electoral Campaign: Valance and Position Dimensions." In Asher Arian and Michal Shamir, eds. *The Elections in Israel 1992*. Albany: SUNY Press, 1995.

Moore, Christopher. *The Mediation Process*. San Francisco: Jossey-Bass, 1986.

Murphy, Richard. "An American Vision of Peace in the Middle East." Address before the Washington Institute on Near East Policy, Washington, D.C. (April 18, 1988).

Naor, Arye. *Cabinet at War: The Functioning of the Israeli Cabinet During the Lebanon War (1982)* (Hebrew). Tel Aviv: Lahav, 1986.

Newman, David. *Population, Settlement and Conflict: Israel and the West Bank*. Cambridge: Cambridge University Press, 1991.

———, ed. *The Impact of Gush Emunim* (New York: St .Martin's Press, 1985.

Palestinian Delegation to the Peace Talks, 'Draft Proposal for a Declaration of Principles, Tunis, May 9, 1993, Document B5, *Journal of Palestine Studies* 22, 4 (summer 1993).

Peleg, Ilan. "The Impact of the Six Day War on the Israeli Right: A Second Republic in the Making?" In Yehuda Lucaks and Abdalla M. Battah, eds. *The Arab-Israeli Conflict.* Boulder, Colo.: Westview Press, 1988.

Peres, Shimon. *Tomorrow Is Now* (Hebrew). Jerusalem: Keter, 1978.

———. "A Strategy for Peace in the Middle East." *Foreign Affairs* 58, 4 (spring 1980): 887–901.

Peretz, Don. "Energy: Israelis, Arabs, and Iranians." In Joseph S. Szyliowicz and Bard E. O'Neill, eds. *The Energy Crisis and U.S. Foreign Policy.* New York: Praeger, 1975.

———. "Israeli Peace Proposals." In Willard Belling, ed., *Middle East Peace Plans.* New York: St. Martin's Press, 1986.

Peretz, Don, and Sammy Smooha. "Israel's Twelfth Knesset Elections: An All-Loser Game." *Middle East Journal* 43, 3 (summer 1989): 389–405.

———. "The Impact of the Gulf War on Israeli and Palestinian Political Attitudes." *Journal of Palestine Studies* 21, 1 (autumn 1991): 17–35.

Peri, Yoram. "From Political Nationalism to Ethno-Nationalism: The Case of Israel." In Yehuda Lukacs and Abdalla M. Battah, eds. *The Arab-Israeli Conflict.* Boulder, Colo.: Westview Press, 1988.

Perlmutter, Amos. "Unilateral Withdrawal: Israel's Security Option." *Foreign Affairs* 64, 1 (fall 1985): 141–153.

Pierre, Andrew J. "Arms Sales: The New Diplomacy." *Foreign Affairs* 60, 2 (winter 1981/1982): 266–286.

Public Papers of the Presidents of the United States, 1983 Washington: D.C.: Government Printing Office, 1985.

Quandt, William. "The Middle East Crisis," *Foreign Affairs* 58, 3 (1979): 450–562.

———. *Camp David: Peace Making and Politics.* Washington, D.C.: Brookings Institution, 1986.

———. "American Proposals for Arab-Israeli Peace." In Willard Belling ed. *Middle East Peace Plans.* New York: St. Martin's Press, 1986.

———, ed. *The Middle East Ten Years After Camp David* Washington, D.C.: Brookings Institution, 1988.

———. "U.S. Policy toward the Arab-Israeli Conflict." In William B. Quandt, ed. *The Middle East Ten Years After Camp David.* Washington, D.C.: Brookings Institution, 1988.

———. "The Middle East in 1990." *Foreign Affairs* 70, 1 (1990/1991): 49–69.

Rabin, Yitzhak. *Pinkas Sheirut* (Hebrew). Tel Aviv: Ma'ariv Library, 1979.

Rafael, Gideon. "Divergence and Convergence of American-Soviet Interests in the Middle East: An Israeli Viewpoint." *Political Science Quarterly* 100, 4 (winter 1985/1986): 561–574.

Reich, Bernard, Noah Dropkin, and Meyrav Wurmser. "Soviet Jewish Immigration and the 1992 Israeli Knesset Elections." *Middle East Journal* 47, 3 (summer 1993): 464–478.

Reiser, Stewart. *The Politics of Leverage.* Cambridge: Center for Middle Eastern Studies, Harvard University, 1984.

Rosenau, James N. "Toward the Study of National-International Linkages." In James N. Rosenau, ed. *Linkage Politics.* New York: Free Press, 1969.

―――. "Theorizing Across Systems: Linkage Politics Revisited." In Jonathan Wilkenfeld, ed. *Conflict Behavior and Linkage Politics.* New York: David McKay, 1973.

Rubenberg, Cheryl A. "The Structural and political Context of the PLO's Changing Objectives in the Post-1967 Period." In Yehuda Lukacs and Abdalla M. Battah, eds. *The Arab Israeli Conflict.* Boulder, Colo.: Westview Press, 1988.

Rubin, Barry. *The Arab States and the Palestine Conflict.* Syracuse, N.Y.: Syracuse University Press, 1981.

―――. "Middle East: Search for Peace." *Foreign Affairs* 64, 3 (1985): 583–604.

―――. "The United States and the Middle East." In Haim Shaked and Daniel Dishon, eds. *Middle East Contemporary Survey,* vol. 8: 1983–84. Boulder, Colo.: Westview Press, 1986.

―――. "The United States' Middle East Policy in 1987." In Itamar Rabinovich and Haim Shaked, eds. *Middle East Contemporary Survey,* vol.11: 1987. Boulder, Colo.: Westview Press, 1987.

Rubinstein, Alvin. "Transformation: External determinants." In Alvin Rubinstein, ed. *The Arab-Israeli Conflict.* New York: HarperCollins, 1991.

Rubinstein, Amnon. *From Herzl to Gush Emunim and Back* (Hebrew). Jerusalem: Shoken, 1980.

Rustow, Dankwart A. *Oil and Turmoil.* New York: W. W. Norton, 1982.

―――. "Realignment in the Middle East." *Foreign Affairs* 63, 3 (1984): 581–601.

Sadat, Anwar. *In Search of Identity.* New York: Harper and Row, 1977.

Safran, Nadav. *Israel, the Embattled Ally.* Cambridge: Belknap Press, 1982.

Sandler, Shmuel. "The Protracted Arab-Israeli Conflict: A Temporal-Spatial Analysis." *Jerusalem Journal of International Relations* 10, 4 (December 1988): 54–78.

Saunders, Harold H. *The Other Wall.* Washington, D.C.: American Enterprise Institute, 1985.

―――. "We Need a Larger Theory of Negotiations: The Importance of Pre-Negotiation Phases." *Negotiation Journal* (July 1985): 249–262.

Schelling, Thomas C. *The Strategy of Conflict.* Cambridge: Harvard University Press, 1966.

Schnall, David. "An Impact Assessment." In David Newman, ed. *The Impact of Gush Emunim.* New York: St. Martin's Press, 1985.

Schueftan, Dan. "Jordan's Motivation for a Settlement with Israel." *Jerusalem Quarterly* 44 (fall 1987): 79–120.

Seliktar, Ofira. *New Zionism and the Foreign Policy System of Israel.* Carbondale: Southern Illinois University Press, 1986.

Shafir, Gershon. "Institutional and Spontaneous Settlement Drive." In David Newman, ed. *The Impact of Gush Emunim.* New York: St. Martin's Press, 1985.

Shaked, Haim. "The Middle East in 1987: A Year of Kaleidoscopic Change?" In Itamar Rabinovich and Haim Shaked, eds. *Middle East Contemporary Survey,* vol.11: 1987. Boulder, Colo.: Westview press, 1989.

Shamir, Michal, and Asher Arian. "The Intifada and Israeli Voters: Policy Preference and Performance Evaluation." In Asher Arian and Michal Shamir, eds. *The Elections in Israel–1988.* Boulder, Colo.: Westview Press, 1990.

Shamir, Shimon. "Israeli View of Egypt and the Peace Process: The Duality of Vision." In William B. Quandt, ed. *The Middle East Ten Years After Camp David.* Washington, D.C.: Brookings Institution, 1988.

Shamir, Yizthak. "Israel's Role in a Changing Middle East." *Foreign Affairs* 60, 4 (spring 1982): 789–801.

Shapiro, Yonathan. "The End of a Dominant Party System." In Asher Arian, ed. *The Elections in Israel–1977.* Jerusalem: Jerusalem Academic Press, 1980.

Shultz, George. *Turmoil and Triumph.* New York: Charles Scribner's Sons, 1993.

Smooha, Sammy, and Don Peretz. "Israel's 1992 Knesset Elections: Are They Critical?" *Middle East Journal* 47, 3 (summer 1993): 444–463.

Spiegel, Steven L. *The Other Arab-Israeli Conflict.* Chicago: University of Chicago Press, 1985.

Sprinzak, Ehud. "Gush Emunim: The Tip of the Iceberg." *Jerusalem Quarterly* 21 (fall 1981): 28–47.

————. "The Iceberg Model of Political Extremism." In David Newman, ed. *The Impact of Gush Emunim.* New York: St. Martin's Press, 1985.

————. "The Emergence of the Israeli Radical Right." *Comparative Politics* 21 (January 1989): 171–192.

————. *The Ascendance of Israel's Right.* New York: Oxford University Press, 1991.

Statistical Abstract of Israel 1992. Jerusalem: Central Bureau of Statistics, 1992.

Stein, Janice Gross, ed. *Getting to the Table.* Baltimore: Johns Hopkins University Press, 1989.

"Talking Points: The Israeli-Arab Peace Negotiations, an Update Following the First Half of the Seventh Round, October 21–29, 1992." New York: Information Department, Consulate General of Israel (November 3, 1992).

Tamir, Avraham. *A Soldier in Search of Peace.* New York: Harper and Row, 1988.

Tillman, Seth. *The United States in the Middle East: Interests and Obstacles.* Bloomington: Indiana University Press, 1982.

Touval, Saadia. *The Peace Brokers.* Princeton: Princeton University Press, 1982.

————. "Frameworks for Arab-Israeli Negotiations—What Difference Do They Make?" *Negotiation Journal* 3, 1 (January 1987): 37–52.

Tung, William L. *International Law in an Organizing World.* New York: Queens College Press, 1977.

U.S. Department of State. *The Quest for Peace: Principal U.S. Public Statements and Related Documents on the Arab-Israeli Peace Process 1967–83.* Washington, D.C.: GPO, 1984.

U.S. House. *Development in the Middle East: Hearing Before the Subcommittee on Europe and the Middle East of the Committeeon Foreign Affairs.* 99th Cong., 1st sess. April 4, 1985, September 18, 1985; 99th Cong., 2d sess. August 14, 1986; 100th Cong., 1st sess. September 15, 1987; 100th Cong., 2d sess. March 15, 1988; 101st Cong., 1st sess. July 12, 1989.

U.S. House. *The Middle East in the 1990s, Hearing before the Subcommittee on Europe and the Middle East, of the Committee on Foreign Affairs.* 101st Cong., 2d Session, April 4; May 8; June 26; and July 17, 1990.

U.S. House. *Post War Policy Issues in the Persian Gulf, Hearings Before the Subcommittees on Arms Control, International Security and Science, and on Europe and the*

Middle East of the Committee on Foreign Affairs. 102 Cong., 1st sess. January 31, February 28, and April 11, 1991, Washington: D.C.

U.S. Senate. *Foreign Operations, Export Financing, and Related Programs Appropriation for Fiscal Year 1992. Hearing before the Subcommittee of the Committee on Appropriation.* 102 Cong. 1st sess.

Weizman, Ezer. *The Battle for Peace.* New York: Bantam Books, 1981.

Yanai, Nathan, ed. *On the Peace Process and Israel's Future* (Hebrew). Tel Aviv: Ministry of Defense, 1988.

Yishai, Yael. "Drafting the Platform: The Territorial Clause." In Asher Arian and Michal Shamir, eds. *The Elections in Israel–1984.* New Brunswick: Transaction Books, 1986.

Young, Oran A. *The Intermediaries.* Princeton: Princeton University Press, 1967.

Zartman, William I. *Ripe for Resolution.* New York: Oxford University Press, 1985.

———, ed. *The 50% Solution.* New Haven, Conn.: Yale University Press 1976).

———. *The Negotiation Process.* Newbury Park, Calif: Sage, 1977.

———. *The Practical Negotiator.* New Haven, Conn.: Yale University Press, 1982.

———. "Prenegotiation: Phases and Functions." In Janice Gross Stein, ed. *Getting to the Table.* Baltimore: Johns Hopkins University Press, 1989.

Index

About the Book and Author

An in-depth study of the effects of Israel's internal struggles on the Arab-Israeli peace process, this book examines how Israel's leaders and citizens have reacted to the various proposals in the post–Camp David era, including the 1982 Reagan plan, the 1988 Shultz initiative, and the 1989 Mubarak and Baker plans. Ziva Flamhaft also analyzes reactions to the signing of the Declaration of Principles in 1993. Focusing on the domestic political scene, she exposes the efforts of Prime Minister Begin to the Reagan plan, the near collapse of the National Unity Government (NUG) in 1987-1988, and the ultimate fall of the NUG in 1990 as a result of the Baker plan.

Flamhaft then looks at how the end of the Cold War and the Gulf War helped to encourage negotiations and evaluates why the Likud Party was replaced by Labor in 1992. Finally, Flamhaft demonstrates the futility of third-party mediation when negotiations are rejected domestically and discusses the essential conditions required for effective mediation.

Ziva Flamhaft teaches in the Political Science Department of Queens College of the City University of New York.